6-11-89

IN-R.

Cooperative Research and Development: The Industry–University–Government Relationship

Cooperative Research and Development: The Industry–University–Government Relationship

Edited by
Albert N. Link
Department of Economics
University of North Carolina at Greensboro

Gregory Tassey
National Institute of Standards and Technology

Kluwer Academic Publishers
Boston / Dordrecht / London

1989

Distributors for North America:
Kluwer Academic Publishers
101 Philip Drive
Assinippi Park
Norwell, Massachusetts 02061 USA

Distributors for all other countries:
Kluwer Academic Publishers Group
Distribution Centre
Post Office Box 322
3300 AH Dordrecht, THE NETHERLANDS

T
175
C65
1989

Library of Congress Cataloging-in-Publication Data

Cooperative research and development : the industry— university—
  government relationship / edited by Albert N. Link, Gregory Tassey.
      p.   cm.
    Includes index.
    ISBN 0-89838-303-X
    1. Research, Industrial.   I. Link, Albert N.   II. Tassey,
  Gregory.
  T175.C67   1989
  607'.2—dc19   88-8547
                                                          CIP

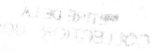

Printed in the United States of America

Contents

Editors' Introduction

We must all hang together or surely we will all hang separately.

Benjamin Franklin

The significant apathy that characterized relationships between industry and universities and the adversarial nature of relationships between industry and government have both faded rapidly in the 1980s as the realities of global competition have surfaced in the United States. Both industry and government leaders articulate a number of constructs for regaining our competitiveness in world markets. One of the more frequent strategies prescribed in this new competitiveness era is cooperation. Different individuals or groups may espouse different definitions, interpretations, or areas of emphasis, but the overall importance of this concept is substantial.

Although examples of cooperative research have existed for several decades, the number and variety of relationships have expanded rapidly in the 1980s as corporations, universities, and governments have embraced this strategy. Joint ventures involving two or three firms increased from under 200 per year in the 1970s to over 400 per year by the mid-1980s. Multiple-firm cooperative arrangements are a more recent phenomenon, made possible by the National Cooperative Research Act of 1984. By mid-1988, 81 of these industry-level consortia had formed under the provisions of the 1984 Act.

The rapid growth in cooperative research and development (R&D) is primarily a response to the pressures of international competition. As a corporate strategy, cooperative R&D meets short-term needs for assets to implement new approaches for coping with intensifying competition. Universities view cooperative research as a means of obtaining funds for more applied research that complements new curricula inspired by the competitiveness agenda. Government growth policies have embraced co-operation as an instrument for shortening the technological life cycle and efficiently transferring early-stage technology. The Technology Transfer Act of 1986 has greatly increased the role of Federal laboratories in cooperative research with industry.

Although cooperative arrangements can have extended lives, one key characteristic is that such arrangements are legally and strategically finite compared to mergers. Cooperative arrangements are also less expensive than the internal investment needed to generate comparable R&D capabilities. The limited life of these arrangements also permits a period of strategy evaluation (the cost of being wrong is generally less than the cost of a permanent commitment made either by a merger or by an internal investment). Cooperation can therefore be viewed in many cases as a transition strategy—a device for cost-effectively and experimentally implementing a new strategy, while the slow and measured accumulation of internal assets takes place.

We have admired the advanced models of industry–government cooperation that the Japanese have evolved over the past several decades and have wondered about the efficacy of long-standing cooperative practices in and between European countries, as described by Rothwell. Still, the United States is inventing its own versions of these models; this is fine as long as we realize that time is of the essence. Leisurely experimentation is unacceptable. Rather, constant planning is required, including careful assessments of past and existing cooperative arrangements. To accomplish these assessments, a meaningful taxonomy is needed—one that can then be used for analyses of the technologies, industry structures, and government policies that affect the feasibility, nature, and timing of a cooperative arrangement.

1. Forms of Cooperative Research

Cooperation can involve one or more of the research, production, and marketing stages of economic activity. It can also take the form of cross-licensing or, more generally, technology sharing. At the research stage, cooperative arrangements are formed for basic research, generic-technology research, and applied R&D. Multiple-firm consortia are frequently used for the early stages of research, while two-firm joint ventures are more common for the applied R&D. These organizational differences are due, in large part, to the difficulty experienced by individual firms when trying to capture the results of the first two stages of research. In addition, infratechnology research—which provides measurement and test methods, scientific and engineering data, etc.—also is conducted by consortia.[1]

University participation is high when basic research is the objective; it is moderate for generic-technology research and low for applied R&D. Government has been participating more broadly during the last several years in basic, generic-technology, and infratechnology research. Most cooperation at the basic and generic-technology research stages is domestic, but, as Mowery has noticed, a trend toward some pairing with foreign firms is taking place in joint ventures for applied R&D and especially for non-research joint ventures (technology sharing, production, and marketing). International cooperation is also appearing in infratechnology research as evidenced by, for example, the number of such projects involving the National Institute of Standards and Technology (formerly the National Bureau of Standards).

The R&D limited partnership (RDLP) and the designated National Laboratory Facility (NLF) are two other forms of interaction involving two or more organizations. They have been included in discussions of cooperative research, as Coursey and Bozeman correctly point out. However, both are at the boundary of what could be called true cooperative research.

An RDLP is a mechanism by which a firm can augment its own research portfolio in return for sharing ownership claims on the research results. The firm usually acts as the active member, or the general partner, of the arrangement. This research is typically funded by a number of limited partners who are passive investors. They hold ownership claims in the form of royalties, or possibly shares of capital gains if the general partnership exercises a frequently included option to buy out the limited partners. Unless more than one general partner exists, the concept of cooperation among users of the research results is not present. The RDLP has been intensively promoted by the Department of Commerce and has been used by small firms to fund and spread the risk of diversification. Venture start-ups are also financed by this mechanism.

A National Laboratory Facility (NLF) is a research facility at a Federal laboratory that, in addition to its primary purpose of conducting public science and technology research, has utility for occasional use by the private sector for proprietary research. NLFs have been designated over the past several years as one means of helping industry conduct research more efficiently. Because these facilities are technically complex as well as expensive, individual firms do not invest in them for occasional use.

Where valuable proprietary research can be conducted, these facilities are being made available to the private sector for a fee (marginal cost to the Government of private use). The Oak Ridge National Laboratory, several Department of Energy laboratories, and the National Institute of Standards and Technology have recently designated such facilities. However, because no more than one firm typically participates in a given proprietary research project, the term *cooperative research* does not seem to apply.

2. Motivations For Cooperative Research

Strategic motivations can include risk reduction; the realization of economies of scale or scope with respect to research, production, or marketing; market entry, including overcoming foreign-market-entry barriers; or shortening the time to achieve any of the above. Costs of cooperation include diversion of internal research funds, coordination costs, and loss of potential competitive advantage. Moreover, competitive structure and behavior can be significantly affected by various forms of cooperation, including research arrangements.

The most commonly used form of cooperation—the joint venture—has been frequently employed (especially in Europe) to attain economies of scale. In the United States, many basic industries fell behind foreign competition during the 1960s and 1970s in product and process technology. To regain a competitive posture, significant restructuring has occurred in the 1980s. One of the fastest ways of catching up has been the use of joint ventures to improve existing technologies.

As pointed out by Rosegger, this form of cooperation, at least the successful examples of it, has a single dominant theme—the combining of complementary assets including product or process technology with such other competitively important variables as management expertise, access to markets, and distribution channels. These needed assets, by virtue of being acquired quickly, can restore or at least maintain market share in the short run. For example, if a firm is deficient in component technology, vertical integration resulting in stable access to the right parts technology can be effected through a joint venture with a parts supplier.

Alternatively, if a firm has insufficient product diversification, horizontal integration with a competitor by technology sharing or a joint production or marketing venture can rapidly expand the product line. Moreover, Mowery observes that the increased burden on marketing in regulated markets (biotechnology) has led the small, innovative firms to make extensive use of joint marketing ventures with large firms experienced in maneuvering through the regulatory process.

Sharing profits is the tradeoff for attaining a cash flow earlier than would otherwise be possible—often at a critical time in a young firm's existence. This cash flow is necessary to acquire the internal production or marketing expertise that will allow the firm to go it alone at a later date. Diversification of the firm's research portfolio is also a requirement for long-run success, and joint research ventures are a mechanism for achieving at least a portion of this objective more rapidly.

While this aspect of restructuring—the use of joint ventures to acquire existing technologies—has helped U.S. industry regain portions of its lost market share, it may nonetheless have a limited long-run utility. The simple reason is that the typical joint venture of the type observed in basic industries transfers existing technology or, at most, achieves marginal improvements. Over time, competitiveness demands the acquisition of new technologies. The complementary assets held by different firms cannot be counted on in the long run to permit dependence on this mechanism as a regular source of technology. A firm must have access to generic-technology research (from which major innovations are derived).

The scope and magnitude of foreign competition greatly affect the appropriability potential of individual firms' own generic-technology research investments, and even the execution of their horizontal- and vertical-integration product strategies. Erdilek makes a case in point by noting that even the large and integrated semiconductor firms have found technological self-sufficiency impossible since the advent of very-large-scale integration (VLSI). As a result, interfirm technological alliances have acquired strategic importance for international competitiveness. Most such alliances involve exchanges or sharing of developed technologies, as opposed to the conduct of joint research. Cooperative research has been occurring at the industry level, with government acquiescence if not direct involvement.

Because the pressures to access new technologies quickly will, if anything, intensify in coming years, the need exists for mechanisms to develop and transfer technologies efficiently. Because technologies are not homogenous entities and because they are developed in stages, with each stage having a different level of property-rights appropriability, different mechanisms must be employed at each stage.

The joint venture can be an efficient mechanism for applied R&D projects with focused product or process objectives. For example, when Hitachi failed in 1986 to obtain a license to manufacture Motorola's 32-bit microprocessor, it immediately formed a joint venture with Fujitsu to develop the technology. For Hitachi, this strategy was a second-best solution, but certainly more efficient in terms of time and cost than going it alone.

However, as the research goals become more generic and the appropriability of property rights declines, two firms will have an increasingly difficult time rationalizing such arrangements. Thus, in recent years industry-level cooperation has arisen in the United States, facilitated by the National Cooperative Research Act of 1984. SEMATECH is one highly visible example. Here, the objective is to attain a large advance in generic processing technology.

From the economist's point of view, generic technology research exhibits significant *public-good* externalities, which become rationales for cooperative research. Specifically, 1) these technologies have a sufficiently broad and, as yet, unspecified set of applications, and so significant appropriability of the research investment is unlikely; 2) the different uses of the generic technology and the considerable additional value added possible through followup applied research and development creates a nonrivalry environment; 3) early-stage research entails high degrees of risk, while foreign competition forces relatively short time periods for conducting the research; and 4) the ability of individual firms to use only portions of an indivisible generic-technology research project results in wasteful duplication of resources.

The result is a significant underinvestment in generic-technology research by individual firms. Even large, integrated firms have experienced this phenomenon in recent years. The main difference between the motivations of large and small firms for cooperation is the coverage of stages in the research process. In the case of SEMATECH, IBM wanted the research agenda limited to generic process-technology research (i.e., through the *proof of concept* stage), while the smaller firms wanted to continue through applied research to achieve the additional step of an actual demonstration of the new process technology.

By spreading costs across a capital-intensive and multidisciplinary research process, not only is time saved (a very important consideration in a time of shorter technological life cycles) but also entry barriers are often reduced. If the capital intensity of applied R&D is less than that of generic technology research, smaller firms, through access to research consortia, will be more competitive in the resulting next generation of the technology. This advantage of research consortia may be surprising to many who have focused on the potential noncompetitive aspects of cooperative research.

Another way in which the economist might characterize the type of research amenable to research consortia is to observe the existence of significant economies of scale and scope. Capital-intensive research is expensive, requiring a large minimum investment. It therefore entails considerable risk. Cost-sharing allows this risk to be spread out. Counteracting the benefits from realizing economies of scale and scope is the fact that these benefits must be shared.

This tradeoff (sharing results) is less of a disincentive in the cases where significant economies of scope are found. Externalities with respect to economies of scope exist because all but possibly the very largest firms do not plan to use the entire scope of the research consortium's output. Thus, less sharing occurs relative to the investment cost to each participant. The Microelectronic and Computer Technology Corporation (MCC)—the first research consortium to file under the 1984 Act—is an example. Member firms buy into individual projects that give these firms property rights to the results of those projects only. However, the conduct of individual research projects presumably benefits from the overall scope of research conducted by MCC, as well as from scale effects of a multiproject research operation.

Three categories of research consortia have evolved from the competitiveness-related motivations described above [2]. One is long-range research conducted in a dedicated facility, staffed by full-time employees. MCC and Bellcore (Bell Communications Research, Inc.) are examples. A second category simply pools funds and issues grants, primarily to universities (for example, the Semiconductor Research Corporation). A third category provides services, including facilities, that test for adherence to standards (the Corporation for Open Systems) or that promote standards for regulation (the Center for Advanced Television Studies).

3. Benefits and Costs

In the university–industry case, Geisler and Rubenstein have summarized a comprehensive set of benefits to universities and to industry. Benefits to industry include exposure to longer-term research in which private firms systematically underinvest, access to unique research skills, and access to a source of highly skilled labor. The university benefits from, among other things, exposure to more applications-oriented research, increased funding, and better insights into curricula development. Indicators of these and other benefits are numerous—some qualitative and some quantitative.

Of course, these rationales, summarized in the previous section, are not unidirectional in that a bounded segment of the evolution of a technology exists for each cooperative mechanism. In particular, as the research becomes more applied in character, the appropriability potential increases, and thus rationales 1 and 2—the nonappropriability and nonrivalry factors—lose their importance. Even rationale 4—the wasteful duplication argument—can be overdone. In fact, a tradeoff exists between removing redundancy and reducing expected rate of return. This tradeoff becomes more unattractive as the research objective becomes more applied.

As Scott reminds us, any policy mechanism can be misused and thereby result in net losses to the economy as a whole. Implementation of the 1984 National Cooperative Research Act has been grounded in a fundamental tradeoff between increased efficiency and reduced competition. For research consortia that are focused on basic research, such as the Semiconductor Research Corporation (SRC), the lack of proprietary content in the research output makes the competitive issue a moot one. Even generic-technology research consortia (those filing under the 1984 Act) can be rather easily rationalized because the efficiency gains cited above are significant. Moreover, considerable value added remains at the applied R&D stage and through production and marketing.

However, the research consortia whose objectives include applied research, and especially development, must receive very careful analysis. While basic research and considerable generic-technology research can easily accept the label *pre-competitive*, a finished development project provides a product ready for commercialization. Although some product engineering may be done by the members, competition is basically limited to production and marketing. The protections of the Act range from basic research only through the prototype stage (i.e., the end of generic-technology research). Once a consortium's research has reached this stage, member firms are expected to take the results, perform their own applied R&D, and compete in a global market.

Uncertainty with respect to the efficiency–competition tradeoff increases for research consortia that include applied R&D as a major part of their operations. An example is the Software Productivity Consortium, which is developing software for large-scale aerospace systems. This consortium will develop generic software modules to permit faster development of specific applications. The sponsors are aerospace firms that have contracts with the Department of Defense. Although these firms have their own internal software-development units to support their defense-contract obligations, they do not appear to have commercial-market strategies for this class of software. They therefore seem to have rationalized the fact that this consortium conducts considerable applied R&D because the software is being supplied to a government agency (Department of Defense), it is not the final product, and the member firms are not competing against each other in commercial markets.

A few examples exist of cooperative production. An evolving experiment in Pennsylvania will consist of a cooperatively owned and operated flexible manufacturing facility. The participating small firms will electronically transmit their designs to the facility for manufacture. This leads one to ask how far cooperation should go. If cooperative research were to be followed by cooperative production, one must ask what is left for individual firms to do in terms of adding value. If economies of scale or scope exist at the production stage as well as at the research stage, one may have to conclude that the minimum efficient size of firm has increased significantly. In such cases, permanent combination (mergers) may be the only alternative.

4. The Government Role

Resource allocation is not a once-and-for-all phenomenon. The process occurs at each of a number of stages, and the optimal level and nature of government participation will vary at each stage. In some cases the optimal level will be high (e.g., basic research) and in others it will be low-to-zero (e.g., product development). Most of us would have little argument with the traditional high subsidies for basic research. And even the allocation mechanisms, although debated on efficiency grounds, are not particularly controversial.

The serious issues in role analyses arise at the stage in a technology's development directly following basic research. Basic research produces scientific and engineering knowledge that is valuable for sets of application, generally unknown at the time the knowledge is produced. When the application process begins, the first efforts are far removed from specific product development. In fact, these initial efforts are focused on identifying the generic performance parameters and obtaining initial specifications of their ranges of possible values. These performance parameters include not only functional characteristics but also architecture and packaging or interface considerations.

An important point regarding efficiency must be mentioned. Because the research objective is generic technology, the results of generic-technology research frequently have a nonproprietary character. This does not mean that a massive government role is warranted, especially when the research is evolutionary with respect to an existing technology. In Japan, the Ministry of International Trade and Industry (MITI) has proven this point many times. Their subsidies for generic-technology research are part of a coordinated cooperative effort with the domestic industry. Semiconductors and optoelectronics are examples. For each stage in the evolution of these technologies, MITI has played an important coordinating and consensus-building role, while providing seed money for emerging technology research. This funding is relatively small compared to the funds committed by industry. As Audretsch points out, MITI has accounted for only about 12% of Japanese Government R&D funding since the 1960s.

In comparison, emerging technologies that do not have an established industry structure require considerable government research support. Biotechnology is a recent example. As biotechnology evolves and products begin to enter the marketplace, large pharmaceutical and chemical companies are making strategic commitments. These larger companies have both the resources and the broader product strategies to rationalize the allocation of funds to generic-technology research, so that future government subsidies will diminish in a relative sense.

Other factors determine the nature of the government role. Audretsch observes that some countries, notably the United Kingdom, have extensively funded cooperative research in mature or even declining industries, whereas Japan's MITI has focused exclusively on emerging technologies. The United States has funded civilian technologies on an ad hoc basis. However, because it does not have an organized and coordinated civilian technology-funding program like its competitors, no strategic character or direction exists, including the funding of research cooperatives. SEMATECH will be the first major commitment of Federal funds to an industry-level research consortia with competitiveness as the objective. Finally, competitiveness is more than a single statement of relative global market positions; bilateral relationships are important determinants of overall competitiveness. In this regard, Ruiz-Mier observes that government incentives to engage in cooperative research can impact upon cross-country trade patterns.

The complex nature of most new technologies creates important roles for government. For many emerging technologies, either an industry structure does not yet exist, or it is immature—populated by small, young firms. Typically, the generic technology is developing and is quite fluid. In such cases, cooperative research is an excellent mechanism for efficiently advancing the generic technology, while affording firms that are considering possible strategic commitments a low-cost opportunity to assess alternatives and determine the nature and magnitude of required investments.

Of course, for these benefits to be realized, the cooperative research program should be established well in advance of the point of commercialization. This usually requires some long-range planning by government, followed by a catalytic or facilitator role through which a combination of coordination and seed money is used to achieve a consensus on the need and timing for a research consortium. The Japanese have become masters at combining the complementary skills of industry and government. In 1979, they set up the first optoelectronics research consortium—long before the importance of this technology even became apparent in the United States. A decade later, the only cooperative U.S. response is a small effort organized in 1985 by Battelle Memorial Institute in Columbus, Ohio.

Another important area of an industry's technology where cooperative research is an increasingly important mechanism is infratechnology. This is the collection of nonproprietary measurement and test methods, procedures, and data that enable the core technology to be developed, produced, and traded. Much of an industry's infratechnology eventually becomes embodied in voluntary industry standards. Industry tends to underinvest in these infratechnologies because they are nonproprietary. In fact, infratechnologies have their maximum impact on productivity, quality, etc., when they are widely and uniformly used.

As with generic technologies, cooperative research arrangements have become increasingly used to improve research efficiency in order to deliver infratechnologies faster. The National Institute of Standards and Technology (NIST) supplies a wide range of infratechnologies (as well as generic technologies). At the end of 1987, NIST had over 1000 cooperative arrangements in place with universities, individual firms, foreign and domestic industries, and foreign governments.

The research objectives of many consortia are what economists call *mixed* public goods. That is, the research output has both public- and private-good characteristics. This fact complicates the relationships among members of consortia, including identification and assignment of property rights. From this issue of public versus private content derives the important problem of distribution of funding responsibility, as Cordes and Watson correctly note. Agreeing on goals, property rights, and cost sharing is difficult enough for a group of private companies with varied organizational structures and market strategies. Separating the public and private components of the research in order to assess the government and industry cost-shares adds more complexity.

In 1988, the Office of Management and Budget (OMB) suggested that the Department of Energy (DoE) have its laboratories consider providing funds to private-sector-initiated cooperatives to leverage its research budget. This device sounds like the MITI seed money approach. OMB stated the necessity for industry's forming the cooperatives and setting the research agenda, and it underscored the government's role as a minority leveraging one by limiting Federal investment in any cooperative to a maximum of 49%.

A final role for government is the provision of information. This can include 1) general guidelines and assistance to industry and assessing options with respect to what type of cooperative arrangement may work best, 2) provision of long-range planning information that is especially useful for timing decisions, and 3) assistance in complying with the filing requirements of the 1984 National Cooperative Research Act. These roles are currently being undertaken by the Office of Technology Policy in the Technology Administration of the Department of Commerce. Government must also continue to document the experiences of existing cooperative research in the United States and in other countries, and to support more formal economic studies of their structure, behavior, and impact.

5. Organization and Management

The negotiation, implementation, and management of cooperative research are complex activities for which a single algorithm has yet to evolve. However, the variety of consortia with respect to motivation, organization, and behavior has been documented and analyzed; in particular, a number of lessons have been learned with respect to university–industry research consortia. This class of consortia has had to deal with a series of problems arising from the distinctly different character and behavior of the university and the participating private firms. Issues ranging from assignment of property rights to funding arrangements to pay scale differentials have been resolved in a number of different and, in some cases, innovative ways.

University–industry research consortia typically focus on basic or very generic technology research, while industry and industry–government consortia are more likely to have advanced generic technology or even applied technology objectives. Thus, in the latter case, the organization and management issues are somewhat different.

One of the more troublesome problems is technology transfer. The success in moving technology within as well as between organizations is people-correlated; that is, the efficiency of technology transfer is dependent on the number and the quality of the people involved in the process of transfer. The involvement of members of the recipient organization in the research is an advantage. However, unless the recipient organization is highly committed to the consortium, neither the staffing nor the quality of the research output is likely to be sufficient to effect efficient transfer.

Erdilek argues that much critical technology in technologically advanced industries is not patented and can be transferred by individuals through regular contact. This is certainly true of infratechnologies and much generic technology. Such contact is readily attained in consortia using a dedicated research facility. However, in some Japanese consortia (their VLSI project, for example), the research was conducted in the participating firms' own laboratories and the results distributed. Such an arrangement elicited strenuous objections from some participants because of the distinct possibility of inequitable transfer.

Other management problems for industry and industry–government consortia revolve around planning. Because the goals of the research more closely resemble individual members' internal research objectives, disputes are more likely over such planning factors as the project content of the research portfolio and time horizons. Property rights and the structure of economic payoffs are also frequently points of contention. A related problem is the difficulty in agreeing on valuation or productivity models for assessing the consortium's performance.

With the focus on the management of the consortium, the frequently inefficient internal decision-making of the member firms is often overlooked. Extended delays in providing input to the consortium's decision-making process negatively affects staff morale as well as the overall efficiency of the consortium's operation. This problem is accentuated when major commitments of resources are required. The Department of Commerce believes that one year is probably the minimum time required to reach agreement on the research agenda and other management issues. For a number of consortia filing under the 1984 Act, such as the Center for Advanced Television Studies, several years have been necessary.

6. Other Competitiveness Factors

The efficiency gains from the effective use of cooperative research are already apparent, especially in the joint-venture mode. Cooperative research at the industry level, by its very nature, will take longer to produce results and thus to be evaluated. Traditional American impatience has already been apparent. One contributing factor is the lack of long-range planning, which has frequently placed the United States in a catch-up mode, leading to frustration and impatience. If we can learn from the Japanese and promote and implement research cooperatives early enough on the evolutionary time path, we will not have this problem.

Of course, while cooperative research is an important strategic mechanism, it is not a sufficient one. Corporate strategy must embody the right mix of product and process technology, improved marketing including customer interactions, and better access to the technological infrastructure.

Government policy must ensure a lower cost of capital and a better-educated work force. Government policy must also encourage a more patient investment community, and promote technology transfer from universities and government laboratories. We must also face the possibility that some of our industries are incorrectly structured for long-term success in global markets; this includes their ability to form and execute cooperative research arrangements.

The seriousness with which U.S. industry is now taking the cooperative-research mechanism is evidenced by the steadily increasing number of research joint ventures and the 81 filings under the National Cooperative Research Act. Even very large, highly integrated firms can benefit if, for no other reason, the quality of their suppliers' products increases. Another benefit, especially to U.S. firms that in the past have tended to go it alone, is the tendency of cooperative research to promote earlier standardization of the nonproprietary elements of a technology. When U.S. standards became international standards, largely by default, neither the timing nor the content of standards were major concerns. Now a growing number of technologically competitive economies are influencing the international standards process. Knowledge of and influence on this standards process, in part through the collective influence of a consortium's members, can be important.

7. Summary

In this decade and especially in the past five years, cooperative research arrangements of various types have proliferated. With only a short lag, economists and policy analysts have begun assessments of the nature and efficacy of this important mechanism. A majority of these analyses have focused on the industry–university interaction. Much less attention has been devoted to the industry–government interaction and the various industry strategies and cooperative research structures to be found in the United States and among its foreign competitors. Therefore, this book focuses on the latter two areas.

Cooperative research is an important tool in the struggle for international competitiveness. The efficiency gains inherent in the use of this mechanism and the ability to share risk are the two most frequently cited advantages of cooperative research. Yet, in an era of shortening technological life cycles, the truncating of the early stages of a technology's development can be a very important factor in determining that industry's future competitive standing. On the other hand, perhaps the greatest risk of failure, especially for multiple-firm research consortia, is the traditional lack of patience on the part of U.S. industry.

Albert N. Link
Gregory Tassey

Notes

1. These various stages in industrial research and polices that affect them are analyzed in [1]. Generic-technology research is the first step beyond basic research. It is therefore the first step in the eventual application of basic scientific knowledge. The objective is *proof of concept*—that is, the determination of the *general* values of performance variables, architecture, and interface requirements. A prototype is often the end product. Applied research successively reduces the variance in each of these categories as specific applications (markets) are targeted. Infratechnologies have the roles of leveraging the core product or process technology that results from the generic technology and applied R&D. They are also used in operational control of production and to efficiently execute (via standards) market transactions.

References

1. Link, A., and Tassey, G. *Strategies for Technology-based Competition: Meeting the New Global Challenge.* Lexington, MA: Lexington Books, 1987.
2. Dinneen, G.P. "R&D Consortia: Are They Working?" *Research and Development* (June, 1988): 63–66.

I THE ROLE PLAYERS

1 A TYPOLOGY OF INDUSTRY– GOVERNMENT LABORATORY COOPERATIVE RESEARCH: IMPLICATIONS FOR GOVERNMENT LABORATORY POLICIES AND COMPETITIVENESS

David H. Coursey and Barry L. Bozeman*

1. Introduction

Industry–government laboratory cooperative research has become increasingly important in competitiveness policy and activity during the 1980s [1, 2]. The focus on government laboratories in improving the U.S. economy is largely attributable to the enormous national investment in their research activities. Approximately 380 federal laboratories expend one fourth of all federal R&D funds and employ one sixth of U.S. researchers [3]. Yet few commercially viable products and processes marketed by U.S. firms are derived from federal laboratory research. Declining U.S. world market

* The authors gratefully acknowledge the cooperation and assistance of officials at Oak Ridge National Laboratory including Marilyn Brown, George Corville, Donald Jared, Jon Soderstrom, and Tom Wilbanks as well as Bill Weiss of the Tennessee Innovation Center and Roger Taylor of the Power Electronics Application Center, Tennessee Center for Research and Development.

3

shares are blamed on the difficulty in transferring laboratory discoveries into commercially viable products [4, 5]. The prominence of cooperative research is predominately attributable to the rise of technology transfer policy as a prescription for U.S. industrial competitiveness woes [6].[1]

Recent legislation, such as the Stevenson–Wydler Technological Innovation Act of 1980 [9] and the National Cooperative Research Act of 1984 [10], has promoted cooperative efforts between government labs and industry. Encouraged by legislative reforms, the federal laboratories have become more active in a wide range of cooperative activities with industry promoting U.S. economic competitiveness. However, industry–government lab endeavors are still curtailed by legal and environmental barriers. One prerequisite to dismantling the barriers to industry–government lab cooperative R&D is simply to understand the range of activities and the functions and possibilities for each type in promoting U.S. economic competitiveness. Yet there has been little effort towards classifying industry–government lab cooperative R&D activity. Towards this goal, this chapter proposes a typology of industry–government lab cooperative R&D activities. Industry–government lab cooperative R&D activities at Oak Ridge National Laboratory (ORNL), one of the Department of Energy's (DOE) multiprogram laboratories,[2] are used as exemplars of each type.

After briefly identifying the four major partners in federal government cooperative research, we present an overview of federal legislation affecting industry–government lab research. We then propose a typology of industry–government lab research activities illustrated by ORNL cases. Roles of the various categories in the innovation process and in developing generic and proprietary technologies are briefly summarized. Finally, we suggest possible improvements in federal policies promoting successful joint activities and outline some of the drawbacks to increased industry–government lab research interaction.

2. Government Cooperative R&D Partners

Cooperative research can be defined as arrangements through which organizations "jointly acquire technical knowledge" [13]. These ventures can be quite formal—for example, developing separate organizations for research activity. They can also be rather informal—for example, sharing acquired technical knowledge in industrial, professional, or academic associations. Cooperative research involving federal government laboratories can be divided into four general categories: research with universities, research for other federal government agencies, research for state and local governments, and research with industry.

Federal cooperative research with universities can be traced to the Morrill Act (1862), which established the land-grant college system, among other early agricultural legislation [4]. Government–university interactions have varied over time and across government agencies. Relationships have been closer in government laboratories located near major universities and involved in less classified research [2]. Such is the case with ORNL and its nearby neighbor, the University of Tennessee at Knoxville, and Oak Ridge Associated Universities, an association of mostly Southern universities. Both have engaged in cooperative R&D with ORNL throughout the laboratory's history.

The DOE laboratories are among the most active government laboratories in cooperative research with universities [2]. The DOE laboratory system, in fact, is a descendent of university-based nuclear research preceding the Manhattan Project. Many of the larger government labs, such as Los Alamos and Lawrence Livermore, are operated by universities for DOE.

Research for other federal government agencies is sanctioned by the Economy Act of 1932 which permits any agency to conduct work for other federal government units.[3] For example, the DOE laboratories conduct work for the Department of Defense, the Nuclear Regulatory Commission, and the Department of Health and Human Services, among other agencies. The emphasis on research for other government agencies varies across government laboratories and their parent agencies.

Historically, national laboratory research for state and local governments is less common. However, Stevenson–Wydler mandated this role. Additionally, Reagan's New Federalism has increased state and local governments' need for technical advice. Since 1980, a few of the labs have engaged in cooperative R&D in some form with state and local governments. Most activity has been limited to technical assistance. For example, Sandia National Laboratory has assisted a New Mexico community in using thermal radiation for sewage treatment [2].

Research with industry has been the primary focus of recent changes in cooperative R&D policies towards improved technology transfer. Traditionally, government labs have performed limited research for industry due to government restrictions in assigning proprietary rights, the basic research orientation of most government labs, inconsistency of labs' research incentives with technology transfer, poor communication with industry, antitrust policies, conflict of interest concerns, and, generally, industry's distrust of government partnerships [2, 5, 14].

Recent changes in federal technology-transfer policies (see [4]), addressing many of the traditional barriers, have promoted industry–government cooperation. For example, Lawrence Livermore National Laboratory (LNL), known for its reclusive weapons research, is developing a new superplastic steel in conjunction with North Star Steel, Caterpillar Tractor, and Ladish [14]. Despite notable successes, significant barriers to industry–government research remain [5] and many government labs are still ambivalent toward cooperative research with industry [4].

The Stevenson–Wydler Technological Innovation Act of 1980 was a bellwether for expanded government–industry cooperative R&D.[4] Prior to this act, NASA was the only federal agency explicitly required to perform technology transfer activities [12]. While some of the act's provisions have not been implemented, the enacted sections have had major implications for industry–government R&D.

Under Stevenson–Wydler, federal agencies operating or directing laboratories must devote 0.5% of the agency's budget to technology transfer activities, and each lab with over a $20 million budget must form an Office of Research and Technology Applications (ORTA) to promote transfer activities, including relations with industry. Section 13 of Stevenson–Wydler enables personnel exchanges between federal labs, universities, and industry. Section 2 of Stevenson–Wydler permits development of cooperative research agreements between federal labs and industry where royalties flow to the laboratories and not the federal treasury [15].

The Bayh–Dole Act [16], also passed in 1980, allowed small businesses and nonprofit organizations to retain title to inventions produced by themselves with federal funds. Additional amendments under the Uniform Patent and Procedures Act of 1983 [17] further expanded the authority to disperse patent rights. Traditionally, federally funded research was seen as public domain. While this view may have been equitable, it hindered technology transfer [12]. Technology available to all often is of no interest to industry because it perceives little hope of gaining a competitive advantage. By offering proprietary rights, government labs gained a sizable incentive for attracting industrial firms for cooperative research.

In 1982, prompted by concerns over the special needs of small businesses and their importance in technical innovation (see, [18, 19]), Congress passed the Small Business Innovation Development Act [19]. The act mandated that federal agencies with sizeable R&D budgets establish small-business research programs facilitating their participation in federal R&D and innovation [15].

In 1984, the National Cooperative Research Act was passed [10]. Among other changes, the act clarified and extended Department of

Justice rulings on R&D joint ventures mostly in relation to antitrust law (e.g., [20]). The act permits joint research between businesses for "theoretical analysis, experimentation, or systematic study of phenomena or observable facts..." [21]. The act's primary influence on industry–government R&D is its promotion of joint business research, which in turn could be linked with government laboratory efforts through industrial consortium or other arrangements such as the Lawrence Livermore National Laboratory superplastic development example.

Two years later, the Federal Technology Transfer Act of 1986 amended Stevenson–Wydler, strengthening cooperative research agreements, between labs and other organizations. The act, in part, formalized the Federal Laboratory Consortium for Technology Transfer and established funding as .005% of the federal laboratory R&D budget. Including more than 100 federal lab representatives and ORTA directors, the consortium's primary mission is developing communication networks promoting technology transfer [12]. The act also authorizes royalty payments of at least 15% from income that labs generate from an employee's invention [4], encouraging lab employees to engage in commercially applicable research activity with private firms.

At this time, significant federal policy activity continues. Executive Order 12591, released in April 1987, expanded the ability of certain federal laboratories to negotiate cooperative agreements. The Technology Competitiveness Act, introduced in 1987 and since absorbed into other legislation[5] proposes the formation of four new national laboratories specifically to assist primarily small- and medium-sized companies in rapid commercialization of new technology. Also pending is the Department of Energy National Laboratory Cooperative Research Initiatives Act [22], which proposes a number of mechanisms for promoting industry–government cooperative R&D in a few selected research areas such as superconductivity and semiconductors. These mechanisms include industry-represented advisory boards, personnel exchanges, and Institutes for Entrepreneurial Studies (offering masters degrees at six universities in association with DOE labs). Section 305 of this act expands on Executive Order 12591 permitting government-owned, contractor-operated labs such as ORNL to negotiate cooperative, semiconductor research agreements without DOE approval.

The storm of legislative activity has not precipitated a thunderous expansion of cooperative industry–government lab research. Considerable activity is occurring at ORNL and a few other labs, but they are conspicuous exceptions [14]. Considerable barriers, remain to industry–government laboratory cooperation. The culture and research activities of many labs still resist industry cooperation. Communication between many government labs and industry is infrequent. Patent and other proprietary rights policies still require lengthy processing procedures [5, 23–25].

Dismantling the barriers and strengthening industry–government lab cooperative R&D greatly depends on understanding the range of activities and usefulness of each type of cooperative R&D activity in advancing U.S. economic competitiveness. Yet there has been little effort towards classifying cooperative R&D activity. Some work has been conducted towards this end, though not specific to industry–government interactions [5, 13, 26–27]. The next section uses cases from ORNL to exemplify a framework for cooperative R&D activities between industry and federal government laboratories.

3. A Typology of Industry–Government Cooperative R&D: Cases from Oak Ridge National Laboratory

Industry–government laboratory cooperative R&D can be defined as any arrangement, formal or informal, whereby at least one government laboratory and one private firm jointly develop and/or obtain technical knowledge. Within this broad definition are several distinctive joint activities. These include

1. Joint research ventures and cooperative research agreements
2. Collaborative research centers
3. Research consortia
4. R&D limited partnerships
5. Subcontracting
6. Advisory boards/Technical review committees
7. Business infrastructure

Industry–government lab cooperative R&D cases illuminate these categories. ORNL, due to its relative success and emphasis on government–industry cooperative R&D, is an excellent choice for explicating the typology. Arguably, ORNL is the most successful government laboratory in technology transfer and cooperative R&D [28]. ORNL, which is part of the Department of Energy's multiprogram laboratory system, employs more than 4000 persons, and its total budget exceeds $450 million [11, 29].[6] Though a government-owned laboratory, ORNL is managed by Martin Marietta Energy Systems.[7]

Phone and on-site interviews with ORNL researchers and technology-transfer employees and with employees of R&D support organizations near ORNL, as well as written documents, were used to develop examples of seven major types[8] (partly overlapping) of industrial cooperative activity, partly based on previous ORNL studies. The following descriptions of ORNL activity exemplify each category of cooperative R&D activity.

3.1. Joint Research Ventures: REMOTEC and ORNL

Joint research ventures have been defined as the formation of a new organization by two or more parent entities [32]. Such arrangements are uncommon in industry–government lab cooperative R&D. A less restrictive definition appropriate to government–industry endeavors is warranted. Industry–government lab joint research ventures can be defined as formal research agreements between government laboratories and at least one industrial firm [5, 13].

Government–industry joint research ventures can take many forms, but usually involve industry funding and marketing of the research and the lab performing the research. An example is ORNL's agreement with Cummins Engine Company in the commercial development of nickel and nickel–iron aluminide alloys as components for high-temperature diesel engines [33]. The closer the technology is towards commercialization, the more industry tends to conduct the research under lab guidance.

Joint research ventures are appropriate as a technology begins to demonstrate feasibility and commercial viability while significant engineering problems remain [5]. Technologies earlier in their life cycle are often viewed as too risky for substantial investment by an industrial firm.

Remote-controlled robots are certainly a commercially viable technology but one with considerable engineering problems. ORNL's most extensive joint venture is with REMOTEC, a world distributor of touch-sensitive robots and an ORNL spin-off company (D. Jared, personal communication). Under its disbanded breeder program, ORNL had spent over $1 million in development of a remote servomanipulator for maintaining contaminated nuclear fuel processing areas. ORNL has established a four-year cooperative agreement for developing a commercializable, remote-controlled robot from the technology under ORNL specifications. ORNL is supplying its entire system and REMOTEC will supply staff and equipment for development and provide ORNL with a commercial device for a small fee [29].

3.2. Collaborative Research Centers: National
Center for Small-Angle Scattering Research

Collaborative research centers are established by the lab to promote collaboration (usually informal) between lab personnel and outside organizations. Industrial and other external groups have access to the lab's expensive and sometimes unique equipment. In turn, the lab can secure user fees and has the opportunity to expose lab researchers to new ideas and perspectives. Industrial groups must submit research proposals for approval. Proprietary research must be conducted at the firm's expense while the DOE labs provide free access for public-domain activity. In every case, full patent rights are maintained by the user [11].

ORNL provides 13 national user facilities in a variety of research areas for industry. Many facilities are among the finest in the world, including the National Center for Small-Angle Scattering Research and the High Temperature Materials Laboratory.

The National Center for Small-Angle Scattering Research (NCSASR) is the ORNL facility most used by industrial firms [24]. NCSASR provides two small-angle neutron-scattering instruments for investigating solid-matter structures in biology, polymer science, materials science, and other research areas [34]. Even though NCSASR was closed for most of 1987, 13 industrial experimentators used the facility that year. The center provides workshops, newsletters, and technical papers in user recruitment [25].

Industrial use of ORNL facilities increased approximately 75% between 1985 and 1986 [24]. In 1986, approximately 100 industrial scientists (17% of all user facility visitors) worked at ORNL [24].

3.3. Research Consortia: Thermomechanical
Model Software Development Center

Research consortia involve multifirm agreements establishing funding for basic and applied research at a government lab. Each member firm pays a membership fee to participate in joint industrial projects. In exchange, participating firms use lab facilities and expertise and can conduct proprietary research [5].

Research consortia are especially useful where technological developments attract several companies, market potential is viewed as great, and the research involves substantial risks beyond those acceptable by a single firm [5]. Since most firms desire proprietary rights to developed products or processes, research consortia are not well suited to prototype and commercial development [5].

The Thermomechanical Model Software Development Center (TMSDC) is the largest of two industrial consortia at ORNL. TMSDC, officially under the Tennessee Center for Research and Development, includes 15 companies (12 U.S. three foreign). Each firm pays $10,000 for two years of development research for a software facilitating use of a highly complex group of element-analysis models for evaluating thermomechanical stresses [24].

3.4. R&D Limited Partnerships: Atom Sciences, Inc.

An R&D limited partnership [RDLP] is a form of business organization using syndicates to raise R&D capital [27]. Though expensive to establish and manage, RDLPs offer development funds and broad participation, and help small- to medium-sized firms conduct research (normally beyond their resources) [5]. RDLPs are primarily applicable to technologies in early manufacturing stages where suitable commercial products or processes are delineated [5]. For government laboratories, the primary usefulness of this cooperative arrangement is sponsoring development of technology originating at the laboratory.

A $1.5-million RDLP has been formed at Oak Ridge with Atom Sciences Incorporated, an ORNL spin-off company, to develop and manufacture a single-atom detection instrument [2]. The instrument, using the patented Resonance Ionization Spectroscopy (RIS), utilizes a narrow-band laser to move atoms from ground state to their unique excited state, or resonance. Once identified, atoms are ionized. The process has commercial potential in semiconductors, electronics, geology, and physiology, among other areas [35]. One application of RIS is the detection of defects in silicon chips where a single, unwanted atom hinders reliable performance.

3.5. Subcontracting: TEMCOR Heat Pump

Subcontracting work to industry has been rapidly increasing among many DOE labs in recent years, in part to offset personnel and budget fluctuations [12]. ORNL industry subcontracts have risen from approximately $1 million in 1980 to $6 million in 1988 and are expected to rise to $9 million by 1993. Subcontracting is useful in two major ways: one, allowing industry R&D management to demonstrate through internal activity the commercial viability of a research area and thereby avoid the "not invented here" syndrome: and two, reducing the firm's risk in developing a research idea into a proprietary product or process by providing financial support.

The TEMCOR heat pump is a good example of ORNL industrial subcontracting. ORNL originally subcontracted with Energy Utilization Systems Incorporated (EUS) among other companies for development and testing work of a heat-pump water heater. The demonstrated success led EUS to continue research beyond the subcontract and bring the heat pump to market as one of their major products [5]. Companies developing heat-pump water-heater models were granted marketing licenses.

3.6. Advisory Boards/Technical Review Committees: Roof Research Advisory Panel

Advisory boards, technical review committees, and other types of industrial groups advising lab researchers help define industrial R&D needs, identify possible joint endeavors, and improve industry–lab communications [27]. These groups vary widely in formality, membership, and purpose. These groups are especially useful in helping set basic and early applied research on a trajectory toward commercial products and processes. Though usually inexpensive to maintain, they are highly vulnerable to promoting special interests of industry groups in lab research [27].

One example of an ORNL technical review committee is the Roof Industry Research Advisory Panel (RIRAP). RIRAP is affiliated with the DOE Roofing Program and the ORNL Roof Research Center, a user facility, conducting research on the thermal efficiency and durability of roofing structures. The Panel meets biannually to help establish industry projects and research priorities as well as to assess the commercial potential of ORNL roofing research. Currently, RIRAP consists of 12 members representing DOE, ORNL's Roof Research Center, various consultants, and industrial firms including Owens Corning and Dow Chemical.

3.7. Business Infractructure: Technology Corridor Development and the Tennessee Innovation Center

Government laboratory resources can provide a substantial supportive infrastructure for local business. ORNL and its contract-operator Martin

Marietta Energy Systems have either directly or indirectly influenced the development of what is a sizable high-tech business community in the Knoxville–Oak Ridge area. Martin Marietta spends 10% of its award fee for operating ORNL on local economic development.

ORNL employees were significantly involved in proposing and arguing for the Technology Corridor, Tennessee's recent answer to Route 128 and Research Triangle Park, located between ORNL and Knoxville (D. Jared, personal communication). Over 6000 acres or public and private land are designated and managed for the special needs of high-tech firms [36]. The Corridor is strategically located near the University of Tennessee–Knoxville (UTK), ORNL, and the Tennessee Valley Authority (TVA). Though no more than six firms are directly on the Corridor (D. Jared, personal communication), several firms are located on connecting roads. Many of the denizens of the Corridor are ORNL spin-off companies. The Corridor offers no tax incentives, only the proximity to ORNL, TVA, and UTK researchers and facilities.

Several support centers are located along the Corridor. The $20-million State Institute of Technology provides all levels of vocational training for local industry employees in a variety of high-tech operations such as laser repair (D. Jared, personal communication). The Tennessee Center for Research and Development (TCRD) is an umbrella organization founded by Martin Marietta, TVA, and UTK. Through its three subunits, the Power Electronics Application Center, Thermomechanical Model Software Development Center, and the Laser Technology Center, TCRD provides a number of business services including market research, training, and subcontracted applied research towards commercial applications (R. Taylor, personal communication). TCRD is governed by a board of directors including private and public representatives [37].

The Tennessee Innovation Center, Inc. (TIC), a wholly owned subsidiary of Martin Marietta Corporation, helps nurture start-up businesses including those using ORNL innovations [38] by providing management, accounting, legal and technical advice, and seed capital [38]. Management support is critical to the survival of new firms [39]. The Center offers between $50,000–$200,000 in seed capital while larger amounts are available through venture capitalists. TIC has financed 14 companies to date. Of those, TIC sold its interest in two at a loss and one is inactive (the investment has been written off). All of the remaining 11 companies are in various stages of growth, some being too new to predict success or failure.

One of TIC's most successful companies is Computational Systems Incorporated, which produces a hand-held device used in preventive maintenance of rotating equipment. Using vibration analysis technology, the device predicts the need for equipment maintenance.

4. Applications for Industry–Government Lab Cooperative R&D

A key for successful industry–government lab cooperative R&D is to determine the strengths and weaknesses of particular approaches and to develop guidelines for choosing among them. ORNL cooperative research with industry illustrates the wide variety of associations possible between government labs and industrial firms. Some, like joint research ventures, require quite formal relationships, while others, such as advisory boards, are usually more informal. Each of the diverse approaches to industry–government lab cooperative R&D seems applicable to certain stages of the innovation process or the particular technology, generic or proprietary, they usually promote.

Soderstrom and colleagues [5] have previously discussed the application of university–industry cooperative R&D activities across the innovation process: research, development, and commercialization.[9] Their recommendations are applicable to government–industry cooperative R&D activities.

For example, joint research ventures seem more appropriate as a technology begins to demonstrate feasibility and commercial viability. It is difficult to attract firms to joint research ventures during a technology's early research and development, when technical and market risks are often sizable. Research consortia, however, entail less risk to individual firms as early development costs are diffused among participants. The closer the technology comes to commercialization, the less attractive consortia become since proprietary technical advantages would be shared among member firms. Collaborative research centers are also useful in early research, offering free access to often prohibitively expensive equipment for industrial research in the public domain. As the technology approaches commercialization, industrial firms can conduct proprietary research at their own expense within these centers. Advisory boards and technical review committees are useful in early research, since they orient laboratory activities towards technologies with significant commercial potential. RDLPs, mostly used in capital formation, are primarily applicable in early manufacturing and commercialization. Business infrastructure activities primarily support commercialization, as is the case with TIC, which assists mostly new entrepreneurial firms with venture capital acquisition and management.

The categories also demonstrate that industry–government lab cooperative R&D promotes not only generic technologies, but proprietary ones as well. Generic technologies, non-proprietary scientific knowledge applied to a functional focus such as design concepts for integrated circuits [13], are traditional products of government R&D. The public-good nature of generic technology discourages its efficient production. Collaborative research centers, research consortia, and advisory boards are supportive of generic technologies by diffusing development costs among firms and government or, as in the case of advisory boards, bringing an industry's firms together to promote development of mutually supportive generic technology, as in the case of ORNL roofing research.

Joint research ventures, R&D limited partnerships, business infrastructure, proprietary use of collaborative research centers, and subcontracting, as in the ORNL heat pump example, promote proprietary technologies. Joint research ventures, under the usual arrangements, permit firms to purchase the scientific expertise necessary for the development of proprietary technology. R&D limited partnerships and business infrastructure support the marketing of proprietary technology. Proprietary use of collaborative research centers reduces the input costs associated with purchasing research equipment in developing proprietary technologies. Subcontracting can help firms avoid the "not invented here" syndrome through on-site demonstration of a technology suitable for proprietary use.

5. Conclusions

The varied categories of industry–government laboratory cooperative R&D have equally diverse applications in promoting U.S. economic competitiveness. Some, such as advisory boards, help orient government lab research towards commercial products and processes while R&D limited partnerships and business infrasture help firms market new technology. The focus in cooperative R&D policy has been on promoting categories and activities nearer the commercialization stage of the innovation process as well as promoting proprietary technologies where benefits are more measurable. The considerable attention devoted to reforming patent and licensing policies exemplifies this orientation. Stressing commercialization and proprietary technology may have considerable short-term benefits, but neglect of generic technology and basic and applied research could be self-defeating. Many high-technology industries are based on generic technology as well as on rapid conversion of basic and applied research into commercial products. Advisory boards, for example, in directing early research towards commercially viable products and generic technologies, will be crucial in such fields as material science and semiconductors, where the research–development–commercialization time span is relatively brief, technology diffusion is rapid, and generic technologies predominate.

Despite the variety of applications, the high level of interest in government lab–industry cooperation, and the push provided by recent legislation, progress has been slow. Even ORNL, perhaps the leading government lab in industry cooperative R&D, shows considerable room for improvement. For example, only one ORNL industrial research consortium is actually functional, and many collaborative research centers are underutilized by industry. Proposals for encouraging industry–government cooperative R&D include providing greater incentives for laboratory personnel to interact with industry, further simplification of patenting and licensing, improving communications, and bridging basic lab research with industrial commercialization interests and short-term profits, among others [25]. Continued analysis of laboratory experiences, successes, and failures in industry cooperative R&D can help determine the relative usefulness of these measures across types of cooperative R&D and technological development stages.

One problem is promoting and nurturing cooperative R&D with government labs; a second is keeping intact a healthy skepticism. While most participants seem to feel that cooperative arrangements have considerable value for all parties, there may be hidden costs. In particular, industrial interactions with government labs may deter basic research programs which, in the long run, may be more vital to U.S. economic competitiveness [4]. Proprietary use of lab staff and facilities may lead to a closed academic environment contrary to the centuries-old openness in scientific research [40]. Industrial sponsorship may make the labs less amendable to conducting research in their primary areas under their parent agency. This is a traditional concern with the DOE labs conducting work for others [31]. Finally, industrial interactions my distract from national research agendas since, as in the case of ORNL, most activity is performed locally.

Currently, a frustration with policies for cooperative R&D is that there is so little standard practice. What is encouraged at one lab is prohibited at another. For example, in some cases, a DOE lab's activity in cooperative R&D is largely a coincidental function of the DOE regional office to which it reports. These frustrations notwithstanding, a blanket approach to government laboratory–industry cooperative R&D would be a mistake.

Government laboratories differ. Some government labs, such as Argonne National Laboratory, have broadly defined missions, while others are small, single-task facilities dedicated to areas such as child nutrition and the development of applications for coal [3]. Even the DOE multi-program national laboratories differ significantly from one another. ORNL is managed by a major corporation and has a long history of concern with commercialization. By contrast, Brookhaven National Laboratory is managed by a university consortium and is a bastion of basic research in high-energy physics. The weapons labs, such as Sandia National Laboratory and Los Alamos, have still different histories, missions, and cultures, avoiding industry interaction due to their defense research. In our view, the success of industry–government lab cooperative R&D will hinge on an understanding of the strengths of particular labs and their unique place in the national system of science and technology providers.

Notes

1. Many more benefits of increased technology transfer and industrial innovation have been explicated [e.g., [7, 8]).
2. Argonne, Brookhaven, Idaho National Engineering, Lawerence Berkeley, Lawrence Livermore, Los Alamos, Oak Ridge, Pacific Northwest, and Sandia National laboratories [11]. For a brief discussion of the evolution and roles of these laboratories, see Bozeman and Fellows [12].
3. The Economy Act of 1932 does pose some restrictions (see, [2]).
4. For brevity, we exclude legislation primarily affecting government research with universities, not-for-profits, state and local governments, and between federal agencies. However, Wilkes and Zerby [15] provide an excellent discussion of this legislation.
5. Trade and International Economic Policy Reform Act of 1987.
6. Also located in Oak Ridge are the Y-12 weapons and K-25 uranium enrichment plants, which are also operated by Martin Marietta for DOE. In total, DOE facilities in Oak Ridge employ 15,000 personnel with an approximate operating budget of $1.07 billion [29].
7. One of the factors contributing to ORNL's success is its contractor's (Martin Marietta Energy Systems) expertise and devotion to technology transfer [30]. Other factors include lab experience in technology transfer, traditional absorption of new missions [31], and research work that, more than many govrnment labs, has considerable short-term commercial potential [12], among other factors.
8. We intentionally do not discuss most informal and individual cooperative agreements, staff sharing, and production activities. Many of these activities could be classified under the typology or more appropriately as technology transfer. See Soderstrom and colleagues [25] for a discussion.
9. Soderstrom and colleagues [5] describe three stages in the innovation process preceding the product life cycle. *Research* includes idea generation, development, and evaluation. *Development* encompasses evaluation and refinement of the product or process, pilot demonstration, and beginning manufacturing. *Commercialization* entails production, sale, and distribution of the technology [see, [5]).

References

1. Morone, J., and Ivins, R. "Problems and Opportunities in Technology Transfer from the National Laboratories to Industry." *Research Management* 25(4) (1982): 35–44.
2. Wilbanks, T. "Relationships of Laboratories with Industry and Universities." In: Oak Ridge National Laboratory (ed.), *The Multiprogram Laboratories of the Department of Energy.* Oak Ridge, TN: ORNL, 1982, pp. 55–67.
3. Barke, R. *Science, Technology, and Public Policy.* Washington, DC: CQ Press, 1986.
4. Rahm, D.; Bozeman, B.; and Crow, M. "Domestic Technology Transfer and Competitiveness: An Empirical Assessment of the Roles of University and Government Research and Development Laboratories." *Public Administration Review,* 48 (1988): 969–978.
5. Soderstrom, J.; Copenhaver, E.; Brown, M.; and Sorensen, J. "Improving Technological Innovation through Laboratory/Industry Cooperative R&D." *Policy Studies Review* (1985): 133–144.
6. Link, A., and Tassey, G. *Strategies for Technology-based Competition: Meeting the New Global Challenge.* Lexington, MA: Lexington Books, 1987.
7. Pavitt, K., and Walker, W. "Government Policies towards Industrial Innovation: A Review." *Research Policy* 5 (1976): 11–97.
8. Hollomon, J., and Members of the Center for Policy Alternatives at M.I.T. "Government and the Innovation Process." In:M. Tushman and W. Moore (eds.), *Readings in the Management of Innovation* Cambridge, MA: Ballinger Publishing Company, 1982, pp. 612–625.
9. Stevenson–Wydler Technological Innovation Act. P.L. 96–480, Title 15, Section 3701–3714, 1980.
10. National Cooperative Research Act. P.L. 98–642, 1984.
11. United States Department of Energy. *Technology '86* (DOE/ER-0192/2). Washington, DC: U.S. Department of Energy, 1987.
12. Bozeman, B., and Fellows, M. "Technology Transfer at the U.S. National Laboratories: A Framework for Evaluation." *Evaluation and Program Planning* 11 (1988): 65–75.
13. Link, A., and Bauer, L. *Cooperative Research in U.S. Manufacturing: Assessing Policy Initiatives and Corporate Strategies.* Lexington, MA: Lexington Books, 1989.
14. Charles, D. "Labs Struggle to Promote Spin-offs." *Science* 240 (1988): 874–876.
15. Wilkes, B., and Zerby, A. "Legal Mandates and Constraints on the National Laboratories." In: Oak Ridge National Laboratory (ed.), *The Multi-program Laboratories of the Department of Energy.* Oak Ridge, TN: ORNL, 1982, pp. 73–83.
16. Patent and Trademark Laws Amendment (Bayh–Dole Act). P.L. 96–517, 1980.

17. Uniform Patent Procedures Act of 1983. P.L. 98–620, 1984.
18. Rothwell, R., and Zegveld, W. *Industrial Innovation and Public Policy: Preparing for the 1980's and the 1990's.* London: Frances Pinter Publishers Ltd., 1982.
19. Small Business Innovation Development Act. P.L. 97–219, 1982.
20. United States Department of Justice *Antitrust Guide Concerning Research Joint Ventures.* Washington, DC: U.S. Department of Justice, 1980.
21. Bozeman, B.; Link, A.; and Zardkoohi, A. "An Economic Analysis of R&D Joint Ventures." *Managerial and Decision Economics* 7 (1986): 263–266.
22. Department of Energy National Laboratory Cooperative Research Initiatives Act. Senate bill 1480, 100th session. Pending, 1988.
23. "Technology for sale." *Scientific American* 256 (May, 1987): 62.
24. Oak Ridge National Laboratory. *FY 1988–1993 Institutional Plan: Oak Ridge National Laboratory.* Oak Ridge, TN: ORNL, 1988.
25. Soderstrom, J.; Copenhaver, E.; Brown, M.; and Sorensen, J. *Enhancing Technology Transfer Through Laboratory/Industry Cooperative Research and Development.* Oak Ridge, TN: ORNL, 1985.
26. Fusfeld, H. *University–Industry Research Interactions.* New York: Pergamon Press, 1984.
27. Snell, S.; Brown, M.; and Zerega, A. *Technology Transfer for DOE's Office of Transportation Systems: Assessment and Strategies.* Oak Ridge, TN: ORNL, 1988.
28. Oak Ridge National Laboratory. *Technology Applications Bulletins.* Oak Ridge, TN: ORNL, Summer, 1988.
29. Charles, D. "Oak Ridge Leads the Way." *Science* 240 (1988): 875.
30. "New Oak Ridge Operator." *Science News* (December 24 & 31, 1983) 405.
31. Teich, A., and Lambright, H. *Redeploying Big Science: A Study of Diversification at Oak Ridge National Laboratory.* Albany, NY: Institute for Public Policy Alternatives, State University of New York, 1975.
32. Grossman, G., and Shapiro, C. "Research Joint Ventures: An Antitrust Analysis." *Journal of Law, Economics, and Organization* 2 (1986): 315–337.
33. Krause, C. "The Technology Transfer Fund: A Status Report on ORNL Projects." *ORNL Review* 4 (1985): 19–30.
34. Oak Ridge National Laboratory. *ORNL User Facilities* [descriptive brochure]. Oak Ridge, TN: ORNL, undated.
35. Atom Sciences Incorporated. *Atom Sciences: Breakthrough Technology in Elemental Analysis* [promotional brochure]. Oak Ridge, TN: Atom Sciences Incorporated, undated.
36. Tennessee Technology Foundation. *Technology Corridor* [promotional brochure]. Oak Ridge, TN: Tennessee Technology Foundation, undated.
37. Tennessee Center for Research and Development. *The Tennessee Center for Research and Development.* [promotional brochure]. Oak Ridge, TN: Tennessee Center for Research and Development, undated.
38. Tennessee Innovation Center. *The Tennessee Innovation Center* [promotional

brochure]. Oak Ridge, TN: Tennessee Innovation Center, undated.
39. Adizes, I. "Organizational Passages—Diagnosing and Treating Lifecycle
Problems of Organizations." In: M. Tushman and W. Moore (eds.), *Readings
in the Management of Innovation*. Cambridge, MA: Ballinger Publishing
Company, 1982, pp. 169–187.
40. Broad, W. "As Science Moves into Commerce Openness is Lost." *The New
York Times* (May 24, 1988): C1–C6.

2 FINANCING INDUSTRY— GOVERNMENT COOPERATION IN INDUSTRIAL RESEARCH

Joseph J. Cordes and Harry S. Watson

1. Introduction

Cooperative research ventures, in which several firms pool their resources in order to develop new technologies, have become more prevalent in recent years. As noted by Link and Tassey, collaborative research among industrial enterprises is not a new phenomenon [1]. For example, firms have supported the research efforts of trade associations since the turn of the century. However, it appears that both the scope and the nature of privately organized cooperative research programs have changed significantly. During the period from 1973 to 1980, there was only one year in which more than 200 joint ventures were reported, whereas in 1982 and 1983 the number had risen to 281 and 348, respectively. Moreover, earlier cooperative research efforts were relatively minor in scope, and not intended, for example, to develop radically new industrial products or processes. By comparison, the more recent cooperative research efforts have been more ambitious.

This rise in the formation of private cooperative research ventures has been accompanied by the establishment of a number of cooperative research ventures involving private industry and government to support research conducted at public research facilities. For example, in the period

21

between 1985 and the present, 15 research consortia have been formed at the National Bureau of Standards, each consisting of a number of private firms who have agreed to share the cost of conducting the research needed to solve a specific scientific and/or engineering problem. This rate of formation may be compared to the period of the 1970s and early 1980s, when only handful of such arrangements were in existence.

Several broad questions are raised by the emergence of cooperative research ventures involving government and private industry: 1) Why have such arrangements become more prevalent in the 1980s? 2) Are such ventures a *desirable* way of organizing and supporting certain types of research that is conducted in the public domain? 3) What factors affect the success of such arrangements? This chapter attempts to shed some light on each of these questions in the specific context of industry–government cooperative research consortia organized through the auspices of the National Bureau of Standards.

2. Emergence of Public–Private Cooperative Resarch Ventures

As in the case of privately organized joint research, cooperation between private industry and government laboratories is not a new phenomenon. For example, there has been and continues to be a long-standing tradition of collaboration between scientists and engineers from private industry and their counterparts at the National Bureau of Standards (NBS).*

However, such participation has consisted largely of arrangements in which scientists and engineers have been *lent out* or *detailed* to work on existing research programs at NBS that have been primarily supported by public funds. By comparison, public–private consortia have been proposed as a means of providing direct financial support for some of this research, thereby relying on *private* financing in the form of cash contributions from consortium participants instead of *public* financing through tax dollars. This particular institutional arrangement appears to have been spawned by the confluence of several different factors. These have been 1) the increasing importance of intermediate technologies that link basic and applied industrial research, 2) the comparative advantage of conducting some of the research needed to develop such intermediate technologies in certain government laboratories, and 3) the changing federal budget environment.

As is noted by Tassey [2], much privately financed industrial research rests not only on basic scientific research, but also on the existence of intermediate technologies that link basic and applied industrial research. One class of such intermediate technologies are *infratechnologies*, which include "scientific data used in the conduct of R&D, measurement and test methods used in R&D, production control, acceptance testing for market transactions, and various technical procedures such as calibrations of equipment" [2]. An example of such an infratechnology would be the existence of widely agreed-upon measurement and calibration criteria for use in evaluating chemical processes.

Another important set of intermediate technologies are *generic technologies*, which "organize fundamental scientific and engineering principles into conceptual and laboratory models from which product and process applications are eventually derived" [2]. An example of such a generic technology would be the development of functional concepts and architectures of a new generation of integrated circuits, including laboratory testing of prototypes.

Each type of intermediate technological input has become increasingly important as part of a strategy of technology-based competition among U.S. firms. However, the research needed to develop both infratechnologies and generic technologies often requires relatively large-scale facilities and has become increasingly complex and multidisciplinary in nature. Hence, *individual* firms may not have the means to conduct the type of research needed to develop a particular infratechnology or generic technology.

Both infratechnologies and generic technologies draw heavily on a common base of basic scientific and measurement research. A considerable amount of such research is conducted at the National Bureau of Standards, which currently performs three basic functions in support of the U.S. economy. *Basic research* is conducted to advance the state of the art of measurement science. *Measurement standards*, which draw on this base, are established and continually updated. Lastly, *measurement science* is applied to provide evaluated data, measurement technologies, and measurement-related technical services to industry [2].

The close relationship between these activities and those needed to develop infratechnologies (which by their very nature are measurement-intensive) is clear. At the same time, with increased emphasis on process and quality control, the development of generic technologies has also come to rely more on applications of scientific measurement.

As a consequence, it would appear that some of the facilities and staff needed to develop both infratechnologies and certain types of generic technologies already exist in the public sector. In the budgetary environment prevailing before 1980, it is likely that this circumstance would have led NBS to *conduct* a certain volume of research *financed* from general tax collections to support the development of these intermediate technologies perhaps with involvement by appropriate research personnel from private industry.

However, the budgetary environment has changed in important ways. Most notably, a heightened awareness of the limits of government and an erosion in the amount of budgetary slack available for modifying existing policies and implementing new ones has prompted policymakers to find ways of implementing policy that do not increase the size of the federal budget deficit [3].

One consequence of this changed environment has been increased pressure to find ways of privatizing hitherto purely public activities. One form of privatizing is contracting-out the provision of some publicly financed goods or services. Another is increasing the share of private financing of publicly provided goods and services.

While there have been no serious attempts to pursue the first form of privatization at the National Bureau of Standards, there has been a discernable shift in the direction of privatizing the sources of financial support for research conducted at NBS. In 1980, roughly 50% of NBS', financial resources came from general tax dollars, 34% from payments for services performed for other government agencies, 10% from in-kind contributions from industry, and 6% from user fees charged to private and public organizations for specific goods or services received from NBS. By comparison, in 1985, roughly 47% of NBS resources came from general tax dollars, 27% from payments for services performed by NBS for other government agencies, 20% from in-kind contributions from private industry, and 6% from user fees. Thus in five years, the share of the costs of NBS activities financed by private sources rose from roughly 16% to 25%.

Under such circumstances, it is not surprising that attempts would be made to devise alternative means of supporting research to develop infratechnologies and/or generic technologies. On the one hand, increased demands for certain types of research at NBS were created by the need to develop certain types of measurement-intensive intermediate technological inputs. On the other, the budgetary environment created incentives to devise arrangements for responding to such demands that relied less than previously on public tax dollars. Public–private research consortia were seen as one way of increasing the share borne by private parties of the financial costs of conducting the desired research.

3. Desirability of Public–Private Researh Consortia

Public–private research consortia are examples of economic activities conducted by a public bureau but financed at least in part by private payments. While such arrangements may have emerged as a budgetary necessity for reasons such as those described above, an important question is whether the combination of publicly supplied but privately financed research will lead to desired policy outcomes.

Two issues are involved here. First, should the research be publicly conducted in the first place, as opposed, for example, to being privately conducted and supported by a mix of private and public funds? Second, if the research is to be publicly conducted, should it be publicly or privately financed?

3.1. Public versus Private Conduct

As is noted by Tassey [2], the three main functions performed by NBS are probably best viewed at minimum as *joint products* that can be produced by a common scientific and technical base, and perhaps more strongly as *complementary production activities*. That is, the quantity and quality of the output of each activity depends in a direct way on the quantity and quality of the othe activities.

Insofar as these activities are either joint products or complements, there are obvious benefits to having them supplied by the same producer. It would make little sense from the standpoint of the most efficient use of society's scarce resources to have each of the three activities new engaged in by NBS performed by different producers—public or private—if this meant that each producer had to replicate the same base-load scientific and technical capacity.

The primary output of basic scientific measurement research is a pure public good in the sense that it benefits a large number of firms in many different industries. At the same time, the human and physical resources needed to conduct such research can at modest additional cost also be used to supply certain types of private services, as well as to support quasi-public research benefiting a smaller number of firms in particular industries.

Calibrating a piece of equipment for a firm is an example of a private good that can be jointly supplied from the NBS research base. To the extent that the calibration relied on basic measurement research conducted at NBS, the resource cost of doing the calibration would be lower at NBS, and hence should be conducted there. Similarly one could argue that NBS would have a comparative advantage in the development of quasi-public infratechnologies and/or generic technologies that were measurement-intensive.

Considerations in addition to those of comparative costs would further support public provision of certain private and quasi-public research inputs. It is essential that the provider of scientific and measurement services be perceived as a neutral third party. This is most likely to occur if the measurements and standards in question can be verified and certified by an independent public body. Moreover, as is noted by Cordes, the complexity of the tasks required to provide such verification and certification is such that these activities can be done most economically if the measurements are publicly conducted in a centralizd facility [4].

3.2. Public versus Private Finance

Whether either calibration services or certain types of quasi-public research should be publicly financed as well as publicly provided is another matter. This is most clearly seen in the case of calibration, where the benefits of properly calibrated equipment accrue in full to the owner of the equipment. In this case, the marginal costs of calibration should be financed by a user fee paid by the firm whose equipment was calibrated, and not by general tax revenues.

Somewhat more complex issues arise in the case of activities leading to the development of infratechnologies and/or measurement-intensive generic technologies that benefit all firms in a particular industry or group of industries, but no other firms. Such activities have characteristics that place them somewhere in between the attributes of a *pure* private good such as calibration, and those of a *national* public research good such as maintenance of the scientific base.

On the one hand, because the benefits of developing these intermediate technologie *are* collectively consumed, the most desirable means of financing their development would not be simple user fees of the sort that could be charged in connection with calibration. Unlike the economic benefits of properly calibrated equipment, which are appropriated in full by the owner of the equipment, the economic benefits from developing an infratechnology or a generic technology would simultaneously benefit a number of different firms. However, no single firm would have a financial incentive to take into account the value of the technology to its competitors. The consequence is that insufficient financial resources would be devoted to the development of otherwise economically beneficial intermediate technologies if these were to be financed by user fees charged to individual firms. This problem would be compounded if, for reasons to be elaborated below, it would be infeasible, and indeed undesirable, to deny access to the technology to firms that failed to pay user fees.

The disadvantages associated with traditional user fees might seem to suggest that intermediate technologies, like more basic research, should be financed with tax dollars. However, the case for doing so is weakened since the benefits from developing a specific infratechnolgy or generic technology spill over among firms in specific industries or groups of industries, but not throughout the entire economy.

Thus, to support the development of, say, a particular infratechnology with public funds would be tantamount to providing a subsidy to particular industries to develop technologies whose benefits would be fully appropriated by the firms in the industry receiving the subsidy. Subsidies of this type would have one important disadvantage. If the subsidy allowed firms in the subsidized industry to escape the economic cost of developing intermediate technological inputs, such firms would earn financial returns that would exceed the true economic return to capital invested in the industry. The upshot would be that resources would flow into favored industries not only in response to the development of a new technology—which would be desirable—but also because the development of the technology was underwritten by the government—which would not be desirable.

Thus, a more appropriate model for organizing the development of quasi-public technologies might be to combine public provision, in order to exploit the aforementioned comparative advantage enjoyed by NBS in supporting the development of such technologies, with a form of private finance that did not suffer from the disadvantages associated with traditional user fees. One way of doing so would be to form a research consortium in which the cost of developing the quasi-public technology was borne by private firms acting as a group, rather than individually, in order to collectively finance the development of the infratechnology or generic technology using government laboratory facilities.

Such consortia could be organized along two basic lines. As in the case of some research consortia involving only private parties, the results of the research could be made available only to participants in the consortium.[1] Alternatively, the results of the research could be made freely available to any party once the research was completed.

In the case of public–private research consortia, practical as well as policy considerations favor the latter alternative. If the research is to be conducted at public laboratory facilities, it would be difficult if not impossible legally to exclude nonmembers from having access to the infratechnology. Moreover, even if exclusion of nonparticipants were legally permissible, doing so would impede the rapid diffusion of the economic benefits of the quasi-public technology once it was developed. Furthermore, excluding noncontributors would detract from the important perception of NBS as a neutral third party, which would be one important advantage of conducting measurement-related research activities at NBS in the first place.

However, as a number of observers have noted, if noncontributors cannot be excluded from consuming the results of research conducted by public–private consortia, potential beneficiaries of such research may behave as free-riders [7, 8, 9]. That is, individual firms will have an incentive either to refrain from joining the consortium altogether or to make smaller financial contributions than would be warrented, given the potential benefits of the quasi-public technology, under the assumption that other beneficiaries will participate and make the required financial contribution.

The presence of such an incentive could make it difficult if not impossible for such activities to receive adequate private-industry support. Thus, while there are important advantages in principle to supporting certain types of research through public–private research consortia, the important question remains of whether such arrangements are financially viable in practice.

4. Participation in Public–Private Research Consortia

The fact that to date 15 public–private research consortia have been formed with just one federal laboratory, the National Bureau of Standards, suggests that at least some firms find participation in such consortia worthwhile, notwithstanding the free-rider motive. However, the record has been mixed, as is illustrated by two examples.

4.1. The Ethylene Metrology and the Supercritical Fluids Projects

Ethylene is a primary chemical feedstock of considerable commercial value, whose primary producers and users consist of the major oil companies and chemical companies. In the mid-1970s, there was a need for more reliable measurement of the rate of flow of ethylene through the pipelines in which it was transported. Among other effects, the absence of such data made it difficult for petrochemical firms to agree about the amount of ethylene that was transmitted and received, leading to a number of complex and costly legal disputes among producers and users of ethylene.

It was therefore proposed to form a government–industry consortium to conduct the research needed to provide more reliable measurement of the flow of ethylene. It was estimated that the research would require a minimum cash outlay of $70,000 per year for five years. Initially, it was proposed that this would be undertaken at NBS if 10 industrial sponsors could be found for the project, with each contributing $7000 per year. A total of 53 firms were invited to participate. Ultimately, the project was undertaken, but with only seven industry sponsors, each contributing a little over $7000 per year for five years, with the difference between the amount contributed and the amount needed to do the research made up by NBS.

This outcome may be contrasted with that obtained in the Supercritical Fluids Project, also organized as a public–private consortium under the auspices of the National Bureau of Standards. In the 1980s there was increased interest in the application of supercritical fluids to chemical engineering separation processes, particularly as alternatives to potentially toxic petroleum-derived solvents and in situations in which chemical separations could be made at low temparatures. Separation processes based on such supercritical fluid extraction were seen to have a wide range of industrial applications, including coffee decaffeination, extraction of natural products, separation of organics from aqueous solutions, polymer processing, low temperature coal liquefaction, tar extraction, and enhanced oil recovery. However, the lack of reliable predictive models for phase equilibrium in nearly critical mixtures posed a significant barrier to the development of commerical applications.

Accordingly, the Center for Chemcial Engineering of the National Bureau of Standards proposed that an industrially funded consortium be established to conduct the research needed to develop such models. In this case, it was determined that a cash outlay of $90,000 per year would be required for three years. It was proposed that NBS undertake research on supercritical fluids if 12 industrial sponsors could be found, with each contributing $7500 per year for each of three years.

The project was undertaken, but the response was better than that for the the ethylene metrology project. The desired level of industrial participation was attained with 13 industrial members, each contributing $7500 per year for three years.

4.2. Determinants of Participation

Whether the policy experiment embodying the two examples of government–industry research consortia represents a successful model for the long term will depend on whether more cases are like the supercritical fluids project than are like the ethylene metrology project. This in turn depends ultimately on whether enough potential beneficiaries have sufficient incentives to become members of government–industry consortia.

The remainder of this section discusses two simple models of the participation decision in order to identify circumstances under which, at least for some firms, the payoff to participation exceeds the payoff to free-riding.

Broadly speaking, the two participation models reflect some important differences between infratechnologies and generic technologies. Infratechnologies are competitively neutral in the sense that successful development of such a technology reduces costs and/or facilitates R&D activities of each of its potential users. Moreover, once an infratechnology has been developed by one or more firms, it is readily accessible to other firms [2]. Both the ethylene metrology and the supercritical fluids project are examples of such technologies.

In contrast, development of a generic technology can, in varying degrees, confer a competitive advantage on firms able to avail themselves of the technology. Furthermore, those who successfully develop a generic technology may be able to appropriate a larger share of the benefits from doing so than those who develop an infratechnology [2]. As will be seen below, because of these differences, the nature of the firms's decision to participate in a government–industry research consortium will differ depending on whether the consortium is formed to develop an infratechnology or a generic technology.

4.3. Participation in Developing Infratechnologies

In evaluating whether to participate in a public–private consortium formed to develop an infratechnology, the firm must weigh the expect payoff it will receive if it chooses to participate against the expected payoff it will receive if it does not. The expected payoff P received by the firm in the event of participation can be defined to be

$$P = sB - C. \tag{2.1}$$

In this equation, s is the probability that the research will be successful given that the firm participates, B is the commercial value of successful research to the firm, and c is the financial contribution to the consortium, assumed to be collected whether or not the research venture is successful.

If the firm chooses not to participate, the expected payoff N can be defined as

$$N = qmG + [1 - q][rE - d]. \tag{2.2}$$

In equation (2.2), q is the probability that the consortium will be formed even if the firm chooses not to participate in the consortium, m is the probability that the research undertaken by the consortium will be successful if the firm does not participate, G is the commercial value of any successful research conducted by the consortium in the absence of the firm's participation, $[1 - q]$ is the probability the consortium will not be formed, r is the probability that the firm could successfully develop the infratechnology on its own, E is the commercial value of any successful research conducted by the firm on its own, and d is the cost of research if it is done by the firm on its own.

Equation (2.2) embodies an important feature of government–industry research consortia—namely, even if the firm chooses not to participate in the consortium it can still consume the results of any successful research conducted by the consortium. Thus an important maintained hypothesis of the remainder of our analysis is that $G > 0$. However, these benefits need not be the same as those derived from a consortium in which the participant is a member. Indeed, a plausible hypothesis is that the (gross) benefits derived from research conducted by a consortium in which the firm was not a participant would be no greater than those produced by a consortium in which the firm was a member, so that $B \geq G$.

Implicit in equation (2.2) is the further-maintained hypothesis that $mG > [rE - d]$, namely that the firm would derive a higher expected gain from acting as a free-rider than from conducting research on its own. If this were not so, it would be economically irrational for the firm to choose to free-ride, even if it could do so. In terms of equation (2.2), such a choice would be tantamount to setting $q = 0$. That is, the expected payoff of not participating would simply equal the expected payoff to the firm of conducting the research on its own.

Equations (2.1) and (2.2) can be combined to form the net payoff to participation, $[P - N]$:

$$[P - N] = [sB - qmG - (1 - q)rE] + [(1 - q)d - c]. \qquad (2.3)$$

In words, equation (2.3) simply states that the net payoff to participation will consist of two components. The first equals the difference between the expected benefits to the firm from the research conducted by the consortium when the firm participates, sB, and the expected benefits to the firm from research either conducted by the consortium or by the firm itself when the firm does not participate, $qmG + (1 - q)(rE - d)$. The second term is the difference between the expected cost of conducting research if the firm does not participate, and the cost of participating in the consortium.

If p is now defined to be the probability that the firm will participate in the consortium, then rational firms can be assumed to make their participation decisions in such a way that

$$p = p(P - N), \qquad\qquad (2.4)$$

or

$$p = p([sB - c] - qmG - [1 - q][rE - d]), \qquad (2.5)$$

where p increases with the value of the term inside the parentheses. That is, the rational firm will be more likely to participate in a public–private consortium the more likely it is that there is a *comparative* advantage to conducting research as a consortium participant.

Equation (2.5) serves to highlight a number of factors that may influence the participation decision. These factors may be grouped into several broad categories.

4.3.1. Comparative Advantage of Consortium Membership. First, it is easily shown that firms will have no incentive at all to participate in a consortium if they could more profitably undertake the research themselves. This can be seen by rewriting equation (2.5) as

$$p = p([sB - c] - [rE - d] - q[mG - [rE - d]]). \qquad (2.6)$$

From equation (2.6) it can be seen that when $mG > [rE - d]$, the third term will be negative, and the firm will have no incentive to participate whenever $[rE - d] > [sB - c]$. If $mG < [rE - d]$, the firm would prefer to conduct research on its own rather than act as a free-rider in any event. In this case too, failure to participate would be the preferred strategy if $[rE - d]$ exceeded $[sB - c]$.

While this conclusion is straightforward enough so as to seem obvious, it nevertheless emphasizes an important point—namely, firms will not join a consortium unless there are true efficiency gains to be realized from doing so. This in turn implies that whenever sufficient private resources are forthcoming to support government–industry consortia, the expected net gain from using public laboratory facilities to conduct the research will be positive. This would not necessarily be the case if the same resources were secured by tax dollars.

Thus, increased reliance on consortia minimizes the risk that research using public facilities will be undertaken when it should not be. However, the simple model also demonstrates that so long as there is some chance that free-rider behavior will succeed (i.e., $q > 0$), consortia may not be formed even though there would be net gains from doing so, if these potential net gains are small enough. As may be seen from equation (2.6), the difference between the first two terms can be positive; that is, there could be a comparative advantage to conducting research through the consortium rather than individually, and yet the expected payoff to participation could still be negative if the gains to acting as a free-rider were large enough.

By comparison, if $q = 0$, so that it is not possible to free-ride, the condition for consortium formation is simply that the comparative advantage of conducting research through the consortium be positive. This result shows that failure to exclude nonparticipants from consuming the benefits of consortium research does come at a price—namely, some consortia promising real though modest benefits may not be organized.

By the same token, however, incentives to participate become stronger the greater the comparative advantage of conducting research through the consortium. Equation (2.5) shows what factors are likely to affect the size of the perceived comparative advantage of participation.

4.3.2. Relative Expected Benefits and costs. Specifically, the comparative advantage to participating in the consortium is more likely to be positive if $s > qm + (1 - q)r$, and if $B > qG + (1 - q)E$. That is, the firm is more likely to become a member of a consortium the more it believes that joining will increase the probability that successful research will be conducted and the more it believes that joining will increase the commercial value of any successful research that ultimately emerges.

It is also easily seen that for given values of q, s, m, r, B, G, and E, the probability of participation will be higher the greater the value of $[(1 - q)d - c]$. That is, the greater the comparative cost advantage of conducting research through the consortium, the more likely the firm is to participate.

4.3.2.1. Uncertainty of Research. The perceived probabilities of success and benefits as well as the comparative cost advantage will, in turn, depend on certain characteristics of the research consortium. For example, it can be shown that for a given value of q, the comparative benefits of participating in the consortium will be higher, the greater the degree of uncertainty about the results of the research to be conducted.

The intuition behind this conclusion is fairly straightforward. If there were no uncertainty at all about the outcome of the research, it would be undertaken successfully with certainty regardless of whether the firm participated in the consortium ($s = 1$), the consortium was formed without the firm as participant ($m = 1$), or the firm undertook the research itself ($r = 1$). Similarly, if the outcome were certain, one could plausibly assume that the gross commercial benefits would be the same regardless of how the research was done, so that $B = G = E$.

Under these conditions, the comparative advantage of participation would reduce to $[(1 - q)d - c]$. That is, participation in the consortium would depend solely on the comparative cost advantage. Moreover, as the probability, q, that the consortium would be formed without the firm's participation approached 1, there would be no economic payoff whatsoever to participation.

In contrast, if the outcome of the research process is uncertain, members of the consortium will derive benefits that are generally not available to nonmembers. So long as consortium participants are given some say in how the research is designed and conducted, membership will provide an opportunity to shape the outcome of the research process. Thus, by joining the consortium, the firm will have an opportunity to see to it that the research succeeds and/or produces commercially useful results, thereby increasing the relative value of s and B as compared to m, r, G, and E.

Moreover, while the research is being conducted, members will be better informed than nonmembers about how it is proceeding. Such information can be of value to the firm precisely because it reduces the amount of uncertainty about the outcome. This would allow the firm to adjust its behavior more rationally and efficiently in response to the anticipated results of the research project, thereby increasing its potential economic payoff.

4.3.2.2. Private Joint Research Products. In addition to providing better and more timely information about the expected *outcome* of the research, it is also possible that participation in the research *process* through designing and monitoring the consortium's research program can provide additional valuable information. For example, in some cases, reports about research in process might provide information to members that would help them conduct their own proprietary research more effectively. Insofar as such information would be made available only to consortium members, the relative value of participation would be enhanced because, in effect, the quasi-public research good would create other forms of private or fully appropriable technical knowledge that would be available only to consortium members. Hence, the comparative advantage of membership would increase as the likelihood increased that the research would provide private research knowledge as a joint product or by-product of the consortium's principal research activities.

4.3.2.3. Absolute Scale of Anticipated Net Benefits. Finally, *when* there is a comparative advantage to participation, it is also likely to increase with the absolute size of the gross benefits of developing the technology. This may be seen by rewriting equation (2.5) as

$$p = p(a[sB - qmG - rE] + [(1 - q)d - c]), \qquad (2.7)$$

where a is a coefficient representing the magnitude of the gross benefits, B, G, and E to be derived from developing the new technology. From equation (2.7) it may be seen that so long as the first term in brackets is positive, for given levels of s, m, r, q, d, and c, firms will be more likely to participate the larger the value of a. Thus, incentives to participate in research consortia increase with the *absolute* level of the commercial benefits of conducting the research.

4.3.3. Probability of Consortium Formation. From equation (2.6) it is also seen that, other things being equal, the perceived net payoff to participation will depend on the probability, q, that the consortium will be formed even if the firm chooses not to participate. Whether firms are more or less likely to act as if the value of q is high or low is closely related to whether firms are more or less likely to form what game theorists have termed *Nash conjectures* about the behavior of others.

4.3.3.1. Assumptions About q. A firm basing its own participation strategy on Nash conjectures will act as if the consortium will be formed regardless of its own behavior. In terms of equation (2.6), this would be tantamount to the firm assuming that $q = 1$. Given this assumption, and the maintained assumption that $[rE - d] < mG$, equation (2.6) reduces to

$$p = p(sB - mG - c). \qquad (2.8)$$

This may be compared to a rearranged version of equation (2.6) when q is not zero, i.e., when the firm decides that there is some likelihood that the consortium will not be formed if it does not join:

$$p = p(sB - [qmG + (1 - q)(rE - d)] - c). \qquad (2.9)$$

From equation (2.8) it may be seen that the firm might still choose to participate in the consortium, even if the firm knew the consortium would be formed regardless of whether it joined. Thus, the forming of strong Nash conjectures about the behavior of other parties does not necessarily make joining the consortium an unprofitable strategy. However, comparing equations (2.8) and (2.9) also shows that so long as $[rE - d] < mG$, joining is relatively less profitable the greater the value of q. Thus, the more a rational firm believed that its own participation did not matter, and hence the closer the value of q is to 1, the less inclined the firm would be to join the consortium.

A number of economists and other social scientists who have studied the provision of public goods have argued that economic entities should be more likely to adopt Nash-type assumptions, i.e., to assume relatively high values of q, when the good to be provided can be shared with a large rather than a small group of beneficiaries. In particular, it has been argued that small group settings will be more conducive to cooperative strategies in which potential participants do not act as if their behavior will have no effect on the behavior of others, but instead expect their actions to be matched by others.

While this particular hypothesis about the effects of group size on individual behavior strikes many observers as reasonable, it has yet to be adequately tested. Moreover, while the conjecture implies that size should matter, it is silent about the precise size threshold at which one is more likely to observe behavior characterized by Nash assumptions.

Nevertheless, given the widespread appeal of the aforementioned hypothesis, one can argue that a firm will face stronger incentives to join a consortium when it is one of a few rather than one of many potential participants. More generally, the discussion above suggests that firms will face stronger incentives to become consortium members if the insitutional environment is such that firms are discouraged from acting as if there is a high probability that the consortium will be formed regardless of whether they join.[2]

4.4. Participation in Developing Generic Technologies

We have noted above that the commercial benefits of developing generic technologies can be quite different from those of developing infratechnologies. An important consequence is that in some cases factors different from those mentioned aboved are likely to influence the firm's propensity to join a government–industry consortium whose purpose is to do research leading to the development of a generic technology.

An important issue is whether successful development of the generic technology confers benefits that are relatively competitively neutral and difficult for any single firm to appropriate. The more competitively neutral and the less appropriable the benefits of developing a generic technology become, the more the firm's decision to participate in a consortium formed to develop such a technology will be conditioned by factors similar to those that would influence its decision to participate in a consortium formed to develop an infratechnology.

However, if the generic technology is such that the individual firm believes it can gain a significant and appropriable competitive advantage from being the first to develop the technology, the comparative benefits of becoming a member versus not joining are of a different character. In such an instance, the firm faces the following tradeoff. It can attempt to undertake the needed research itself, hoping thereby to succeed and reap all or a major share of the commercial benefits of developing the new technology. Alternatively, it can join a consortium that will undertake the needed research. Such a consortium may lower the costs of doing the research, and may also reduce the probability of not being able to share in the benefits of successful R&D. However, its members must also agree to share the new technology with everyone.

The incentives facing potential consortium participants under such circumstances are best analyzed in the context of an *appropriation game*, rather than the *public-goods participation model* described in section 4.3. In such a game, R&D is conducted in order to win a prize, in the form of higher profits [10]. If any single firm succeeds and wins the prize, it is allowed to appropriate all of the gains. Conversely, if it loses, the gains accrue to some competitor. Moreover, while increased R&D activity by all participants may increase the overall probability of discovering the prize, some portion of each firm's effort duplicates that of other rivals, so that the marginal social gain of an additional $1 spent by a single firm is less than the marginal private gain to the firm.

It is useful first to describe briefly the outcomes of such a game if it is assumed that all firms are identical and that a firm that successfully discovers the prize on its own can appropriate all of the gains. Results from a simple simulation model show that under these assumptions, if a consortium can be formed, those who join will earn greater expected profits than they would if all firms competed against each other to win the prize.[3] This results from the fact that the consortium reduces duplication of effort among its participants, thereby reducing costs of conducting R&D.

However, the simulation results also show that *if* a consortium is formed, firms can earn even higher expected profits if they are not members. As a nonmember, the firm can compete against the consortium and continue to invest its own resources in seeking the research prize; and if the firm is successful, it can appropriate all of the gain. At the same time, nothing is lost if instead the consortium wins, because it must share the prize with everyone, including nonmembers. In effect, then, any single firm has nothing to lose and everything to gain by not participating, and hence has a very strong incentive to remain outside the consortium.

Similar results are obtained when variation among firms is introduced in the costs of conducting R&D, and hence in the likelihood of winning the prize. That is, when the cost of R&D is allowed to vary among firms, the simulation results continue to show that if the consortium is formed, any single firm can do better by not joining. However, the incentive to remain outside the consortium is found to be stronger among firms with low R&D costs that have a relatively high probability of winning the prize, and weaker among firms with relatively high R&D costs that have relatively low probabilities of capturing the prize.

Of course, such behavior is rational only if the consortium is formed. And since each firm will have an incentive to behave in the manner just described, the appropriation game reduces to a classic example of the prisoner's dilemma—namely, firms would be better off if a consortium were formed, but it is privately rational for each firm to act in a way that prevents this option.

While behavior of this sort has the same effect as the type of free-riding that could be observed in the public-goods participation model, there is an underlying difference. In the case of developing an infratechnology, the firm has an incentive to remain outside the consortium if it believes it can share in the benefits of the new technology without having to bear the costs of its development, rather than because the firm desires to undertake research on its own. In the case of the simple appropriation game, the firm has an incentive to remain outside the consortium not because it expects to share in the prize if the consortium wins, but because it hopes to win all of the prize by remaining outside the consortium and conducting research on its own.

4.4.1. Motives for Joining.   In some cases, these distinct motives for nonparticipation will nonetheless lead to similar predictions about when firms are more or less likely to participate. For example, both the public-goods participation model and the appropriation game predict that membership will be encouraged by increasing the amount of benefits the firm shares with the consortium when it is a member as compared to the amount it shares when it is not a member.

In other instances, these distinct motives for nonparticipation imply that different factors are likely to be important in influencing the firm's participation decision. We have shown that in the case of an infratechnology, the firm will be more apt to join if it believes that doing so will increase the probability of successfully developing the technology. This is not the case in the appropriation game. In this instance, joining increases the resources available to the consortium for conducting research, thereby raising the probability that the consortium will win the prize. But by joining, the firm also foregoes the chance, however small, of winning the entire prize on its own. In this case, the fact that the consortium may have a lower probability of winning if the firm does not join is an advantage rather than a disadvantage.

Similarly, in the case of an infratechnology, there is a relatively straight-forward relationship between the probability of participation and the cost to any given firm of undertaking research in the absence of the consortium. Namely, the incentive to join will be stronger the more costly it is for each firm to conduct research on its own.

In the appropriation game, the relationship between the cost of one's own R&D and the likelihood of participation are more complex. Higher costs of R&D increase the effort that each firm must expend to win the prize. This in turn increases the benefits of conducting research through a consortium rather than independently. However, given that the consor-tium is formed, the presence of higher costs simultaneously reduces the chance that either the consortium or any firm remaining outside the con-sortium will discover the prize. When all firms are assumed to have identical costs of R&D, the net effect seems to be that increasing the cost of R&D does not reduce the relative gain of remaining outside the consortium so long as the costs of each identical firm rise by the same amount. However, when firms face different costs of R&D, raising the cost of R&D among firms with relatively high costs of R&D lowers the gain of remaining outside the consortium for such firms.

These simulation results have one interesting policy implication. So long as consortia organized under the auspices of government research labo-ratories are required to share the results of their research, they are unlikely to be successful vehicles for developing generic technologies with benefits that are relatively appropriable and competitively nonneutral. One re-sponse might be to restrict access to the technology developed by such consortia to members only. However, for reasons given above, it may be undesirable for other policy reasons to do so in the case of publicly or-ganized consortia. Hence, in such instances, privately organized consortia may ultimately prove to be a more successful arrangement for conducting such research, though government laboratories could still play a useful role by making their facilities available under contract to such private consortia.

5. Conclusions

Recent growth in cooperative research arrangements among private parties has been mirrored by increased interest in forming consortia to undertake research at public research facilities funded in whole or in large part by private industrial sponsors. The formation of such consortia can be viewed as an attempt to take advantage of the distinctive capabilities of certain public research facilities, such as those at the National Bureau of Standards, while at the same responding to fiscal constraints imposed by changes in the federal budget environment.

This chapter has focused on the financing of such ventures by their industrial sponsors. Two broad issues have been considered. First, is it desirable in principle to finance some research through government–industry research consortia? Second, is this form of finance viable in the long run?

With regard to the first question, the answer is clearly affirmative. Real savings in the form of reduced duplication of facilities and effort can be achieved through such consortia, relative to the alternative of each firm conducting research on its own.

Moreover, if adequate financing can be secured from private sponsors, it is also desirable to place greater reliance on private sources of support relative to the alternative of funding such research out of general public revenue. A necessary though not sufficient condition for membership is that the net payoff of research conducted by the consortium be greater than that to research conducted by each potential member acting on its own. Hence, greater reliance on government–industry consortia reduces the chance that scarce public laboratory facilities will be devoted to research that could just as easily be conducted in the private domain.

However, because it is unfeasible as well as undesirable to prevent the results of research conducted by such consortia from being widely disseminated to nonmembers, there is reason for concern that adequate voluntary support may not be forthcoming. Thus, some consortia may not be formed at all, or may be supported at less than desired levels, even though there would be a real economic payoff to cooperative government–industry reserch. However, at least where infratechnologies and nonappropriable generic technologies are involved, the problem may not so severe as to fundamentally limit the the viability of at least some amount of public–private cooperative research.

First, we have noted that the incentive to act as a free-rider, at least in the case of developing an infratechnology, becomes weaker the greater the comparative payoff is to research conducted by the consortium, and also the more uncertain the research outcome is. Hence, when there are difficulties in organizing government–industry consortia, one reason may be that the comparative advantage of organizing research in this fashion is modest to begin with. Another may be that the research to be conducted is fairly low-risk. In effect, placing greater reliance on government–industry consortia is less likely to screen out *high payoff/high risk* than *low payoff/ low risk* projects.

Moreover, there are several ways in which both the process by which consortia are formed and the structure of the consortia themselves can be used to foster a strategy of participation. If in the process of forming the consortium, potential members can be made to feel that failure to participate will have an impact on whether the consortium comes into existence, or on the ability of the consortium to support an adequate research program, the payoff for acting as a free-rider is reduced. Similarly, even though the results of the research must be shared widely, input into the design and conduct of the research can be restricted to members only. Members can also be entitled to receive regular reports on the progress and direction of the research in order to permit them to modify their own research and production decisions in a timely manner. Finally, where possible, the proposed research can be structured so that it complements the existing research activities of potential members.

It should be emphasized, however, that these observations are most applicable to the cases of infratechnologies and generic technologies, where it is difficult for a single firm to appropriate all of the gains from developing the technology. When it is possible to capture all or most of the gains from developing a generic technology, the incentive to remain outside the consortium derives not so much from the potential gain from acting as a free-rider in the traditional sense, but rather from the possibility of capturing a potential prize that may not have to be shared.

In such cases, requiring that the results of research conducted by the consortium be shared with all parties my be a serious obstacle to adequate levels of participation, even though all parties would be better off if they could agree to conduct research cooperatively rathe than individually. Accordingly, privately as opposed to publicly organized research consortia may be a more viable means of supporting such research, with government research laboratories limiting their role perhaps to making facilities available to private consortia on a contractual basis.

Notes

* Since completing this paper, the National Bureau of Standards has been renamed the National Institute of Standards and Technology (NIST).

1. Consortia of this type, as well as research joint ventures, are discussed and analyzed in [5] and [6].

2. A description and results of the simulation model are available upon request from the authors.

3. Some preliminary empirical tests of the model presented in [11] have produced pro-

mising results and suggest that the factors described in the text do affect the decisions of firms to participate in publicly organized research consortia.

References

1. Link, A., and Tassey, G. *Strategies for Technology-Based Competition: Meeting the New Global Challenge.* Lexington, MA: D.C. Heath and Company, 1987.
2. Tassey, G. "The Economic Role of the Bureau of Standards." *IEEE Transactions in Engineering Management* 33 (August, 1988) 162–171.
3. Cordes, J.J., and Steuerle, C.E. "The Effect of Tax Reform on Budget, Tax and Social Policy Making." *Proceedings of the 80th Annual Conference of the National Tax Association-Tax Institute of America*, 1988, forthcoming.
4. Cordes, J.J. "Government Funding vs. Government Supply of Public Services: A Survey of the Literature With Special Emphasis on Contracting Out." Mimeo, prepared for the Program Office, National Bureau of Standards, June, 1985.
5. Bozeman, B.; Link, A.; and Zardkoohi. "An Economic Analysis of R&D Joint Ventures." *Managerial and Decision Economics* 7 (1986): 263–266.
6. Link, A., and Bauer, L.L. "An Economic Analysis of Cooperative Research." *Technovation* 6 (1987): 246–260.
7. Grossman, G.M., and Shapiro. "Research Joint Ventures: An Antitrust Analysis." *Journal of Law, Economics, and Organization* 2 (2) (Fall, 1986): 315–337.
8. Katz, M.L. "An Analysis of Cooperative Research and Development." *Rand Journal of Economics* 17 (4) (Winter, 1986): 527–543.
9. Olson, M. *The Logic of Collective Action: Public Goods and the Theory of Groups.* Cambridge MA: Harvard University Press, 1965.
10. Cordes, J.J. and Watson, H.S. "Strategic Behavior and Participation in Cooperative Research." Mimeo, The George Washington University, 1988.
11. Cordes, J.J. "Some Preliminary Evidence on the Determinants of Participation by Private Companies in Industrial Research Consortia at the National Bureau of Standards." Mimeo, prepared for the Program Office, National Bureau of Standards, January, 1988.

3 UNIVERSITY–INDUSTRY RELATIONS: A REVIEW OF MAJOR ISSUES

Eliezer Geisler and Albert H. Rubenstein*

1. Introduction

The relationship and the collaboration processes between universities and industrial companies have been the subject of increased interest in the past decade. Several workshops have been conducted, some sponsored by Federal agencies [1, 2, 3], others by universities and commercial entities [4, 5, 6, 7]. The National Science Foundation conducted and funded major efforts in industry–university cooperative research [8, 9]; such programs include the recently established engineering research centers in several universities. In other such programs, the Industry–University Collaborative Research Centers (IUCRC) involve multicompany arrangements in which each company pays a participant annual fee [10, 11].

Although there is a relatively limited *research* literature on this topic, there are many reports, proceedings of symposia, think pieces, and

*Research for this study was funded, in part, by International Applied Science and Technology Associates, Inc.

descriptions of existing and planned collaborative relations between universities and industry.

In approaching the topic, academics and practitioners alike tend to concentrate on issues perceived to be major barriers to the initiation, implementation, and successful consummation of university–industry relations. Some of the issues emphasize differences in the culture, policies, expectations, and rules of conduct between universities and their industrial partners. Moreover, in much of the literature we reviewed, euphemisms abound for what appears to be a very central issue for both parties to potential cooperation: financial viability[1] [12, 13].

Why do universities and industry choose to cooperate? A 1982 NSF survey of 400 cases of university–industry research relations [18] identified 12 main reasons. Industry respondents listed access to students and professors; access to technology for problem-solving or obtaining state-of-the-art information; prestige; economical use of resources; support of technical excellence; and proximity and access to university facilities. University researchers listed access to scientific/technical areas where industry has special expertise; opportunity to expose students to practical problems; use of ear-marked government funds; and potential employment for graduates [17, 19, 20].

In the review of current literature, we have identified six major issues or categories of key factors impinging upon the following questions: Why do universities and industry cooperate? What are the more effective mechanisms for such cooperation? What are the main barriers to such cooperation? (1) Inherent differences in mission and objectives 2) differences in organizational structure and policies; 3) differences in orientation and interests of individual researchers; 4) effectiveness of university–industry arrangements and mechanisms for collaboration; 5) benefits versus costs; and 6) how to evaluate university–industry interaction. Table 3–1 summarizes these and the subissues of university–industry relations.

2. A Review of Major Issues

2.1. Inherent Differences in Mission and Objectives

2.1.1. Research Orientation, Time Horizon, Methods. Historically, the differences in the social-economic mission and the division of labor between university and industry were relatively clear and free of conflict. Universities were destined to contribute to general knowledge, and industry's mission was to use it. This clear division, ironicially, may have

Table 3–1. Major Issues in University–Industry Relations

---

1. *Inherent Differences in Mission and Objectives*
   1.1 Research orientation, horizon, and method [5, 6, 13, 17]
   1.2 Free inquiry versus confidentiality [14, 21]
   1.3 Exclusivity in utilization of research results [14, 21]

2. *Differences in Organizational Structure, and Policies*
   2.1 Conflicting structural formats
   2.2 Compensation for university researcher [14, 21, 22, 23]
   2.3 Consulting relations [24, 25, 26, 27, 28]
   2.4 Funding the cost of research [6, 17, 29]
   2.5 Diversity of interests and values [17, 30, 31, 32]

3. *Differences in Orientation, Philosophy, and Interests of Individual Researchers*
   3.1 Conflict of commitment and interests [8, 33, 34]
   3.2 Promotion policies and constraints [16, 35, 36]
   3.3 In-house capabilities versus external help [3, 23, 27]
   3.4 Perceptions and attitudes [1, 17, 37, 38, 39, 40, 41]

4. *Effectiveness of University–Industry Arrangements and Mechanisms for Collaboration*
   4.1 Industrial extension services [1, 42]
   4.2 Procurement of services [23, 43]
   4.3 Cooperative research [3, 44]
   4.4 Research parks [1, 11, 34]

5. *Benefits versus Costs*
   5.1 Benefits to industry [8]
   5.2 Benefits to universities [45]
   5.3 Costs [3, 14, 39]

6. *How to Evaluate University–Industry Interaction*
   6.1 Overall evaluation of benefits and success [13, 15, 17]
   6.2 The use of indicators in the evaluation [46]

---

generated a perceived mismatch between the university orientation toward long-term research versus industry's preoccupation with short-term, product-oriented research [29]. Universities have chosen a role in society with the primary mission of educating future scientific and technical cadres, and of conducting research at the frontiers of science. Industry has practical problems to solve, with a short-term horizon. Thus, such inherent differences produce differences in style, behavior, and policies for inter-organizational interaction [15, 38, 47]. Moreover, each organization has developed different methods for interaction with its environment. Universities prefer cooperation; industry opts for competition and confrontation.

When cooperation is called for, the different approaches and their methods may prove to be incompatible and to an extent inadequate.

2.1.2. Free Inquiry versus Confidentiality.   In a discussion of the issue of free inquiry, A. Bartlett Giamatti, then Presideent of Yale University, suggested in 1982 that universities rely on certain principles with implications for their policies that tend to "strongly influence their propensity for external linkages" [14]. Universities insist on the freedom to publish, without any restriction or infringement, including oral communication of the results of academic research. Giamatti suggested that universities do allow for an industrial sponsor to apply for a patent or a license. In a recent survey, Fowler [29] reported that the *right to publish* was perceived by universities to constitute a major barrier to collaboration, but was not viewed as an impediment by industry respondents [29].

2.1.3. Exclusivity versus Broad Utilization of Research Results: Who Owns the Fruits of R&D Innovation?   Many universities tend to disapprove of exclusive rights to one company, although in certain circumstances, universities do grant exclusive licenses [14, 16, 21]. The issue seems to be even more generalized and involves this question: Who owns what in a university–industry relation? When industry provides uncommitted support for basic research, such as charitable contributions to education and research, the issue is less of a problem than when something useful results from more focused research. An example is the 1980 Interferon lawsuit [48], but other disputes have arisen as to who owns inventions [49, 50], technical data and test results [42], research equipment [37], manufacturing know-how [43], drawings, unpublished reports, and new methods, concepts and techniques.

Universities are pulled in several directions on this issue [13, 51]. Idealistically, many academics feel that the fruits of their research should be made available for the public good, regardless of the sponsor [30]. However, many inventors in universities want to benefit personally from potentially commercial research results [52]. In the biotechnology area, Congress has voiced concern over university faculty "holding equity positions in commercial ventures that coincide with their academic endeavors" [34].

There may be no clear solution, since both sponsors and doers of research seem to have legitimate claims. Each situation requires negotiation on the merits of the relationship, within a general policy framework and the legal environment of patent and invention rules [17, 21] and the emerging legal and ethical views of intellectual property.

2.2. Differences in Organizational Structure and Policies

This category of issues includes those factors that, acting as barriers or facilitators, impinge upon the behavior and the attitudes of scientists and managers on both sides of the university–industry interaction.

2.2.1. Conflicting Structural Formats. There is a contrast between the structure formats of a university research group and that of an industrial concern as perceived by both groups. Figure 3–1 shows such structural contrasts. There are several relevant potential difficulties in creating a lasting interaction. The basic difficulty on the industrial side seems to be the relative rigidity of the decision and communication channels. On the university side, the amorphous structure generates barriers to swift and unambiguous decision processes. Individual researchers who try to engage in on-going relations would thus confront these and the following problems.

2.2.2. Compensation for University Researchers. How will the university faculty members be compensated for work with industry? If the university allows payment in stock options, such a policy may raise ethical issues

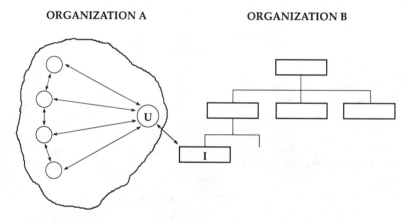

ORGANIZATION A   ORGANIZATION B

Source: Rubenstein [17].

Figure 3–1. Conflicting structural formats between university and industry. Individuals U and I are trying to find each other, and/or cooperate, and/or make a decision, and/or strike a deal. Organization A = University structure as perceived by industrial researchers. Organization B = Industrial structure as perceived by university researches.

and trigger problems of conflict of interests [14, 22, 23]. Most universities, in their patent policies, allow for certain percentages of the proceeds from inventions and discoveries to be paid directly to the inventor [21]. However, the complexity and, in many ways, inadequacy of such patent, licensing, and compensation policies can create biases, voids, and unclear situations that tend to be perceived as barriers to the interaction.

2.2.3. Consulting Relations.

Universities tend to allow faculty members to conduct limited consulting activities (usually one workday per week), and these activities are perceived to be beneficial to both the researcher and the institution [24]. Academic consultants can play a number of roles in contributing to industrial R&D, For example as idea generators, working team members, information sources and gatekeepers to literature or unpublished research results, linkages with the scientific community and leading universities, and reviewers of scientific work in the company [13, 17].

Many companies, however, have not learned to use academic consultants effectively. Some of this is because many consultants come in only occasionally, throw in some radical new idea or a bit of advice, and then leave with little or no followthrough. In addition, there are often psychological problems for industrial researchers who resent consultants who behave in a distant and superior manner [13].

On the other side of the interaction, universities tend to impose organizational limitations on the time expended and the scope or content of such consulting relations [28]. Some universities assess the consulting efforts in terms of their effects on the intellectual climate and balance in the academic department, particularly when consulting requires more than the personal time of the individual researcher [14]. Most universities formally require the faculty member to obtain permission of the dean or the chairperson, potentially adding a bureaucratic hurdle to the initiation and the maintenance of university–industry interactions [25, 26, 27].

2.2.4. Funding the Cost of Research.

Industrial companies tend to be reluctant to fund the total cost of joint research ventures, particularly with regard to the university's indirect costs [6, 29]. Rigorous time allocation of key faculty personnel to the university–industry interaction is not always possible, and there are differences between the university and the company on what constitutes the real cost of research. In addition, outstanding university researchers, who have become used to large government grants, may be less than enthusiastic about industrial support, usually for applied research, at much lower levels of funding and with as many or more strings attached [17].

A general problem that may not be obvious to people outside the university community is that the value system of the university community is far from monolithic [30, 47]. The competing objectives of obtaining funds for general university purposes versus obtaining funding for very specific research projects of individual faculty members are a source of potential conflict [11, 53]. In one form, this potential conflict may be exacerbated by block grants to universities for subsequent dispersal internally. University research centers and interdisciplinary programs have been used as dispersal mechanisms in this connection. Some faculty members, especially those who may not have had much experience or success in raising outside project funds themselves, may prefer this two-step procedure. Others— including perhaps the more entrepreneurial practitioners of grantsmanship —may be negatively inclined toward this system. They may see it as reducing the amount of money they can get for their own programs from a given source [1, 22]. This problem is sometimes prevalent in the planning and operation of science parks and innovation centers [15, 29].

The view of the university administrator and the trustees is likely to be more focused on general operating revenue with as few strings attached as possible. As discussed above, individual research-oriented faculty members may strongly prefer funds earmarked for research. These differences also apply at the departmental level, where conflicts abound over division of available resources between general purposes and specific research projects. The industrial partner to a relationship with a university would do well to become familiar with these potential differences and be prepared to negotiate within that context [17, 28]. On the other hand, such differences tend to create barriers in cooperation between university departments or even research groups across departments.

2.2.5. Diversity of Interests and Values. As mentioned earlier, within universities, as in industry, there is hardly a unified system of values and interests [30, 47]. The different interests of entrepreneurial faculty and those within academic fields that are hard to sell or not as glamorous may create conflicts and barriers to the propensity of universities and their faculty to cooperate with industry [1, 50, 54].

2.3. Differences in Orientation, Philosophy, and Interests of Individual Researchers

2.3.1. Conflict of Commitment and Interest. Many university researchers encounter difficulties in adjusting their commitments to the institution (primary duties) with their desire to be involved with external research, particularly with industry [8, 33, 34]. They tend to perceive the primary duties as teaching, publishing, and research, whereas practical involvement with industrial settings and problems (albeit scientifically challenging) seems to conflict with such duties in competing for faculty time [30]. Moreover, although many university faculty are essentially lone-wolf individualists, with specialized interests and insulated areas of scientific curiosity, they nevertheless develop institutional loyalties. Thus, they tend to organize their activities in the best interests and in conjunction with the objectives and the mission of their university. In some respects, working with industry represents a distraction and taxes faculty resources.

Industry researchers, on the other hand, find it even more difficult to allocate their time to interactions with univeristy. Their commitment to company priorities tends to collide with the more academic and exploratory aspects of university research [53, 55].

2.3.2. Promotion Policies and Constraints.

Faculties in research universities are required to conduct basic research and to publish the results. Such research outputs are then used in promotion and compensation decisions. Therefore, when working on industrial-type problems, faculty may feel constrained by limitations of time and by the publishability of the research they undertake. This is particularly the case with junior faculty, reluctant to join an industry-sponsored project that demands time but may not hold much promise of academic outputs and rewards [16, 35, 36].

2.3.3. In-House Capabilities versus External Help.

Many industrial scientists tend to have a psychological barrier against the employment of university consultants. They may feel that their in-house capabilities are sufficient to carry out the necessary tasks. In addition, R&D units in industry undergo periodic assessments of their performance, thus having to justify cooperative effort with universities and the spending of scarce resources for the acquisition of skills and capabilities that they may feel they already do or should possess [3, 23, 27].

2.3.4. Perceptions and Attitudes.

Individual researchers, on both sides of the university/industry interaction, have formed certain attitudes that tend to foster a culture gap or lack of understanding, even in those interactions that have a reasonable level of success. Industry researchers perceive faculty as unable to "effectively perform directed research" [14]. University faculty tend to perceive industrial research as oriented towards nonacademic problem-solving [1, 38, 47]. These attitudes and perceptions can create a somewhat self-imposed division of labor, accentuating the gap between so-called *exploratory* and *applied* research agendas [17, 37, 39, 40, 41] and thus making a smooth transition or technology transfer more difficult.

2.4. Effectiveness of University–Industry Arrangements and Mechanisms for Collaboration

There are several general types of university–industry arrangements and a variety of specific mechanisms designed to initiate and to maintain the interaction. In each such arrangement, many of the aforementioned issues may be relevant factors in the initiation, continuation, and success of the interaction.[2] In addition, each arrangement and specific mechanism is influenced by other factors and issues. Table 3–2 provides a description of types of university–industry arrangements and illustrative mechanisms associated with these arrangements.

Table 3–2.   Types and Mechanisms of University–Industry Relations

Type of Arrangement	*Modes of Interaction and Some Mechanisms*
1. Industrial Extension Services	1.1 Information transfer and consulting [17, 46, 56].
	1.2 Workshops, classes [9, 28]
	1.3 Undirected corporate gifts to university funds [27, 31, 39]
	1.4 Capital contributions to university departments, centers, laboratories [29, 37, 42]
	1.5 Industrial fellowships [9, 16, 57]
2. Procurement of Services	2.1 By university from industry. Prototype development, fabrication, testing, on-the-job training for students, theses topics and advisors, specialized training [26, 38, 58, 59]
	2.2 By industry from university. Education and training of employees (degree programs, continuing education); contract research, consulting services [17, 60]
	2.3 Industrial associates. Industry pays fee to university to have access to total resources of the university [2, 7, 13]
3. Cooperative Research	3.1 Joint research planning and execution [10, 13, 17, 53]
	3.2 Faculty and student participation [1, 61, 62]
	3.3 Cooperative research projects: direct cooperation

Table 3–2.   (*continued*)

Type of Arrangement	Modes of Interaction and Some Mechanisms
	between university and industry scientists on projects of mutual interest; usually basic, nonproprietary research. No money changes hands; each sector pays salaries of own scientists. May involve temporary transfers of personnel for conduct of research [1, 17, 50, 57, 63]
	3.4 Cooperative research programs: industry support of portion of university research project (balance paid by university, private foundation, government); results of special interest to company; variable amount of actual interaction [53, 64, 65]
	3.5 Research consortia: single university, multiple companies, basic and applied research on generic problem of special interest to entire industry; industry receives special reports, briefings, and access to facilities [11, 13]
4. Research Parks	4.1 Research cooperation on frontiers of science and technology [32, 56]
	4.2 Informal interactions [13, 17]
	4.3 Increased sharing of research facilities and participation in consulting, seminars, and continuing education [11, 39, 53]
	4.4 Contractual arrangement—specific and detailed; both parties contribute substantially to the enterprise [44, 48, 66, 67]

As the table shows, university–industry interaction may range from a one-shot transfer of information to a complex and long-term relationship, as in a research park or a cooperative research center [31, 55].

The more complex, long-term, and binding the type of arrangement, the more complex may be the issues involved. In complex relationships, such as the joint research park, issues such as commitment of researchers and sharing of funding become crucial to the continuation and the success of the enterprise [15, 19, 68]. Furthermore, as the contacts between researchers on both sides become more frequent and more intense, differences in the culture and other misconceptions may be accentuated, or they may be diminished, due to an increased understanding on both sides. The general belief is that the outcome depends on the individual conditions and circumstances of each case [1, 3, 23, 42, 43, 44].

The *range* of mechanisms and forms of relationships can provide a facilitator to cooperation in that high flexibility can help in selecting a potentially effective mechanism. It can also present a barrier in terms of delays and decision-making and extended studies of the best way of cooperating. In many instances, the search for the optimal pattern may be self-defeating, since most mechanisms have their limitations and advantages. A healthy relationship should involve multiple mechanisms and linkages between the firm and the university. One-shot deals for a specific piece of technical cooperation may be of short-run benefit to a particular industrial project or a particular university financial need, yet may not build the kind of relationships that can help in the long run. Rather than search for the optimal means of cooperation, several apparently attractive linkages should be tried for a period of time to see which ones survive. This means avoiding an initial approach that leads to a rigorous test of whether a firm and a university can work together. In order for relationships to develop and mature and for mistakes to be made and overcome, long time periods are needed, sometimes on the order of several years.

2.5. Benefits versus Costs

Several academic and industry researchers and managers have written on the topic of what can be gained from university–industry interaction [2, 3, 35, 36, 38]. Table 3–3 summarizes various benefits that may accrue to industry and universities as the result of the interaction.

2.5.1. Benefits to Industry.   In a 1984 study, the National Science Foundation (NSF) surveyed 226 university and industry principal researchers [8]. The study found that both university and industry respondents felt that the joint effort improved their ability to cooperate with each other. University respondents showed more optimism than industry researchers with regard to "likelihood of tangible benefits occurring to the firm" [8].

2.5.2. Benefits to Universities.   Universities appear to interact with industry primarily to acquire funding for basic research and to support the university's facilities [45]. Industrial support is seen by universities as requiring a lesser amount of reporting requirements than government grants, and is a source for consulting opportunities for individual faculty members.

2.5.3. Costs.   The costs associated with the interaction, on the part of the university, seem to be in terms of potential disequilibrium of the research agenda [14] and the orientation of faculty away from its primary mission

Table 3–3.   Potential Benefits from University–Industry Interactions

1. *Benefits to Industry*
   — Window to technological state-of-the art [1, 14, 45]
   — Systematic review of faculty research results [7, 21]
   — Specific skills and knowledge provided by faculty consultants [22, 23, 29, 56]
   — Training of industrial scientific/technical personnel–part-time, full-time,
      on-site, night courses [26, 27]
   — Participation of faculty members in industrial conferences [29]
   — Source of highly skilled scientific/technical employees [6]
   — Increased rate of technological progress in fields of lagging technology [6, 17]
   — Solving specific problems for industrial projects [24, 25]
   — Joint effort, start-up businesses, economic payoffs [31]
   — Access to university facilities [5, 14]

2. *Benefits to University*
   — Practical updating of faculty and students [3, 23]
   — Funding for research as well as capital investments [1, 37, 38]
   — Development of university curricula [6]
   — Summer employment and other opportunities for students [6, 23, 26]
   — Industrial membership on university advisory committees [39]
   — Access to industrial facilities and equipment [1, 23, 37, 43]
   — Ability to utilize government funds for applied research with industry [23,
      34, 43]
   — Joint effort, start-up businesses, economic payoffs [31, 32]

of teaching and publishing. For industry, a major cost is the possibility of industrial scientists becoming too involved with basic research and "losing sight of practical solutions" [3]. Another cost is part of the evaluation of the cost-effectiveness experienced by the company as a consequence of its monetary outlays in the interaction, related to the question: Are we getting our money's worth? [39].

2.6. How to Evaluate University–Industry Interaction

The multifacets and the longer-term aspect of university–industry interaction are the prime difficulties in arriving at an agreed-upon mechanism for its evaluation [17]. There are two major approaches to the evaluation of such interactions: 1) overall evaluation of benefits and success [15], and 2) the use of specific indicators to evaluate levels of accomplishment of selected dimensions or aspects of the interaction [5, 46, 69].

2.6.1. Overall Evaluation of Benefits and Success. As in many interorganizational interactive processes, university–industry interactions may be evaluated on the basis of the overall success and the benefits resulting from the process. Overall success may be determined by surveys of key participants and their judgment as to success or failure [3, 9]. A variant approach may include the identification of the needs and expectations both partners have, followed by the subsequent comparison with actual or perceived satisfaction of these needs, once more by surveying key partipants [7, 13, 40].

The problems with these approaches are 1) differences between industry and university key participants on the definition of the success of the interaction, including differing views of what constitutes a successful or beneficial outcome; and 2) the relatively long term usually required for an interorganizational cooperation to be declared accomplished so that judgments may be made regarding its accomplishments. Moreover, attempts to evaluate individual stages of the process are usually opposed by key participants from both sides of the interaction with the pretext of "It's too early to tell," or "Give it more time" [15, 19, 20].

2.6.2. The Use of Indicators in the Evaluation. Perhaps a more useful approach is the use of selected categories of quantitative indicators to measure the level or, in some instances, the intensity of the interaction, subject to a subsequent judgmental assessment of the indicators by key participants.[3] The main advantage of this procedure over the previously mentioned overall evaluation is the utilization of quantitiative indicators of the process and outcomes of the interaction as the basis for a judgmental assessment, as well as qualifiers to such an assessment, e.g., by virtue of documented factual indices.

An initial list of potential indicators is given in table 3–4. The list has been composed from the literature and from the authors' experience in research and consulting. The first category of indicators focuses on dimensions of the conduct of university–industry interaction. The indicators are operational measures of selected occurrences in the life of the interaction and can be collected by periodic access to files and reports. Additionally, some indicators provide a qualitative or judgmental assessment. These can be collected through surveys of participants at given dates and occasions.

The second category contains indicators of short-term outcomes from the interaction, primarily those we consider critical to any successful interaction. The third category includes indicators of the longer-term outcomes, where the more lasting impacts of the interaction may be observed and measured. Finally, we propose a fourth category of indicators of the type

Table 3–4.   Initial List of Potential Indicators of University–Industry Interaction

1. *Indicators of the Process of Interaction*[1]	2. *Immediate (Short-Term) Outputs/ Outcomes from Interaction*
Potential Indicators[2]	*Potential Indicators*
1.1 Number of contacts between parties at each stage of the interaction	2.1 Change in probability of interaction in the future
1.2 Organizational level of contacts	2.2 Number of commitments made: monetary information and personnel exchange, access to facilities
1.3 Duration/intensity level of contacts (brief conversation, meetings, etc.)	2.3 Number of agreements drawn up (grants, licenses, joint ventures)
1.4 *Flavor* of contact (pleasant, stressful)	2.4 Number of contracts signed
1.5 Focus of contact (administrative, technical)	2.5 Amounts of money changing hands
1.6 Type of participants in contact (individuals, groups, researchers/administrators)	2.6 Number of technical problems solved
1.7 Usefulness of information content of contacts (by survey of participants)	2.7 Number of reports delivered
1.8 Perceptions of the *seriousness* or *integrity* of the other party in participating in contact	2.8 Number of conferences, workshops, symposia, and joint seminars conducted
1.9 Number of decisions made in contacts	2.9 Number of fellowships established
1.10 Organizational level at which decisions were made	2.10 Number of faculty hired as consultants to industry
1.11 Resources initially allocated to contacts (people, facilities)	2.11 Number of graduate students hired by industry
	2.12 Number of joint projects established
	2.13 Number of industrial researchers as guest lecturers at university
	2.14 Number of patents, inventions, and innovations in joint effort

3. *Longer-Term Outputs/Outcomes from Interaction*	4. *Type and Pattern of Interaction*
Potential Indicators	*Potential Indicators*
3.1 Number of faculty accepting employment with industry	4.1 Time to fruition of interactions (days, weeks, years to research agreements or research results)
3.2 Number of spin-off enterprises	4.2 Levels of each organization involved in a given interaction
3.3 Number of consortia developed	
3.4 Number of third-party	

involvements (government, venture capital firms)

3.5 Level of third-party involvement ($)

3.6 Level of satisfaction with interaction among participants

3.7 Impacts on teaching

3.8 Level of industrial support for research centers and programs

3.9 Changes in percent or number of faculty with industrial contacts

3.10 Changes in patent and licensing rules and other procedures to accommodate needs of other party to interaction

3.11 Changes in general perception of needs, quality, and motives of other party

3.12 Developing of networks: change in average number of regular contacts

3.13 Changes in production rates, sales, productivity, profits, and other indicators of success attributed to interaction

4.3 Degree of institutionalization of contacts (multiyear agreements, permanent committees formed, etc.)

4.4 Formation of Advisory Boards and degree of formalizing interaction mechanisms

---

[1] *Process* includes, but is not limited to, such aspects of the interaction as inputs of resources, professional activities, and decision and other managerial processes.

[2] Possible measures for the indicators may range from *number of* (as included in some indicators), to *degree of: usefulness, intensity, etc.*, to be provided by surveying key participants and entering responses on a scale.

and pattern of interactions. These indicators are related to the four modes of interaction shown in table 3–2, in that they indicate the degree of formalization or institutionalization of the relationship, from the short-term, one-shot extension or consulting service, to the longer-term establishment of research parks.

Such relations are illustrated in table 3–5.

The table suggests a correspondence between the short-term relations and indicators that measure the process of interaction and the immediate outputs. The longer-term arrangements, such as cooperative research and research parks, are evaluated by indicators of longer-term outputs.

Table 3–5 may thus be a preliminary framework for the evaluation of

Table 3–5.   Illustrative Examples of Indicators to Evaluate Selected Types of
University–Industry Relations

Type of Arrangement	Illustrative Indicators
1. Industrial Extension Services	1.1 Change in probability of interaction in future 1.2 Number of technical problems solved 1.3 Number of fellowships established 1.4 Amounts changing hands 1.5 Number of symposia, seminars, etc.
2. Procurement of Services	2.1 Number of patents, inventions, innovations 2.2 Number of faculty hired by industry 2.3 Number of training programs established 2.4 Number of joint projects
3. Cooperative Research	3.1 Number of research consortia developed 3.2 Size and shape of research consortia 3.3 Number of spin-off enterprises 3.4 Changes in general perceptions of needs, quality, and motives
4. Research Parks	4.1 Degree of institutionalization of relations 4.2 Number and level of third-party involvement 4.3 Level of continuing (multiyear) industrial support 4.4 Level of satisfaction with interaction

different types of university–industry relations, by providing indicators of
outputs from the relation.

3. Conclusions

Universities and industrial companies interact despite many barriers and
differences in their objectives, organizational structure, and policies, including orientation, philosophy, and interests of researchers. Successful
interactions provide lasting benefits to both parties. Researchers and their
managers, from both sides of the interaction, may evaluate the progress
and the outputs of the interaction by using a combination of quantitative
indicators and judgmental assessments.

Although short-term, one-shot relations may prove beneficial to the
parties, the longer and more lasting cooperation seems to bear the more
positive and beneficial outcomes to both industry and universities because
of the psychological, organizational, and social aspects of the interaction.

Notes

1. Many university and industrial researchers believe that an important factor driving universities to closer relations with industry is their need for financing to remain solvent, as pressures mount due to falling government support coupled with significant increases in costs of operations, research, salaries, and maintaining campus facilities [13–17]. Additionally, recent concerns about the possible effects of Gramm–Rudman–Hollings may significantly contribute to increased university–industry contacts.

2. Industry and university leaders have conducted several joint conferences since 1980 to discuss general contractual arrangements, including the pioneering Pajaro Dunes conference of March 1982 [14] and the Philadelphia meeting of December 1982 [34].

3. Such judgmental assessment may be required for lack of established and agreed-upon norms of acceptable or successful levels of the interaction, as measured by the various indicators.

References

1. Barker, R. "Bringing Science into Industry from Universities." *Research Management* 28 (6) (November–December, 1985): 22–24.
2. National Science Fundation and The Society of Research Administrators. "Industry–University Research Relations—A Workshop for Faculty." The University of Texas at Dallas, April 11, 1983.
3. National Science Foundation. *Industrial Innovation Processes: Implications for Public Policy.* Proceedings of the 1983 Conference on Industrial Science and Technological Innovation, Skokie, IL, May 2–4, 1983.
4. Bruce, J., and Tamaribuchi, K. "MIT's Industrial Liaison Program." *Journal of the Society of Research Administrators* 12 (Winter, 1981):
5. Eveland, J., and Hetzner, W. "University–Industry Cooperative Research Centers: Dimensions of Initial Development." Paper presented at the Annual Meeting of ORSA/TIMS, San Diego, CA, October 26, 1982.
6. Kiefer, D. "Forging New and Stronger Links Between Universities and Industrial Scientists." *Chemical and Engineering News* (December 8, 1980): 38–51.
7. Lien, A. "What Industry Needs and Expects from Universities." In: *Proceedings of the National Conference on the Availability of New Technology to Industry from American Universities and Technological Institutes,* Chicago, IIT (April 2–5, 1973) 1–2.
8. National Science Foundation. *Cooperative Science. A National Study of University and Industry Researchers.* Volume I, November, 1984.
9. National Science Foundation. *Cooperative Science: A National Study of University and Industry Researchers.* Case Studies, Volume II, November, 1984.
10. Colton, R. "Status Report on the NSF University–Industry Cooperative Research Centers." *Research Management* 28 (6) (November-December, 1985): 25–31.

11. Walsh, J. "New R&D Centers will Test University Ties." *Science* 227 (January 11, 1985): 150–152.
12. Norman, C. "The Growing Corporate Role in University Budgets." *Science* 220 (February 25, 1983): 939.
13. Rubenstein, A.H. "Mechanisms for Industry–University Cooperation in R&D Innovation." Paper presented at the TMS/ORSA Meeting, Colorado Springs, Colorado, November, 1980.
14. Giamatti, B. "The University, Industry and Cooperative Research." *Science* 218 (December 24, 1982): 1278–1280.
15. Gibb, J.M. (ed.). *Science Parks and Innovation Centers: Their Economic and Social Impact.* Proceedings of the Conference held in Berlin, 13–15 February, 1985. New York: Elsevier Science Publishing Co., 1985.
16. Headlum, A. "Connecting University Research with Industrial Technology— The role of the Research Administrator." *SRA Newsletter* 15 (5) (March/April, 1983): . . . .
17. Rubenstein, A.H. "Some Issues in Research Relations Between Universities and Industry." Paper presented at the Northwestern–NSF Conference on Innovation, May, 1983.
18. Norman, C. "Audit May Cost UC Millions." *Science* 216 (April 16, 1982): 279.
19. Segal, Quince, Wicksteed & Partners. *The Cambridge Phenomenon: The Growth of High Technology Industry in a University Town*, 1985.
20. Sparks, J. "The Creative Connection: University–Industry Relations." *Research Management*, 28 (6) (November-December, 1985): 19–21.
21. Northwestern Unviersity. *Patent and Invention Policy.* September 30, 1974.
22. Azaroff, L. "Industry–University Collaboration. How to Make it Work." *Research Management* 25, (3) (May, 1982): 31–34.
23. Marshall, E. "NYU's Malaria Vaccine: Orphan at Birth?" *Science* 219, (February 4, 1983): 466–467.
24. Edelen, M. "Faculty Urged to Freelance." *Lehigh Horizons*, September, 1983.
25. Fox, J. "Retiring Frees NIH 'Guest' to Consult." *Science* 224 (June 1, 1984): 966.
26. Marshall, B. "Government-University Relationships" (letter to editor). *Science* 215 (1982): 1564.
27. Norman, C. "Chip Makers Turn to Academe with Offer of Research Support." *Science* 216 (May, 1982): 601.
28. Rothwell, R. "The Commercialization of University Research." *Physics in Technology*, September, 1982.
29. Fowler, D. "University–Industry Research Relationships." *Research Management* 27 (1) (January–February 1984): 35–41.
30. Lepkowski, W. "Academic Values Tested by MIT's New Center." *Chemical and Engineering News* (March 15, 1982): 7–12.
31. Prager, D., Omehn, G. "Research, Innovation, and University–Industry Linkages." *Science* 207 (January 23, 1980): 379–384.
32. Smith, L., and Karlesky, J. (eds.). *The State of Academic Science: The*

Universities in the Nation's Research Effort. New Rochelle, NY: Change Magazine Press, 1977.

33. Culliton, B. "Academic and Industry Debate Partnership." *Science* 219 (January 14, 1983): 150–151.
34. Culliton, B. "New Biology Foundation Off to a Good Start." *Science* 220 (May 20, 1983): 803.
35. Norman, C. "Pentagon Seeks to Build Bridges to Academe." *Science* 228 (April 19, 1985): 303–305.
36. U.S. Dept. of Commerce. *A New Climate for Joint Research.* Conference Proceedings, May 13, 1983.
37. Chakrabarti, A. "University–Industry Cooperative Research: Some Lessons in Insitution Building." Paper presented at the WPI/NSF Conference, May, 1983.
38. National Academy of Engineering. *Issues in Engineering Education.* Washington, DC, April, 1980.
39. Roberts, E., and Peters, D. "Commercial Innovations from University Faculty." *Research Policy* 10 (1981): 108–126.
40. Tamaribuchi, K. "Effectively Linking Industry with a University Resource: A Survey of University–Industry Liaison Programs." Paper presented at the WPI/NSF Conference on Management of Technological Innovation, May, 1983.
41. Whiteley, R., and Postma, H. "How National Laboratories Can Supplement Industry's In-House R&D Facilities." *Research Management.* (November, 1982): 31–42.
42. "Business and Universities: A New Partnership." *Business Week* (December 20, 1982): 58–61; and "Corporations Bet on Campus R&D." *Business Week* (December 20, 1982): 61–62.
43. Conway, L. *The MPC Adventures, Experiences with the Generation of VLSI Design and Implementation methodologies.* Xerox, Palo Alto Research Center, 1981.
44. Walsh, J. "NSF Sets Ground Rules for Enterprising Grantees." *Science* 220 (June 3, 1983): 1029.
45. National Science Foundation. "University–Industry Research Relationships." 14th Annual Report to the National Science Board, October 1, 1982.
46. Rubenstein, A. H., and Geisler, E. "The use of Indicators and Measures of the R&D Process in Evaluating Science and Techonlogy Programs." In: J. Roessner (ed.), *Government Policies for Industrial Innovation: Design, Implementation, Evaluation.* New York: St. Martin's Press, 1988, pp. 185–204.
47. Abelson, P. "Differing Values in Academia and Industry." *Science* 217 (September 17, 1982): 4656.
48. Wade, N. "University and Drug Firm Battle over Billion-Dollar Gene." *Science* 209 (September 26, 1980): 1492–1494.
49. A. B. T. Associates *Factors Affecting University Spin-Off Firm Establishment.* Cambridge, MA, 1984.
50. Clauser, H. "New University Research Centers Linked to Industry." *Research Management*, perspectives, (January, 1981): 2.

51. Hise, R.; Futrell C.; and Snyder, D. "University Research Centers as a New Product Development Resource." *Research Management* 23 (6) (May, 1980): 25–28.
52. Newport, J. "Waiting for Lightning: Will Professor's Research Pay Off for University Patents?" *Fortune* (April 15, 1985): 105–106.
53. Sirbu, M.; Treitel, R.; Yorsz, W.; and Roberts, B. *The Formation of a Technology Oriented Complex: Lessons from North American and European Experiences*, CPA 76–8. Cambridge, MA: MIT, December, 1976.
54. Robertson, A. "Are Academic Inventions Wasted?" *The Business Graduate* 12 (1) (Spring, 1982):
55. Smith, D. "Contracts on the Campus." *Physics Bulletin* 28 (2) 2 (December, 1977):
56. U.S. Congress, House, Subcommittee on Science, Research, and Technology of the House Committee on Science and Technology. *Government and Innovation: University–Industry Relations, Hearings.* July 31-August 2, 1979, Government Printing Office, 53-868, 1979.
57. Hunt, N. "University–Industry Linkage." Paper prepared for the UNIDO, 1984.
58. Battenburg, J. "Forging Links Between Industry and The Academic World." *Journal of the Society of Research Administrators* 12 (Winter, 1981).
59. Rodman, J. "A Model for Inter-Institutional R&D Administration and Industry/University Relations." *Journal of the Society of Research Administrators* 13 (3) (Winter, 1982).
60. Peters, L., and Fusfeld, H. *University–Industry Research Relationships.* Washington, DC: Superintendent of Documents, US GPO, 1983.
61. Block, E. "Some Comments Concerning Industry–University Relationships in the 80's." *Journal of the Society of Research Administrators* 16 (1) (Summer, 1984):
62. Brodsky, N.; Kaufman, H.; and Tooker, J. *University–Industry Cooperation.* Center for Science and Technology Policy, NYU, 1980.
63. Cannon, P. "A Model for Industry–University Minority Doctoral Engineering Programs." *Research Management* 23 (4) (July, 1980): 21–23.
64. Johnson, E., and Tornatsky, L. "Academia and Industrial Innovation." In: G. Gold (ed.), *New Directions for Experimental Learning: Business and Higher Education—Toward New Alliances.* San Francisco: Jossey Bass, 1981, pp. 47–63.
65. Kerr, R. "Texas A&M to Direct Deep Sea Drilling." *Science* 220 (April 15, 1983): 287.
66. Wade, N. "Harvard Marches Up Hill and Down Again." *Science* 210 (December 5, 1980): 1104.
67. Wade, N. "La Jolla Biologist Troubled by the Midas Factor." *Science* 213 (August 7, 1981): 623–628.
68. MacKenzie, I. W., and Phystoner, R. P. *Commercialization of University Research.* London: Imperial College, 1983.
69. Dietrich, J., and Sen, R. "Making Industry–University Government Collaboration Work." *Research Management* 24 (September, 1981): 23–25.

II NATIONAL STRATEGIES

4 HISTORICAL AND ECONOMIC PERSPECTIVES OF THE NATIONAL COOPERATIVE RESEARCH ACT

John T. Scott*

1. Introduction

The National Cooperative Research Act of 1984 (NCRA) [1] codified U.S. public policy toward joint ventures in research and development (R&D). It provided, inter alia, that the behavior of a research consortium, if challenged under the U.S. antitrust laws, would be judged under a rule of reason asking whether the alleged restraints of trade were ancillary to the pursuit of efficiency. For those research ventures notifying the government of their participants and purposes, any subsequent antitrust violation would be assessed single, not treble, damages. The historical context of the NCRA is important; the act was passed during a dramatic redirection of U.S. government policy toward business combinations. Uncritical pronouncements about the efficacy of such combinations abounded.

The Reagan administration expected much good from business combinations. The declining international competitiveness of U.S. industrial

---

* This chapter has benefited from comments by William L. Baldwin, Meredith O. Clement, Theodore A. Gebhard, Albert N. Link, Geoffrey Woglom, and Everett W. Wood.

products added importance to the expectations. The claims of advocates of change in antitrust laws led to new laws and proposals for still more new laws championing combinations among U.S. industrial competitors as ways to promote efficiency and meet the challenges of international competitors.

That historical context of the NCRA, reviewed in section 2, implies that the act would have passed even if it were not sound economic policy. Section 3 reviews economic theory explaining why the NCRA may not promote desirable R&D behavior. In section 4, the administration of the NCRA is juxtaposed with the economics and the unique historical context to suggest that the policy is not based on serious evaluation—probably because policy-makers have been blinded by their uncritical assessments of the efficiencies of business combinations. The ventures encouraged by the NCRA may nonetheless promote desirable behavior. The evidence reviewed in section 5, however, does not hold much promise for that sanguine conclusion.

2. The Historical Context

The NCRA encourages research combinations among competitors. To establish the context of uncritical advocacy of business combinations, this section provides an overview of the Reagan administration's antitrust initiatives, describes its policy toward horizontal and conglomerate mergers, and explains the similarities in the approach to them and the NCRA's approach to R&D ventures.

Government regulation commonly denotes policies as diverse as the regulation of a public utility and the enforcement of our antitrust laws. Perhaps as a result, policies proscribing certain combinations among competitors are often considered unwarranted interferences with markets. The regulation of a public utility is direct regulation in which a regulatory authority prescribes prices and services. In contrast, our antitrust laws establish indirect regulation under which firms are free to compete according to the rules of the game legislated by the antitrust laws. The Department of Justice (DOJ) and the Federal Trade Commission (FTC) enforce those laws, and the courts interpret them. Such laws most prominently proscribe competing firms' colluding to set price or merging if competition would decrease.

The Reagan administration was tough on price fixers, but it was more relaxed than past administrations about other business combinations. Often that was good; some combinations promote efficiency. Undoubtedly in the past, antitrust enforcement *blocking* mergers at times went too far.[1] But the enforcement policies of the Reagan administration may have gone too far in *promoting* combinations. If so, the desire to promote U.S. international competitiveness and to reduce government regulation stimulated the excesses. Understanding the uncritical reorientation of antitrust policy toward business combinations is crucial for interpreting the NCRA and its enforcement.

2.1. New Directions for Antitrust Policy

William Baxter, antitrust chief at DOJ in the early years of the Reagan administration, initiated many important antitrust policies. As an Assistant Attorney General heading DOJ's Antitrust Division, he played a key role in antitrust policy. Baxter considered many Supreme Court rulings "rubbish," "wacko," or "ludicrous" [3]; he set out to instruct courts on proper application of the law. By simply not bringing cases that would traditionally have been brought, he could to a large extent make the administration's view the law. Policy was redirected for mergers—horizontal, vertical, and conglomerate—and for vertical restraints such as resale price maintenance. Published guidelines codified these new enforcement policies.[2]

President Reagan's first FTC chairman, James Miller, dramatically changed the focus of the Commission's work from its traditional orientation and the orientation of the Commission under the previous chairman, Michael Pertschuk, who had been appointed by President Carter. Many observers believe that under Pertschuk there was too much consumer activism. Apart from that possibility, broadly, the FTC was transformed from an agency that looked for inefficient markets where performance could be improved by government action to one that sought cases where government intervention in the marketplace had decreased economic performance.[3]

We have new laws promoting business combinations as well as new enforcement policies. The Commerce Department championed and won passage of new law—The Export Trading Company Act of 1982—promoting formation of export cartels by U.S. firms. Commerce and Justice promoted and won passage of the act that is the focus of this essay—the NCRA, which encourages research joint ventures among firms. In 1986, the Reagan administration's antitrust establishment proposed the enactment of five new laws that, among other things, would have codified its view of appropriate merger policy and reduced the damages that plaintiffs in certain types of antitrust suits could win from firms found in violation of the law [6].

These initiatives share a common philosophical foundation—namely, the belief that the performance of the economy will be improved if government interference with business behavior is lessened. Antitrust laws aim to set out rules of the competitive game, which, if followed, can allow a system of markets to work well. The question is how stringent those rules should be. In the area of mergers, should we begin to worry about a lack of competition, and therefore single out mergers for further scrutiny when the number of sellers in the industry would be decreased to say seven or eight, or four or five, or two or three? At what point should we begin to worry about the concentration of an industry's resources in the control of a few sellers (called seller concentration)? What other factors must we examine to estimate the potential for less competition?

An important theme, subsumed in the Reagan administration's general philosophy that government interference with the market should be lessened, is that policy should be less concerned with business combinations, whether via merger or joint venture. One can argue that the new policies regarding horizontal mergers, conglomerate mergers, and joint ventures in research and development show too little concern about business combinations. More importantly, as documented below, the Reagan administration—surely at least in part because of its concern with declining competitiveness of U.S. firms in global markets and in part because of its desire to deregulate markets—justified these policies by extraordinarily selective reference to theories and facts.

2.2. Horizontal Mergers

The new policy for a horizontal merger (one between firms competing in the same product and geographic market) explicitly weighs evidence of potential efficiencies from a merger against the likelihood of increased market power. But the U.S. Supreme Court's rulings under the current version of section 7 of the Clayton Act state that if a merger is likely to increase market power (the ability of the new firm, or the industry's firms together, to control price), the fact that it also increases productive efficiency (lowering costs) cannot make it legal. Potential operating efficiencies provide no defense for a merger that is otherwise illegal because of its probable effect on competition. "Possible economies cannot be used as a defense to illegality. Congress was aware that some mergers which lessen competition may also result in economies but it struck the balance in favor of protecting competition."[4]

Yet administrative procedure has now diverged from the precedent embodied in the Court's opinions. Baldwin's review [7] traces the evolution of merger policy. Since the Merger Notification Act of 1976, firms involved in a prospective merger above a certain size must notify both DOJ and the FTC. Notification is followed by a waiting period before the merger can be consummated. If either enforcement agency questions the proposed merger, a negotiated settlement is typically reached during the waiting period. Thus, most challenged mergers are no longer fought in the courts after the fact. As Baldwin [7] emphasizes, the decisions about whether mergers are allowed are not being made so much by the courts in a legal setting as by the current administration's departments and agencies, most notably DOJ and the FTC.[5] The Reagan administration accepted greater levels of postmerger concentration than would have been accepted by earlier administrations, and it explicitly incorporated an efficiency defense for otherwise illegal mergers.

Undoubtedly, if we *could* confidently identify the efficiencies of a merger, the absence of an efficiency defense for an otherwise illegal merger *would* in some cases lessen economic welfare, because gains from cost savings can outweigh losses from increased market power. But such efficiencies are difficult to establish, yet very easy to allege. Witness the uncertainties faced by the Reagan administration in its handling of the LTV–Republic Steel merger.[6]

Further, most potential economies could be achieved by internal expansion, which is often procompetitive and evidently far more likely to achieve efficiency than a merger [11, 12]. Nothing in antitrust law prevents the internal growth of firms that provide better products or produce at lower costs, although section 2 of the Sherman Act has been interpreted as proscribing internal growth to dominance not achieved by chance or better products or lower costs. Case law under section 2 of the Sherman Act has made clear that internal growth resulting from innovation is accepted under the rules of the game. Finally, for example in the 1945 Alcoa case and the 1962 Brown Shoe case, the courts have interpreted the antitrust laws as embodying the desires of Congress to promote not only economic efficiency narrowly construed, but also to ensure the dispersion of social and political power—to fulfill the Jeffersonian ideal of decentralized power. The courts have therefore been willing to give up the uncertain efficiencies a merger might bring, in return for the lower seller concentration maintained by blocking the merger. Yet the Reagan administration repeatedly said that the antitrust laws were intended to promote economic efficiency only. According to antitrust chief Baxter, "The sole goal of antitrust is economic efficiency" [3].[7]

In introducing DOJ's 1984 Merger Guidelines, Attorney General William French Smith referred to what he called "the latest legal and economic learning—recognizing that most merger activity does not threaten competition, but actually improves our economy's efficiency and thus benefits all consumers" [4]. In these guidelines, the Reagan administration,

although it claimed otherwise, made efficiency a defense to a challenge by
the enforcement agencies, whatever the courts might hold. In the statement
accompanying the release of the revised merger guidelines, the Department
claims that "...efficiencies do not constitute a defense to an otherwise
anticompetitive merger but are one of many factors that will be considered
by the Department in determining whether to challenge a merger" [4]. In
the guidelines themselves, the Department states,

> Some mergers that the Department otherwise might challenge may be reason-
> ably necessary to achieve significant net efficiencies. If the parties to the merger
> establish by clear and convincing evidence that a merger will achieve such ef-
> ficiencies, the Department will consider those efficiencies in deciding whether to
> challenge the merger....The parties must establish a greater level of expected
> net efficiencies the more significant are the competitive risks....[4].

Clearly, DOJ now weighs efficiency gains (from lower costs) against any
loss in efficiency (from higher prices) resulting from a merger. Further, one
of the proposed laws sent to Congress in 1986, the Merger Modernization
Act of 1986, would have amended section 7 of the Clayton Act to require
weighing efficiencies against any possible increase in market power. The
new language implied illegality would require a probability of increased
market power greater than required under the current law.

The reorientation of policy has been based on unsubstantiated claims,
and this reorientation and similar faith in combinations underlie the
NCRA. The Conference Report on the NCRA [13] describes the rule of
reason that is to be applied to antitrust evaluation of R&D joint ventures.
The same weighing of losses from market power versus efficiency gains is
required. Again, especially with R&D ventures, this is sensible in principle. Yet, given the enforcement agencies' uncritical advocacy of business
combinations, joint ventures may pass muster even when unwise from a
social standpoint.

On what evidence did the Reagan administration change the course of
merger law? To quote the late Secretary of Commerce Baldrige,

> Economists now believe that the positive relationship between industry profit-
> ability and concentration is due to the comparatively greater efficiency of larger
> firms in the industry rather than collusion. Recent studies show that firm profit-
> ability in a given line is related to its market share regardless of whether or not
> the industry is 'concentrated.'...This is powerful evidence that the larger firm
> has achieved profitability through economies of scale rather than collusion.[8]

There *is* evidence [16, 17], especially from the mid-1970s, supporting the
late Secretary's position. But what is of importance for objectively analyz-
ing the reorientation of antitrust policy, including the new policy embodied

in the NCRA, is the way that the Reagan administration supported its position while ignoring contrary evidence.

Many observers in addition to the late Secretary have interpreted the evidence he cited as suggesting that better products or lower costs have resulted in expansion and profitability of certain firms, and thus relatively large shares of an industry, and that therefore the profits associated with concentrated industries have resulted from the efficiency associated with market share, not from the price-raising inefficiency allowed by mutual dependence recognized (tacit collusion) among concentrated sellers. The evidence they see says that large-share firms have high profits whether concentration is high or low, while low-share firms have low profits regardless of the level of industry concentration. Concentration appears to have no profit-increasing effect.[9]

There are two problems with this popular interpretation of the evidence. First, the evidence about the profitability of high-share firms could be interpreted quite differently. The conventional dominant-firm model associates market power with high profits for the large-share firm (or a group of leading firms), while a competitive fringe without such power does less well. Shepherd [19] interprets the relation between share and profit in that way. Salop and Scheffman [20] explain that large-share firms may increase their profits by carrying out socially wasteful policies that raise smaller rivals' costs, decreasing the output from the smaller firms and ultimately increasing the market share and profits of the leading firm or firms. Caves and Porter [21] hypothesize segmented industries, with a market-power problem for some segments of the industry but not others, with barriers to the mobility of resources preventing entry into the segments of the industry where excess profits are earned. In none of these hypotheses is market power necessary for efficiency.

The second problem is that the very data the Reagan administration marshaled in its favor suggest an opposing view [22]. The mid-1970s were turbulent times for our economy, and oligopolistic consensus is expected to be difficult to maintain during periods when demands and costs are unstable. Such consensus should be especially likely to break down if sellers have high fixed costs, tempting them to undercut their rivals' prices in an attempt to spread fixed costs over more sales, but ultimately causing a collapse of the industry price. Using measures of seller concentration that include the impact of foreign firms, it appears that the evidence on which the Reagan administration relied, the evidence showing no positive effect of concentration on profits and hence suggesting that the concentration problem is no problem, is the result of averaging the low profits of high fixed-cost concentrated industries, where oligopolistic coordination had evidently broken down, with the high profits of the remaining concentrated industries.

More importantly, none of the structural variables that are so important in the policy debate appear to be very important in terms of explaining variance in line of business profitability. Yet, unidentified firm and industry variables are quite important, explaining a large part of that variance. Thus, the results cited by the Reagan administration are quite likely driven by the unidentified variables, which have been left out of traditional specifications that have informed the policy debate. The data, then, do not support a revolution in policy regarding the traditional concern of antitrust with the oligopoly problem caused by the concentration of sellers in an industry.

2.3. Conglomerate Mergers

New policy toward conglomerate mergers also illustrates a willingness to ignore the potential problems of business combinations. The policy is relevant here both as another example of unsubstantiated claims about the effects of business combinations and because joint ventures often combine the resources of firms doing R&D in different manufacturing industries. Assistant Attorney General Baxter believed that "During the 1960's, in its general hostility to conglomerate mergers, the Supreme Court cooked up a variety of esoteric and totally baseless theories about the harm caused by conglomerate mergers" [3].

It does not appear that those theories were baseless. But in any case, Baxter's view became the official view of the enforcement agencies. Assistant Attorney General for Antitrust Douglas Ginsburg stated that

> In the case of a purely conglomerate merger, on the other hand [as contrasted with horizontal mergers in concentrated markets], no serious anticompetitive problems arise because the firms involved in the deal, by definition, do not actually compete with one another in any relevant market. One exception to this occurs in cases where one firm is properly characterized as a potential competitor of the other....[23]

This belief is embodied in the Justice Department's current merger guidelines.

The current received wisdom about conglomerate mergers is mistaken because theory and evidence suggest such mergers can, in some circumstances, significantly enhance the likelihood of noncompetitive behavior and performance in industry. Consider two markets, each with only two sellers. In the first and second we find seller A. In the first, we find seller B competing with seller A. In the second, seller A competes with seller C. If sellers B and C merge, even though they are not competitors, the merger creates a situation in which the tacit cooperation, the communication needed to overcome myopic behavior of a prisoners' dilemma game, is more easily attained. There are twice as many opportunities to come to understand one another, because the same set of sellers now meets in two markets. The process of reaching a consensus on price is facilitated because there is more contact. Also, the costs and strategies of the two sellers in each market are now more symmetric, making tacit agreement easier.

Fellner [24] described behavior in markets where sellers are few as akin to negotiation, even though the sellers do not sit down at a bargaining table and break the law (section 1 of the Sherman Act). He described the process of testing the waters, and noted that once some pattern of behavior becomes the norm, it is *as though* a bargain had been negotiated. Such behavior is quite legal, as was recently made clear when the FTC lost, in a U.S. Court of Appeals, the Ethyl–Du Pont case [25]. The FTC's original decision was, significantly, over the objection of the new Reagan-appointed Chairman Miller [26].

Even in the absence of *facilitating practices* making consensus more likely, oligopoly theory teaches that wholly "independent" profit-maximizing behavior in the context of recognized mutual dependence among a few sellers may result in prices considerably greater than the competitive ones. The conglomerate merger of sellers B and C would (because of the increased multimarket contact) make the market-power-inducing understandings that follow from recognition of mutual dependence more likely, yet the merger would not be challenged given the new policy.

Do we have any evidence that a conglomerate merger such as the merger of the hypothetical firms B and C might matter? Most of the evidence about the multimarket contact of sellers shows no effect on behavior. But some research [27] suggests that this is because the effect of multimarket contact works in opposite ways in concentrated and unconcentrated markets. When seller concentration is high, as in our example above, high multimarket contact can enhance the ability to coordinate behavior legally, and can result in high prices and excess profits. But when seller concentration is low, diversification across many industries is expected to increase sellers' awareness of profitable opportunities and their ability to quickly redeploy resources in response to those opportunities, thus competing away economic profits especially rapidly. So if we just ask the data if multimarket contact increases profits, the answer is expected to be no. *On average*, there is no such effect. But when markets were divided into those that are concentrated and those that are not (accounting for foreign firms' U.S.

sales when measuring concentration), it was found that, as hypothesized, multimarket contact increases profits in the former and decreases them in the latter.

2.4. Can Mergers Among Competitors Strengthen Our Competitiveness?

The Reagan administration proposed the Promoting Competition in Distressed Industries Act [6], which would have precluded antitrust action against any merger granted exemption because the International Trade Commission had found that an increase in imports had injured, or was likely to injure, an industry. Again, the rationale for the mergers was that they would promote efficiencies and lower costs, thus allowing the injured domestic firms to regain their previous share of the domestic market.

The strong dollar prior to the last years of the Reagan administration helped the United States avoid inflation even while running a huge federal deficit, but the competitiveness, in domestic and foreign markets, of U.S. industrial products consequently suffered. The lack of international competitiveness of U.S. industrial products strengthened policymakers urging changes in policy toward competition in our industrial markets. The overall thrust of such recommendations was quite wrong. A microeconomic policy was proposed to remedy problems caused in large measure by unsound macroeconomic policy. True, under some circumstances market power in an export industry could improve the exporting country's position vis-à-vis other countries—for example, by converting foreign consumers' surplus into domestic producers' surplus. However, exploiting such possibilities could, because of retaliation, ultimately undermine international trade or prove the first step in undermining the static and dynamic efficiency of the industries in the country promoting market power.

An essential problem was one of the macroeconomic distortions stemming from the Federal deficit and to some extent from the trade policies of our international trading partners. It needed macroeconomic remedies. The available evidence (which includes the impact of foreign sellers' U.S. sales on seller concentration) suggests that the microeconomic merger policy that was championed (as a response to the *globalization of markets*) would make U.S. industry less competitive, not more competitive. The combination of firms in the name of efficiency might not significantly reduce costs but just reduce the number of leading competitors (including foreign firms) in U.S. industries. The reduction in competition could make U.S. industrial products more expensive and less innovative.

3. R&D Cooperation and the Extent of Innovation

Firms competing in R&D are in many important cases undoubtedly unable to appropriate all of the social returns of their innovative investments. Appropriability of returns is especially likely to be difficult for basic research and generic applied research [28]. If the private marginal value of research is less than its social marginal value, then the private sector will invest too little in research, and there is a priori reason to believe that "cooperative industry research organizations" [28] and government support for basic and generic research are appropriate [28, 29]. Indeed, explaining strategies to revive U.S. productivity growth, Link and Tassey [30] emphasize the importance of joint ventures and government support for generating and capitalizing on generic research.

On the other hand, under some circumstances industry may, even without joint ventures, willingly support basic and generic research that is difficult to appropriate, because all firms share in the public knowledge and benefit from the process when successfully exploiting it for proprietary projects [31]. Further, although it is often reasonable to assume that the total private value of research falls short of its social value, even then it is not obvious that private marginal value is strictly less than social marginal value [32]. As Nelson [29] observes, the situation is complex and competitors may actually spend too much on R&D. Barzel [33] explains that *incomplete* appropriability in and of itself may lead to too little R&D investment by a monopolist free from the competitive pressure of an R&D race, while competitive pressure given a high enough degree of appropriability may cause too much R&D. Thus, in a world of *incomplete* appropriability, a monopolist may do too little while competition may result in roughly the right amount of R&D, especially when, in the sense of Nelson [34], parallel paths are optimal. Thus a firm is discouraged from doing R&D by the prospect that much of the return may go to others who imitate the innovation, but the fear of having a competitor be the first to introduce the innovation is a stimulus to R&D. To the extent that R&D joint ventures allow monopoly power *in R&D*, one can conclude, therefore, that R&D joint ventures protected by the NCRA may decrease desirable R&D spending.

That possibility is especially likely given that the cooperative research protected by the NCRA combines R&D across industries in ways similar to the previously existing diversified R&D of individual firms [35]. Joint ventures combining multi-industry research are quite likely to occur in areas where a monopolist of the R&D investment would undertake too little R&D. Consider the ratio of net social value to net private value of innovative investment as the multi-industry nature of the innovation increases. The ratio is expected to increase because of spillovers to consumers and other firms not conducting R&D in the area. The proportion of returns to R&D that is not appropriated by the firm doing the R&D is expected to increase as the multi-industry span—the extent—of the innovation increases, because more areas of technology are involved and the possibilities for applications other than those controlled by the firm increase.[10]

Barzel [33] explains that if the monopolist appropriates a constant fraction of the social return, the innovation is not pursued to the socially optimal extent. Granting the ratio of net social value to net private value of innovative investment increases, the conclusion that a monopolist will not pursue multi-industry innovations to the socially optimal extent follows a fortiori. Let z measure directly the extent—the multi-industry nature—of the innovation. Net social value $N_s(z)$ is assumed to be greater than net private value $N_p(z)$ because of incomplete appropriability of the returns from innovation. The ratio of net social value to net private value is a function $f(z)$ of the expected value of the measure of the extent of innovation. So, $f(z) = [N_s(z)/N_p(z)]$, and our discussion implies that $f'(z) > 0$.

The optimal extent of innovation from society's standpoint is $z_s{}^*$ such that $N_s' = 0$ and $N_s'' < 0$, while the optimal level from the private perspective of a monopoly is $z_p{}^*$ such that $N_p' = 0$ and $N_p'' < 0$. At the monopolist's optimal extent of innovation,

$$f'(z) = (N_p N_s' - N_s N_p')/N_p{}^2 = N_p N_s'/N_p{}^2 > 0$$

and thus $N_s' > 0$. Therefore, z is too low; the extent of innovation is less than socially optimal. Conversely, at the socially optimal extent of innovation,

$$f'(z) = -N_s N_p'/N_p{}^2 > 0$$

and thus $N_p' < 0$. Therefore, from the monopolist's perspective, the extent of innovation is greater than optimal. Thus, if the ratio of net social value to net private value of innovative investment increases as the multi-industry nature of the innovation increases, a monopolist will do too little investment in innovations spanning multiple industries.

Now, precisely such innovations are likely to be pursued by research consortia. Consortia are putting together R&D efforts that span sets of industries, and further, those sets have been combined previously by individual diversified firms investing on their own [35]. Such consortia then could be improving private returns to R&D by eliminating competition that is socially optimal. Competition can stimulate firms to undertake strategies increasing the expected multi-industry span—the extent—of innovation toward socially desirable levels that would not be reached in the absence of competition.

Whether the concern is for the optimal extent of innovation, or simply for the optimal expenditure on an innovation particular to a given industry [33], given that even a consortia would be unable to appropriate all of the returns to its innovative investment, the overbidding (from the private perspective of the firms) of competitors can move R&D investment toward the social optimum. Whether or not it does depends on the extent to which competition entails truly wasteful, duplicative efforts (rather than optimal multiple trials in the context of uncertainty) and the extent to which competition erodes the competitors' appropriation of returns.[11]

4. Screening Cooperative R&D[12]

DOJ and the FTC have "essentially ministerial" duties in processing the notifications of R&D joint ventures. "Neither agency is authorized to 'certify' or 'approve' the conduct described in a notification." [13]. However, the enforcement agencies are responsible, under their more general mandates, for screening cooperative R&D to be protected by the NCRA, yet from our discussion of the historical context, neither DOJ nor the FTC are likely to be objective evaluators. Indeed, the record suggests that the Reagan administration's position of advocacy regarding business combinations clouded its scrutiny of the economic consequences of the ventures. DOJ's assessments of cooperative R&D were in fact rather uncritical.

DOJ has said that it wants to preserve competition and will block ventures that lessen it significantly. For example, stating in a business review letter its enforcement intentions regarding one of the cooperative projects, the Department observed that

> Joint R&D ventures generally are procompetitive, and are condemned by the antitrust laws when they have a net negative effect on competition. Generally, R&D joint ventures rarely will raise competitive concerns—[they will do so] only when the venture's membership is "overinclusive," because an insufficient number of entities are left outside the venture to perform competitive R&D, or when the venture results in a significant restraint on competition that precludes or retards the production or sale of goods or services that do not employ the technology developed by the venture. [37]

But review [35] of the cooperative R&D that is granted NCRA protection shows that the projects appear to have quite inclusive memberships, sometimes even when one does not look for a particular niche in the general area of research. The administration had neither developed nor applied a careful, sufficiently complete model within which each actual case could be evaluated.[13]

For example, the business review letter quoted above concerned a venture that included the U.S. and foreign leaders in the area of research. But there could be problems even when only U.S. leaders are combined. For example, in aerospace, foreign competition for our defense establishment's dollars is not of great interest. Further, significant reduction in competition is possible even when many other U.S. firms do similar research. For example, if leading aerospace firms combine to do software research, although innumerable U.S. firms do similar research, there may be no viable competitors in developing applications in aerospace. Also, firms outside aerospace that develop software applicable to aerospace, and then need to license the technology to aerospace firms, would be licensing to the set of firms in the venture who would then have bargaining power that could lessen the value of the license to the innovator, perhaps retarding the pace of innovation. The Software Productivity Consortium, which is developing complex computer software, illustrates both of these potential problems. To be sure, numerous organizations not party to the venture conduct R&D in this area. However, at the time of review for NCRA protection, the venture included the largest (by sales or R&D) eight firms listed in *Business Week*'s aerospace category. Other important firms in aerospace are also included in the venture, but did not appear in *Business Week*'s aerospace category because of their diversified sales. It appears that the United States policy establishment was too willing to look at an R&D venture and find that "apparently numerous organizations and firms not currently members. . . , both in the U.S. and in other countries, can and do perform R&D that competes with the R&D performed under [the venture's] sponsorship" [37]. The willingness to overlook the possibility that R&D performance would be less good because of cooperation can be understood in the historical context described in section 2.

Given the historical context, there is reason for concern about the thoroughness and the seriousness of the policy establishment's evaluation of consequences of cooperative R&D. But is there any evidence that the ventures formed are nonetheless of the sort we would want to see? This seems unlikely, as explained in section 5.

5. Evidence on the NCRA Cooperative R&D

Championed by the Reagan administration, the NCRA was passed to promote cooperation in research among competitors. The aim is to encourage R&D efforts by overcoming fears of antitrust liability that might inhibit combinations that reduce R&D costs by eliminating wasteful duplication of

R&D efforts and allowing realization of scale economies, and that make it easier for firms to appropriate higher fractions of the returns from their innovative investment, returns that might otherwise be competed away by a host of patentable substitutes.

The Reagan administration actively supported such coordination of competitors' R&D. The support for the NCRA legislation, revealed in the Conference Report[14] on the bill and in the statements of advocacy by DOJ and the Commerce Department, does not persuasively demonstrate that policymakers appreciate the magnitude of the potential problem arising from the bill—namely, as explained in section 3, a priori theory suggests that cooperation could worsen performance in the area of technological change. Given our expectation that under monopoly the appropriation of returns to innovative investment will be incomplete, from society's standpoint even a monopolist is likely to underinvest in research and development. Two characteristics of competition in R&D can correct such underinvestment. First, in the uncertain world of innovative investment, some duplication afforded by the parallel paths of competitors can be shown to be optimal. Second, competitors fear preemption and also consider only their individual profits rather than total profits in the market. Consequently they have a tendency to overinvest, from a monopolist's private value-maximizing perspective, in innovative investment. That tendency can offset the lessened appropriability in competitive markets. Competition in R&D may get us closer to the socially optimal level of innovative investment.

In addition to the a priori reasons to suspect that combining firms' research efforts may not improve the pace of technological progress, we do have some evidence. The research of this author casts doubt on the assertions about the benefits of business combinations in R&D. Earlier research, and some subsequent research using new data but old techniques, finds evidence that, up to a point, R&D intensity increases with seller concentration, but at high levels of concentration, the R&D intensity falls. Such evidence could be used to support the moderate amounts of concentration of resources for research promoted by the new law.

However, it appears that, we have no general cross-sectional evidence that concentration of research resources matters one way or another. Once new data, and the methodology they allowed, were used to control for firm effects (some firms, perhaps with better research scientists or with better financial resources, do more R&D than others even when they conduct research in the same industry categories) as well as for the broad industry category effects (some industry categories, such as the pharmaceutical industry, offer more opportunity for R&D than others, regardless of the level of seller concentration), seller concentration (the extent to which a few sellers dominate a market, with foreign as well as U.S. sellers' presence measured) had no effect on R&D intensity, although without the controls, the effect found by others was clearly present [39]. Evidently, differences among firms in the value, cost, and opportunity for R&D, entirely apart from those differences that may arise from differences in the concentration of R&D resources, determine the differences in R&D intensity observed across firms and industries. Whether one looks at R&D spending or various elements of that heterogeneous total, the relative importance of opportunity differences and the relative unimportance of seller concentration has been repeatedly documented in a variety of empirical studies [32].

Further, a study [35] of the cooperative R&D projects that have filed for protection under the NCRA suggests that the cooperation fostered by the act may well lower social economic welfare rather than increase it. First, are the cooperative projects predominantly in unconcentrated industries where joint ventures might be needed to overcome fragmentation of R&D effort? No: using concentration measures that account for import competition, the ventures are occurring in the more concentrated industries. Second, are the cooperative projects predominantly in relatively low productivity-growth industries where joint ventures would perhaps improve productivity? No: the ventures are occurring in the relatively high productivity-growth industries. Third, are the cooperative projects occurring predominantly in industries where we have not observed purposive diversification and where the appropriability advantages from such diversification could not have been able to offset appropriability problems caused by competition in R&D? No: joint ventures are more likely to be found in industry categories combined with others by firms purposively diversifying their R&D activity. Fourth, are the cooperative projects occurring predominantly in industries where company-financed R&D intensity has been low and where extra stimulus might be needed to get innovative investment? No: the ventures are occurring in high-R&D-intensity industries. And we are not simply observing that cooperation is most likely where R&D is most likely when we compare in the same sample old traditional or smokestack industries with high-technology industries. The relation between R&D intensity and cooperation holds throughout the sample, even for the leading quartile of industry categories ranked by R&D intensity. Fifth, there is no evidence that the cooperative R&D is in categories where there have been significant appropriability problems. In all, it seems quite likely that the joint ventures will increase the profits of the firms involved but that society will lose because the reduction in competitive pressures was not necessary to get the firms to invest in productive R&D.

Notes

1. See, for example, the dissenting opinion in *U.S. v. Von's Grocery Company*, 384 U.S. 270 (1966) and the discussion of the case in [2].

2. For the most recent versions, see [4, 5].

3. Evidently, the new FTC had no trouble finding such cases. For example, it decided that the costs imposed by its own line-of-business data-collection program were greater than any benefits, in the face of convincing evidence to the contrary, and killed the program. The Commission believed that the private sector of the economy would generate the information if it were worthwhile. In addition to reorienting research, the FTC has taken a new view of the mergers on which it rules—emphasizing the potential for efficiencies and for entry of new competitors to mitigate any adverse consequences of market power.

4. *FTC v. Procter & Gamble*, 386 U.S. 568 (1967). Baldwin [7] discusses the origins of the precedent in the *Bethlehem–Youngstown* decision.

5. There has been some resurgence of court challenges to the agencies' decisions. See, for example, *FTC v. Owens–Illinois, Inc., et al. and Brockway, Inc.*, February 18, 1988, in which the U.S. District Court for the District of Columbia denied the FTC's request for a preliminary injunction blocking Owens–Illinois Inc.'s proposed takeover of Brockway, Inc.

6. See [8, 9]; more generally, the evidence suggests that we are unlikely to gain much in the way of production efficiencies when we allow mergers of competitors. After all, if two inefficient production facilities (say the plants are too small) are merged, we typically still have two inefficient facilities. There are possibilities such as product run-length economies which, by rearranging production tasks across plants, could allow lower unit production costs than those attainable in each plant. Most of the potential efficiencies, though, would be multiplant efficiencies in nonproduction activities—central-office activities such as advertising, R&D, or finance. The evidence does not support the importance of such economies in the cases of the prominent mergers of concern here. Scherer et al. [10] find that seller concentration in U.S. manufacturing typically far exceeds what is necessary to realize important plant- and multiplant-scale economies.

7. The Reagan administration's focus on market power (the ability to increase price above competitive levels for significant periods of time) and the extent to which it is offset by lowered costs may not be the most important focus for antitrust. The difficulties posed by what economists call the theory of second-best or big-think questions about social and political implications of market concentration are worthy of evaluation. But even if one accepts the administration's premise that policy should consider only economic efficiency and block business combinations only when they lessen efficiency, the new policy toward combinations may be a mistake. In a world of perfect knowledge about the economic implications of merger, the new policy would *not* (using the narrow view of antitrust) be a mistake, but the world is not that perfect. There is surely a potential tradeoff that must be addressed: heightened market power versus lower costs. But in the enthusiasm of advocacy, the new policy provides the groundwork for grave problems.

8. The quote is from [14], provided to me by David M. Barton and discussed and cited by Baldwin [15]. Baldwin provides much more evidence about the historical context of the shift in antitrust policy.

9. The evidence that market share, not seller concentration, is associated with high profit rates has received widespread publicity. *Business Week* [18] reviewed the evidence and proclaimed

Ever since Adam Smith, economists have held that when an industry is dominated by a few companies, they will stifle competition, keep prices uncompetitively high, and garner monopoly profits. This view has long been used to justify stringent government limits on mergers. But studies based on new Federal Trade Commission data are beginning to provide some evidence that this tenet may be wrong. The studies will buttress the arguments of a growing number of economists, both liberal and conservative, who are calling for a substantial easing of antitrust laws. And they support the Reagan Administration's decision to liberalize the guidelines the government uses to decide if potential mergers harm competition within an industry.

10. Mansfield et al. [36] provide a way to test that expectation. Mansfield et al. find in their sample of industrial innovations that the gap, which is typically positive, between social and private rates of return increases, ceteris paribus, with the significance of the innovation. They measure the extent to which the innovation is major rather than minor by its annual net social benefits. With a larger sample of innovations that provided adequate variance in the extent to which the innovations spanned multiple industries, one could test whether the ratio of net social to net private value increased with "the extent" of innovation. In such a sample, however, it would be quite difficult to carry out their methodology.

11. Scott [35] provides a simple graph comparing the investment by competitors and a venture combining them and illustrating the effects of wasteful duplication, overbidding from a private perspective, and appropriability conditions.

12. This section is taken, with some important modifications, from Scott's article comparing diversification and cooperation in R&D [35].

13. Katz [38] holds the promise that such a model useful for policy could be developed.

14. See [13]; it does have a lot of material about the need for a sufficient amount of competition in R&D, but taken in the context of the act itself and the behavior of the enforcement agencies, the language about the need for R&D competition does not seem to reflect a serious commitment to ensure it.

References

1. U.S. 98th Congress. *National Cooperative Research Act of 1984*, Public Law 98–462, October, 1984.
2. Pitofsky, R. "Coke and Pepsi were Going Too Far." *New York Times* (July 27, 1986): 2F.
3. Taylor, R.E. "A Talk with Antitrust Chief William Baxter." *Wall Street Journal* (March 4, 1982): 7–8.
4. U.S. DOJ. News release and *Merger Guidelines*. June 14, 1984.
5. U.S. DOJ. *Vertical Restraints Guidelines*. January 23, 1985.
6. U.S. DOJ. News release with the Reagan Administration's five proposed new antitrust laws with statements by the Attorney General and the Secretary of Commerce, fact sheets, and the proposed bills. February 19, 1986.
7. Baldwin, W.L. *Market Power, Competition, and Antitrust Policy*. Homewood, IL: Irwin, 1987.
8. U.S. DOJ, Statement of J. Paul McGrath about the proposed merger of LTV Corporation and Republic Steel Corporation, news release. February 15, 1984.

9. "An Antitrust About-Face on Republic and LTV." *Business Week* April 2, 1984): 31–32.
10. Scherer, F.M., et al. *The Economics of Multi-Plant Operation: An International Comparisons Study.* Cambridge, MA: Harvard University Press, 1975.
11. Mueller, D.C. "The Corporation: Growth, Diversification and Mergers." *Fundamentals of Pure and Applied Economics*, Volume 16. London: Harwood Academic Publishers, 1987.
12. Ravenscraft, D.J., and Scherer, F.M. *Mergers, Sell-Offs, and Economic Efficiency.* Washington, DC: The Brookings Institution, 1987.
13. U.S. 98th Congress, House of Representatives. *National Cooperative Research Act of 1984: Conference Report.* Report 98–1044, September 21, 1984.
14. U.S. Department of Commerce. "Remarks of Malcolm Baldrige, Secretary of Commerce, before the American Bar Association, Section of Antitrust Law. July 11, 1985.
15. Baldwin, W.L. "Giving Economics a Bad Name." *Antitrust Law & Economics Review* 17 (1985): 22–26.
16. Gale, B.T., and Branch, B.S. "Concentration versus Market Share: Which Determines Performance and Why Does It Matter?" *Antitrust Bulletin* 27 (1982): 83–106.
17. Ravenscraft, D.J. "Structure-Profit Relationships at the Line of Business and Industry Level." *Review of Economics and Statistics* 65 (1983): 22–31.
18. "Attacking the Test that Curbs So Many Mergers." *Business Week* (November 16, 1981): 151–152.
19. Shepherd, W.G. "The Elements of Market Structure." *Review of Economics and Statistics* 54 (1972): 25–37.
20. Salop, S.C., and Scheffman, D.T. "Raising Rivals' Costs.' *American Economic Review* 73 (1983): 267–271.
21. Caves, R.E., and Porter, M.E. "From Entry Barriers to Mobility Barriers: Conjectural Decisions and Contrived Deterrence to New Competition." *Quarterly Journal of Economics* 91 (1977): 241–261.
22. Scott, J.T., and Pascoe, G. "Beyond Firm and Industry Effects on Profitability in Imperfect Markets." *Review of Economics and Statistics* 68 (1986): 284–292.
23. U.S. DOJ. "Statement of Douglas H. Ginsburg before the Committee on the Judiciary, U.S. House of Representatives." News release, March 5, 1986.
24. Fellner, W. *Competition Among the Few.* New York: Knopf, 1949.
25. *Trade Regulation Reports*, No. 639. Report on E.I. du Pont de Nemours & Co., CA-2, 65,881. March 13, 1984.
26. "FTC Expands Interpretation of Antitrust Law. *Wall Street Journal* April 4, 1983): 8.
27. Scott, J.T. "Multimarket Contact and Economic Performance." *Review of Economics and Statistics* 64 (1982): 368–375.
28. Nelson, R.R. "The Simple Economics of Basic Scientific Research." *Journal of Political Economy* 67 (1959): 297–306.

29. Nelson, R.R. "Government Stimulus of Technological Progress: Lessons from American History." In: R.R. Nelson (ed.), *Government and Technical Progress*. New York: Pergamon Press, 1982, pp. 451–482.
30. Link, A.N., and Tassey, G. *Strategies for Technology-based Competition: Meeting the New Global Challenge*. Lexington, MA: Lexington Books, D.C. Heath, 1987.
31. Nelson, R.R. "The Role of Knowledge in R&D Efficiency." *Quarterly Journal of Economics* 97 (1982): 453–470.
32. Baldwin, W.L., and Scott, J.T. "Market Structure and Technological Change." *Fundamentals of Pure and Applied Economics*, Volume 17. London: Harwood Academic Publishers, 1987.
33. Barzel, Y. "Optimal Timing of Innovations." *Review of Economics and Statistics* 50 (1968): 348–355.
34. Nelson, R.R. "Uncertainty, Learning, and the Economics of Parallel Research and Development Efforts." *Review of Economics and Statistics* 43 (1961): 351–364.
35. Scott, J.T. "Diversification versus Cooperation in R&D Investment." *Managerial and Decision Economics* 9 (1988): 173–186.
36. Mansfield, E., et al. "Social and Private Rates of Return from Industrial Innovations." *Quarterly Journal of Economics* 91 (1977): 221–240.
37. U.S. DOJ. News release with accompanying letter of June 25, 1985 by Charles F. Rule, Acting Assistant Attorney General. June 26, 1985.
38. Katz, M.L. "An Analysis of Cooperative Research and Development." *Rand Journal of Economics* 17 (1986): 527–543.
39. Scott, J.T. "Firm versus Industry Variability in R&D Intensity." In: Z. Griliches (ed.), *R&D, Patents, and Productivity*. Chicago: University of Chicago Press for the National Bureau of Economic Research, 1984, pp. 233–245.

5 TECHNOLOGY POLICY AND COLLABORATIVE RESEARCH IN EUROPE

Roy Rothwell*

1. Introduction: European Policy Evolution

Governments in Europe have, for many years, been involved in implementing mechanisms designed to stimulate scientific advances and industrial technological change. Between 1945 and the mid-1970s, the two main tracks of policy were *science policy* and *industrial policy*. Science policy included scientific education and research funding in universities and public sector laboratories. Industrial policy included industrial restructuring, capital grants, R&D subsidies and subsidized collective industrial research infrastructures. In terms of firm size, emphasis was placed mainly on industrial agglomeration and the creation of national flagship companies, in areas such as computers, that were capable of competing on a world scale. In all European countries, very little venture capital was available during this period to fund the formation and growth of new technology-based firms (NTBFs).

---

*The author would like gratefully to acknowledge the financial support of the Leverhulme Trust during preparation of this chapter.

In general, science and industrial policies were formulated and implemented by different government departments and progressed in a largely uncoordinated manner. For example, in the UK, basic research, funded by the Department of Education and Science, focused mainly on *big science* (e.g., radio astronomy and particle physics), and engineering research was largely ignored; most of this research was not seen to be relevant to industrial needs, and university–industry technology transfers were minimal. This occurred during a period in which there was little collaboration between the DES and the Department of Industry.

During the latter half of the 1970s, following the energy crisis and associated world recession, European public policies began to change in a number of respects. Faced with growing budgetary constraints, governments began to seek to gain greater economic benefit from their considerable R&D funding. In the UK, for example, there was a progressive restructuring of basic science funding towards more industrially relevant *small* science and an increase in the proportion of funding going to engineering research. At the same time, governments began to question the notion that more R&D was equivalent to more industrial innovation. It began to be recognized that there was considerably more to the successful commercialization of technological change than simply developing the requisite technological know-how, and governments began to introduce *innovation policies* that tackled a broader range of the activities encompassed by the industrial innovation process than just R&D. During this period, interdepartmental cooperation and coordination improved in a number of countries.

A further significant change in government policy was a shift of resources towards small and medium-sized firms (SMFs). This was based on a growing belief that SMFs were potentially a more suitable (endogenous) vehicle for the economic renewal of less developed regions than were the branch plants of large firms (the traditional vehicle of regional policy); that they were more efficient employment generators than their larger counterparts; and that SMFs had a higher potential for innovation than larger firms [1].

During the 1980s, there have been three important shifts in European policy. First, based on the realization of the close links between basic research and strategic industrial technological needs in certain key areas (e.g., semiconductors, biotechnology), science policy is again being emphasized. Second, based largely on the recognition of the important role that NTBFs played in the emergence of new, high-technology sectors in the United States (e.g., semiconductors, computer-aided design, microcomputers) during the postwar period [2, 3, 4], public policies in Europe have focused increasingly on stimulating the creation of NTBFs. And third,

European governments have been involved in the creation of so-called *technology policies* of collaborative precompetitive research at both the national and European Community levels. The evolution of European research and technology development policies, as described above, is summarized in table 5–1.

2. Collaborative Research Infrastructures

Before describing national and EEC technology policies, in this section we will summarize briefly collaborative industrial research infrastructures and related initiatives in the UK, France, and West Germany [5].

2.1. United Kingdom

Although a number of government research institutes and laboratories perform collective industrial research in the UK, by far the greatest amount is undertaken by the Industrial Research Associations. The first RA was funded with government support in 1917, and by 1980 RAs numbered 42, the majority being industry-specific, mainly in traditional areas, although some, like the Production Engineering Research Association, perform cross-sectoral R&D.

Up to the mid-1960s, the main source of RA funding (about 60%) was membership subscriptions, with an additional 30% deriving from government in the form of grant in aid. After 1971, following the adoption of the Rothschild Principle, the so-called *customer–contractor principle* (i.e., if a piece of research is to be done, there must be a customer who is prepared to pay and a contractor to do it), the RAs were required to "sell" their facilities to government who, as a customer, contracted with an RA to perform a specified piece of research in a given time at a preestablished fee. Under this scheme, the government acted as a proxy for the public and, in order to enable it to perform this function, a number of Research Requirements Boards were established. Following the introduction of the customer–contractor principle, government funding dropped to about 15% of the total, membership subscriptions to 35%, and direct fee income increased to 50%. In other words, the RAs became more market-oriented and began more vigorously to sell their services directly to firms on both an individual and a collective basis.

In June 1986, following the merger of the Association of Independent Contract Research Organizations and the Committee of Directors of

Table 5–1. Evolution of Public Research and Technology Development Policies in Europe

Year	Science Policy	Industrial Policy	Firm Size Emphasis	Financing
1950s and 1960s	— Scientific education — University research — Basic research in government labs — Little coordination or active collaboration	— Grants for R&D — Equipment grants — Industrial restructuring — Support for collective Industrial Research — Technical education and training, etc.	— Emphasis on large firms and industrial agglomeration — Creating national flagship companies, e.g. in computers	— Little venture capital available
Mid-1970s		*Innovation policy* — Grants for *INNOVATION* — Involving collective research institutes in product development — Innovation-stimulating public procurement etc. [increased interdepartmental coordination]	— Increasing emphasis on small firms	— Little venture capital available
1980s	— Increased emphasis on science policy	*Strategic Innovation Policy* (Technology Policy) — Selection and support of generic technologies and high-technology product groups — International (EC) collaboration [interdepartmetal initiatives]	— Emphasis on NTBFs and interfirm collaboration	— Increase in the availability of venture capital

Source: R. Rothwell and W. Zegveld, [4] and R. Rothwell (in [14]).

Research Associations, the Association of Independent Research and Technology Organizations (AIRTO) was formed. In 1987, AIRTO had 45 research and technology organizations (RTOs) in its membership employing 8700 staff, and an aggregate turnover of £230 million.

The Department of Trade and Industry (DTI) has for some years been shifting resources from individual company projects to the support of *research consortia* or *clubs*, of which it now has over 100. Some of these clubs conduct collaborative research programmes, while others concentrate on spreading awareness and promoting technology transfer. Examples are as follows:

- The Chemical Sensors Club, established by the DTI in 1985, has nearly 70 members drawn from industry, universities, and research establishments. It was designed to promote the development of new and better chemical sensors and to encourage their wider use throughout UK industry. It is jointly run by the Laboratory of the Government Chemist and the Warren Springs Laboratory.
- The Biosensors Research Club, based at the United Kingdom Atomic Energy Establishment at Harwell, is research-based and has 11 members.
- Biosep (founded in 1984) works on bioseparation (mainly membranes and chromatography). It is based at Harwell and Warren Springs and has 50 members, mainly pharmaceutical and food companies.
- The British Electrotechnical and Allied Manufacturers Association is, in conjunction with the DTI, currently establishing an advisory service to inform companies of available expertise and sources of information. The aim is to encourage companies (particularly SMFs) to undertake R&D work and to alert them to the help available.

2.2. France

The system of collective industrial research in France is based primarily on the 15 sectorally based Industrial Technical Centers (ITCs). These are similar in many respects to the RAs in the UK and offer a wide range of services, including R&D, technical consulting, information, training, standards, and quality control. The ITCs have more recently become increasingly involved in the French technopole networks and are placing an increasing number of technological consultants in the regions to provide assistance particularly to SMFs. Between 50% and 80% of ITCs' income derives from compulsory subscriptions by industry via a parafiscal tax. They are also supported from public funds.

The Centre National de la Recherche Scientifique (CNRS) is the principal organization in France for fundamental scientific research. During the 1980s, CNRS increasingly became decentralized along a structural theme. Through its Industrial Relations Committee, a number of industrial clubs have been established in specific scientific themes, groups of special interest have been set up, and groups for cooperative research have been established.

An important public policy tool for collaboration and technology transfer at the regional level is the Centres Regionaux d' Innovations et de Transfer de Technologies (CRITT). In 1983, 15 CRITT were in place; by 1986 there were 40. They aim to encourage interaction between research bodies and industry and to assist SMFs to master new technologies and utilize innovative equipment. They help to promote the development of new products and production processes. They bring together universities, engineering schools, large industrial groups and SMFs, and chambers of commerce and industry, to form a comprehensive network of technology transfer and a comprehensive and diverse body of skills and competences [6].

2.3. West Germany

Germany's considerable industrial strength has traditionally been in the medium-technology engineering industries in which SMFs have played an important role. Because of this, there has been a long-standing emphasis on establishing collective industrial research infrastructures and stimulating infrastructure–industry technology transfers. As a consequence, collective industrial research is well established in Germany. Under the umbrella of the Germany Federation of Research Associations, established in 1954, there are 63 institutes and 93 affiliated institutes operating in 32 branches of industry. In 1986, about 25% of funding for collective industrial research derived from government sources, a total of DM137 million. Most of the research is performed on behalf of SMFs.

A second important collective research institution is the Fraunhoffer Society, which has 30 institutes throughout Germany. Contract research income is matched DM for DM with a government subsidy to cover infrastructural maintenance and development costs. In addition, there is a public subsidy that amounts to 40% of the cost to small firms of the projects they commission at Fraunhoffer institutes. This is designed to encourage small firms to utilize the services available through the Fraunhoffer Society.

3. National Collaborative Technology Policies in Europe

As indicated in table 5–1, during the 1980s European governments began to initiate *technology policies* in the form of programs of precompetitive research in generic technologies involving firm–firm and university–firm collaboration. These were largely triggered by the announcement in 1981 of the Japanese Fifth Generation Computer Development Project. A major feature of the Japanese initiative was that it represented an explicit attempt on the part of the Japanese to leap ahead of their Western rivals in the vital area of artifical intelligence, thus breaking away from their established image of being imitators rather than original innovators.

Governments of the major European nations reacted to the Japanese initiative by setting up special programs in the Information Technology (IT) area. The programs initiated by the British, French, and German governments are outlined briefly below. (Fuller details are contained in the comprehensive reports of Mackintosh (1984), English and Watson-Brown (1984), and Arnold and Guy (1987) [7, 8, 9].

3.1. The United Kingdom

Successive British governments have for many years been involved in areas of industry that bear some relationship to the general field of information technology. In the 1960s, for example, the British government was instrumental in the creation of ICL, the national flagship company in the computer area, and in 1978 the National Enterprize Board set up the semiconductor company Inmos. In addition, between 1978 and 1982, 13 separate publicly funded support schemes were established that were designed to stimulate the development and diffusion into industrial use of microelectronics-based devices, the most important of these being the Microelectronics Industry Support Scheme and the Microelectronics Applications Scheme. The total allocation to the 13 schemes amounted to some £300 million.

The UK government's response to the unveiling of Japan's fifth-generation computer program was the establishment of the Alvey Committee on advanced information technology, which produced the so-called Alvey Report in 1982 [10]. The Alvey Committee identified a number of main priority areas in which the UK should build up technical strengths as a basis for commercial exploitation. These major *enabling technologies* are software engineering, very-large-scale integration (VLSI), intelligent knowledge-based systems (IKBS) and the man–machine interface (MMI).

The Alvey Program cost £350 million over five years. Of this, £200 million was committed by the government, with participating companies providing the remainder. Some £60 million was originally designated for the support of research and training in academe. Regarding the rest of the program, carried out in industry, government funds were intended to cover 90% of the costs of those projects in which wide and open dissemination of research results is required, and 50% of the cost of other projects. Some £58 million was earmarked for demonstration projects linked to particular advanced applications of information technology.

The main aim of the Alvey Program was to facilitate interfirm and industry–university collaboration at the precompetitive research stage, leaving commercial exploitation in the hands of individual companies. It was hoped, however, that firms would capitalize on potential technical and market complementarities where these existed. The Alvey Committee recognized that while there existed considerable technical potential in the UK in the general field of IT, the effort was widely fragmented. The interface between the research community and industry in Britain was nowhere near as productive as in the U.S., and British companies generally did not collaborate on basic research to the same extent as in Japan. Thus, the Alvey Program was designed as an important linkage mechanism, linking basic university research to industry and linking the research efforts of companies. In order to facilitate collaboration between the different institutions involved and to coordinate the various projects (i.e., to achieve program coherence), a new directorate, the Alvey Directorate, was established within the Department of Trade and Industry. In addition, a number of independent academic research groups were given the task of evaluating the effectiveness of the Alvey Program on an on-going basis.

While the evaluations of the effectiveness of the Alvey Program have yet to be published, Land [11] has made a number of interesting criticisms. One of these is that the programme essentially was one of *technology push*:

> All but one of the non-civil service members of the committee represented suppliers or research interests. Of the 115 organizations which are listed as having provided substantive inputs to the committee, only three can be said to represent the user rather than the supply or research side of the industry. The three were ICI, the CEGB and the hospital for nervous diseases. The outcome of this selection is bound to be a one-sided viewpoint of the problems, and a set of proposals which favour certain kinds of solution over others.[11]

A second criticism leveled by Land was the omission of communication technology from the list of enabling technologies:

> Communication technology, such as fibre optics, satellite communications, communication protocol and private networks, have a central role in the computer

systems of the future. The communication industry is an important national resource. All other technologies selected by Alvey interact with communication technology. [11]

It was recognized by the Alvey Committee that the long-term implementation of the program would require an increase in the supply of graduates with high-level skills in fields relating to information technology. Accordingly, the University Grants Committee agreed to increase the number of teaching and research posts in information technology. According to data from the Department of Trade and Industry published in 1985, however, the shortfall in information-technology graduates was then 1500 which, with the then-current levels of commitment, was conservatively expected to rise to 5000 by 1987–1988. This growing skills shortage, it was felt, could seriously impede the longer-term implementation of the research results arising from the Alvey initiative.

3.2. France

Just as in Britain, the French government has for many years been involved in supporting developments in areas relating to information technology. The French route, again like the British, has focused on the support of flagship companies in the areas of computing (Compagnie des Machines Bull) and semiconductors (Thompson and Matra). Since 1966, the French government has set up a number of Plans Calculs designed to establish a viable and significant computer industry, and in 1977 the first Plan Composants was launched aimed at developing a semiconductor components industry. This involved a planned expenditure of FF600 million over five years, with an additional FF200 million being allocated towards the costs of establishing new industrial groupings in integrated circuits. While the first Plan Calcul was designed to establish a purely French computer industry, under the Plan Composants French firms were encouraged to forge links with U.S. firms to promote the transfer of LSI technology.

In September 1981, the French government established the Farnous Commission (La Mission Filiere[1] Electronique) to identify the specific needs of the electronics industry. The Farnous Report, published in March 1982, formed the basis for the Programme d'Action pour la Filiere Electronique (PAFE), announced in July 1982. According to President Mitterrand, the prime aim of PAFE was to place France on an equal technological footing with the U.S.A and Japan. The PAFE initiative was, essentially, the French response to the Japanese fifth-generation program.

Outlined in PAFE was a total expenditure of FF140 billion between

1982 and 1987, with FF60 billion of this deriving from government sources (Ministeries of Defence, PTT and Industry and Research). PAFE was designed to tackle four main areas of policy intervention—research, education, industry, and microelectronics applications—in a coordinated manner. Of the total financial allocation, 40% was to go towards developments in telecommunications and professional electronics and 43% to components, consumer electronics, and information. The first seven projects launched under PAFE were in the areas of microcomputers, large computers, CAD for VLSI, software engineering, CADCAM, computer-assisted translation, and image processing.

By all accounts, PAFE did not progress altogether satisfactorily. Among the most important of the reasons identified by English and Watson-Brown [8] as contributing to this poor performance were shortage of skilled manpower; budget cuts; lack of market awareness amongst French administrators; over-ambitious targets; too few small entrepreneurial companies; and bureaucratic control of R&D. (The Mitterrand administration nationalized the French IT industry, and the government controls some 75% of R&D expenditure.) The French government tackled these problems through reduced interference at the company level, encouraging improved research–industry links and attempting to encourage a more market-oriented approach on the part of administrators.

3.3. West Germany

Policymakers in West Germany have long striven to strike a balance between the stated commitment of successive administrations to a free-market philosophy and the need for public intervention in certain high-technology areas. Given its federal structure, there exists a considerable level of decentralization in West Germany (e.g., the universities are controlled by the Lander), which would make it difficult, even if the political will existed, for the federal government to implement integrated, indicative policies of the kind traditionally adopted in France. Despite this situation, the federal government has intervened in the electronics sector for a number of years. English and Watson-Brown [8] have identified a number of the most significant trends in federal support to German industry:

- Between 1968 and 1980, overall R&D spending increased in real terms by 60% and formed 2.3% of GNP in 1984.
- The proportion of R&D expenditure going to electronics since 1969 has, on average, been 30% higher than in other European nations.

- During 1981 and 1982, the BMFT spent DM300 million on data processing. This support has gone to fund specific projects in a large number of companies, which contrasts with the more generalized support offered during that period in the UK and France.

In general, public electronics R&D support in Germany has traditionally emphasized applications. In other words, there has been considerable emphasis on the *diffusion* of electronics into the basic engineering sectors in which Germany enjoys comparative national strengths.

In 1984, the Kohl administration announced a four-year program in information technology with a total financial allocation of DM3 billion. This program represented a more unified approach than was the case with previous federal initiatives and, for the first time, involved the coordination of funding between the BMFT, the Bundespost, and the Economics Ministry.

Many of the projects previously funded have been continued under the umbrella of the Informationstechnic program, and the amount of extra money involved appeared to have been modest. However, the degree of coordination between the existing projects, and between projects subsequently initiated under the program, has been increased significantly. As with previous initiatives, the Inforamtionstechnic program emphasized technology diffusion. It emphasized in addition the use of public procurement to stimulate innovation, and it aimed to stimulate the involvement of small- and medium-sized companies. The main areas covered by the new program were components (including submicron technology and integrated optics), data processing (including new computer structures and software), industrial automation (including robotics and FMS), telecommunications (including optical technology and broadband netwroks), improvements in the research infrastructure (research networks), and education. Unlike Alvey, the Informationstechnic programme laid relatively little emphasis on artificial intelligence or fifth-generation computer techniques, which was probably the result of its continuation character. In other words, it was less of a radical departure from existing support projects than was the case with Alvey.

Despite the convergence in the use of technology policies in Britain, France, and West Germany, some differences in policy emphasis are evident, and the size, form, and organization of the three programs vary considerably. These differences are illustrated in table 5–2 [12]. Table 5–2 shows that the French program is by far the largest, but that the British program has a stronger focus on basic research than the French, which is more developmental in character. The British Alvey program is strongly technology-pushed, with few overt market linkages; the French PAFE

Table 5–2. Government IT Program in Europe in 1984

	Size (ECU m.)	Basic Research	Applied Research	Tech. Pushed	Market Linked	Technological and Program Novelty
UK	285	25%	75%	HIGH	Overtly few links	HIGH Radical technologies New initiatives
France	824	8%	92%	MEDIUM	Strongly with telecomms	MEDIUM Some radical technologies 'Filiere' approach continues
FRG	236	—	—	LOW	Strongly with telecomms Diffusion oriented	LOWER Existing projects coordinated under a new inter-ministerial umbrella

Source: Adapted from Mackintosh International [7] and Arnold and Guy [9].

program has strong downstream linkages with telecommunications, an area which is seen as the core carrier sector for the new technology; the German program not only has strong links with the telecommunications sector, but also lays considerable emphasis on the diffusion of IT to existing sectors in which Germany has strong competitive strengths, and in this respect it is strongly market-linked.

In terms of program *novelty*, the British program ranks high on two counts: it focuses on four radical new technologies, and it represents a new style of initiative for the UK. While the French program also tackles a number of radical technologies, it continues the well-established *filiere* approach to technology development. In technological terms, the German program represents mainly a repackaging of existing projects, but it does so under a coordinating interministerial umbrella, which is a new departure within the West German policy system.

4. Programs of the European Community

Collaborations between countries within Europe on various aspects of science, technology, and industrial development have been taking place for many years. Sharp and Shearman [13] have listed the following examples:

- The European Coal and Steel Community (ECSC), established under the Treaty of Paris in 1951;
- The European Atomic Energy Commission (EURATOM), established under the Treaty of Rome in 1957;
- The European Airbus project—the British, French, and West German governments signed a Memorandum of Understanding in 1967 to develop the A300 aircraft;
- The European Launcher Development Organization (ELDO), established in 1962, and the European Space Research Organization (ESRO); and
- The Anglo-French Concorde project of the 1960s.

A marked feature of the 1980s has been the establishment by the European Commission of a number of EEC-wide technology development programs. Sharp and Shearman [13] have provided the following reasons to explain this trend:

Prior to the 1980s the underlying assumption was that market size was required mainly to secure the necessary economies of scale in production. Only in computers was the issue of R&D the dominant one. By the early 1980s, however, R&D had become a prime concern of many European industries, faced as they were with the globalization of competition, U.S. predominance and Japanese success. The logic behind this new industrial collaboration was therefore based on the need to spread both costs and the market-entry risks for new products at a time when technologics were converging, the pace of technological development was accelerating and development costs were rising.

A second factor was the French commitment to the idea of European collaboration, especially information technology and telecommunications. France had been foremost among European governments in campaigning for a United European front in the struggle to gain a larger share in the global electronics and information processing markets, and it had called for the creation of strategic telecommunications alliances, the liberalization of procurement policies and the harmonization of standards. [13]

Table 5–3, taken from Sharp and Shearman [13], lists a number of the major European Community technology oriented programs introduced between 1982 and 1986. The Biomolecular Engineering Program (BEP), launched in 1982, had a total expenditure of only 15 million ECU while its successor, the Biotechnology Action Program (BAP), launched in 1986, has a much larger budget of 50 million ECUs [14, 15].

4.1. Esprit

Partly as the result of a growing EEC trade deficit in IT products ($10 billion in 1982), and partly as a response to the Japanese fifth-generation computer initiative, Etienne Davignom (then President of the European Commission) brought together the 12 leading European IT companies to plan a collaborative EEC program in IT. This resulted in the European Strategic Program for Research and Development in Information Technologies (ESPRIT), which was approved in February 1984 with a five-year budget of 1.5 billion ECUs (about $1.25 billion), 50% of which would derive from the Commission and 50% from participating companies. The four main aims of ESPRIT are

- to ensure that research teams achieve the critical mass to obtain results;
- to enable optimization of resources that will result in reducing duplication and widen the spectrum of research tackled;
- to reduce the time-leg effect caused by reliance on imported technology; and
- to pave the way to the definition and adoption of standards of European origin.

Table 5–3. Sample of Major European Community Programs

Program	Date	Duration	Budget	Emphasis	Future Plans
Bep	1982	4 years	15 mecus	Promotion of academic/industrial links; support of posdoctoral training and exchange	Succeeded by Bap
Esprit	1983 (Pilot phase)	1 year	11.5 mecus	Microelectronics, software technology, advanced information processing, office systems, computer integrated manufacture	Phase 2 (5 years)
	1984 (Phase 1)	5 years	750 mecus		
Race	1985 (Definition phase)	18 months	40 mecus	Establishment of a technological base for the introduction of a Community-wide IBCN telecommunications infrastructure and services	Phase 2 (5 years)
	1987 (Phase 1)	5 years	Currently being decided		
Brite	1985	4 years	125 mecus	Development of advanced technologies to support traditional industries within the EC	
Bap	1986	5 years	50 mecus	Promotion of research and training and contextual developments in enzyme, genetic, and protein engineering	
Comett	1986	4 years	80 mecus	European network of university–industry training partnerships	Phase 2 (3 years)

Compiled by Claire Shearman, February 1987.

Source: Margaret Sharp and Claire Shearman [13].

The program includes five areas of technology: advanced microelectronics, software technology, advanced information processing, office automation, and computer-integrated flexible manufacturing. Central to ESPRIT is its focus on precompetitive research, and a major criterion for participation is a cross-national partnership between at least two research groups, one of which must be commercially oriented.

Under ESPRIT there are two types of project: type A projects (these account for 75% of the budget), which are long-term and systems-oriented and which require large-scale resources; and type B projects, which are small-scale and of shorter-term perspective. By 1984, 104 collaborative, cross-border projects had been set up under ESPRIT: 27 in advanced microelectronics, 14 in software engineering, 21 in information processing, 23 in office systems, and 19 in compter-integrated manufacturing. These 104 projects involve 344 company collaborations, 97 research institute collaborations, and 107 university collaborations.

Finally, in addition to the five areas of technology mentioned above, funds are being allocated to activities that influence the overall effectiveness of ESPRIT. These are the establishment of an information exchange system, the establishment of common standards, and the creation of systems for information acquisition and dissemination (English and Watson-Brown, 1984). Whether or not ESPRIT will be successful in placing the European IT industry on a comparable technological level with the U.S. and Japan remains to be seen. Perhaps in the longer term its outcome will be judged less on a technological basis and more on a cultural basis, i.e., on the degree to which it succeeds in establishing a tradition of cross-border R&D collaboration between European companies and research groups.

5. Conclusions

The brief description of recent European technology policy initiatives given above indicates some convergence between major European nations in the types of policies currently being pursued. In the first case, there is a strong trend towards the explicit choice of certain key enabling technologies, specifically information technology (and also biotechnology) [16]. In the second case, there is a common trend towards the setting up of major national technology programs with a growing degree of central coordination in the IT field. While central coordination is a long-established tradition in France, it has been much less prevalent in the past in the UK and even less so in West Germany. In the area of IT, national policies have been complemented by European-wide policy initiatives undertaken by the European Commission in Brussels. (The same is true of the biotechnology field.) Despite these general commonalities in approach to technology policy, as has been indicated, a number of national differences exist on a more detailed level.

It seems clear that the national technology policies currently being pursued in Europe are designed to tackle a number of problems common to most European nations. The most significant of these are fragmented and uncoordinated R&D effort; lack of interfirm R&D collaboartion; and too few contacts between universities and industry. At the European level, EEC policies are designed to stimulate cross-national R&D collaboration in order to attain technology threshold levels to match those in the U.S. and Japan; to stimulate internation information exchange and cooperation in order to reduce R&D duplication; and (perhaps most importantly) to establish common standards and regulations to create a truly common market for high-technology products. Regarding the latter point, little real progress has been made to date, although the single market will be in place in 1992.

Notes

1. Filiere is a French concept that applies to the chain of activities from components supply through manufacture to end use.

References

1. Rothwell, R., and Zegveld, W. *Innovation and the Small and Medium Sized Firm*. London: Frances Pinter, 1982.
2. Dosi, G. *Technical Change and Industrial Transformation*. London: Macmillan, 1984.
3. Kaplinsky, R. *The Impact of Technical Change on the International Division of Labour*. London: Frances Pinter, 1982.
4. Rothwell, R., and Zegveld, W. *Reindustrialization and Technology*. Harlow (UK): Longman, and Armonk, NY: M. E. Sharpe Inc., 1985.
5. Rothwell, R.; Dodgson, M.; and Lowe, S. *Technology Transfer Mechanisms: A Report to NEDO—Part I: United Kingdom* and *Part II: The USA, Japan, France and West Germany*. Science Policy Research Unit, University of Sussex, UK, 1988.
6. Sunman, H. *France and Her Technopoles*. Cardiff, UK: CSP Publications Ltd, 1986.
7. Mackintosh, I. *A Survey of Community Support Programmes and Strategies in Information Technology*. Luton, UK: Mackintosh International Ltd, 1984.

8. English, M. and Watson-Brown, A. "National Policies in Information Techno-
    logy: Challenges and Responses." *Oxford Surveys in Information Technology* 1
    (1984): 55–128.
9. Arnold, E., and Guy, K. *Parallel Convergence: National Strategies in In-
    formation Technology*. London: Frances Pinter, 1986.
10. Department of Trade and Industry. *A Programme for Advanced Information
    Technology*. London: Department of Trade and Industry, 1982.
11. Land, F. "Information Technology: The ALVEY Report and Government
    Strategy." Inaugural Professorial Lecture, London School of Economics,
    1983.
12. Rothwell, R. *Public Innovation Policies: Some International Trends and Com-
    parisons*. Papers in Science, Technology and Public Policy, No. 12, Science
    Policy Research Unit, University of Sussex, UK, 1986.
13. Sharp, M., and Shearman, C. *European Technological Collaboration*. Chat-
    ham House Paper 36. London: Routledge and Kegan Paul, 1987.
14. Sharp, M. "National Policies Towards Biotechnology." In: R. Rothwell
    (ed.), *Technology Policy*. Special issue of *Technovation* 5 (4) (1987): 281–304.
15. Sharp, M. "Biotechnology: Watching and Waiting." Chapter 6 in: M. Sharp
    (ed.) *Europe and New Technologies: Six Case Studies in Innovation and Ad-
    justment*. London: Frances Pinter, 1985.
16. Sharp, M. *The New Biotechnology: European Governments in Search of a
    Strategy*. Sussex European Paper No. 15, European Research Group, Science
    Policy Research Unit, University of Sussex, UK, 1985.

6 JOINT R&D AND INDUSTRIAL POLICY IN JAPAN

David B. Audretsch

1. Introduction

Referring to American policy, Link and Bauer [1] observed, "The economic rationale for public support of innovation, particularly industrial R&D, is based on the argument that innovation involves the process of creating information, and information has at least some characteristics of being a public good." While this idea is currently being debated in the U.S.,[1] it has long been accepted in Japan that R&D output contains at least an element of a public good, and therefore provides convincing motivation for undertaking programs that exploit the public-good aspect of R&D. Thus, both cooperative R&D programs, and the targeting of resources by the government to support such programs, have played an important role in the overall Japanese R&D policy.

This chapter has three purposes. The first is to describe the role of Japanese industrial policy in cooperative R&D. The second is to examine the actual Japanese experience and record in supporting joint R&D programs. The third is to provide an evaluation of cooperative R&D within the context of the overall Japanese R&D policy.

In Japan, R&D, and particularly cooperative R&D programs, can be

103

understood only within the context of the broader relationship between business and government policy. Not only is a general approach that relies upon cooperative endeavors more characteristic in Japan than in, say, the U.S., but also cooperative R&D in Japan is firmly rooted in those industrial policies implemented during the first three decades following the Second World War. Essentially, the principle underlying Japanese industrial policy was what Pugel [2] terms as the *infant industry* rationale, characterized by "...underdeveloped domestic industries with little competitive power under government's active interference to build up a large-scale production system while limiting entry into the domestic market of foreign enterprises with already established mass production systems and restricting the competition of foreign manufacturing in the domestic market" [3]. The Foreign Investment Act of 1950 enabled the MITI (Ministry of International Trade and Industry) to exercise considerable control over imported technology by requiring government approval of all transactions involving foreign currency.[2] This enabled the government to display "...an extraordinary ability to organize and adopt modern technology" [4].

Other instruments of industrial policy promoting Japanese R&D have included tax policy, especially the depreciation tax. The Enterprise Rationalization Law of 1952 enabled the Ministry of Finance to grant generous depreciation rates to targeted industries, with the major goal being the promotion of technological change [5]. Another important industrial policy instrument was the selective allocation of funds to key industries, using an approved network of financial institutions. Similarly, institutions such as the Japan Development Bank have served as vital instruments of Japanese industrial policy. Since the late 1960s, the Bank has allocated over $300 million per year in subsidized loans to promote technological progress [6].

During the 1950s and 1960s, these industrial policy instruments provided Japan with "...the capability to borrow technology and to absorb more advanced production methods, along with an activist role for the government in the process" [7]. Thus, as joint R&D programs became increasingly important in the 1970s, it was natural that "Japanese technology policy worked alongside market forces rather than replacing them with the political process. This approach was successful in the sense that it contributed to the promotion of technological progress and a high rate of economic growth" [8]. In fact, it was the Japanese government's support of cooperative R&D programs, as wll as its overall R&D policy, that led the U.S. International Trade Commission [9] to conclude the following:

> Recently, some have asserted that while direct funding of industrial research by the Government is often relatively low, it is aimed at particular industries at crucial moments and thus affords the firms in those industries important advantages

not otherwise available in the free market. It is this precise, well-orchestrated Government aid that is most frequently cited as the primary concern of U.S. competitors regarding Japanese industrial targeting, particularly in rapidly growing, high-technology industries where sustained and high levels of investment can be a key element in maintaining a competitive advantage.

2. Cooperative R&D in Japan

There are reasons particular to Japan why cooperative R&D plays such an important role. At the heart of these reasons is the chronic scarcity of natural resources. Japan can produce only 0.3% of its requirement for petroleum products, 15% of its energy needs, and 75% of the minimal amount of food required to feed its population [3]. As a result, Japan has had to rely upon success in exporting fabricated products in order to facilitate the procurement of needed inputs. During the last two decades, the application of advanced technological methods resulting from R&D has proved to be the greatest source for promoting the competitive advantage of Japanese firms and industries vis-à-vis their American and European counterparts [10]. The importance of Japanese R&D is indicated by an average rate of return on R&D of 20% both between 1966 and 1973 and between 1974 and 1982 [11]. In fact, recent evidence suggests that additional increases in R&D in Japan promote the Japanese trade advantage more than equivalent additions of American R&D promote the U.S. trade position [12]. That Japan has evolved to rely on R&D as its major source for trade advantage is hardly surprising when considered from the perspective of a nation deficient in natural resources. Its only viable alternative in achieving prosperity has been to concentrate on developing human and technological resources. By doing so, it was able to transcend the constraints inherent in a country with limited natural resources.

One of the national policies implemented to maximize the return from scarce R&D resources has been the promotion of cooperative R&D programs. While joint R&D in the U.S. has been limited to the largest firms involved in projects on a somewhat grandiose scale [13], cooperative R&D in Japan has included both large and small enterprises. Cooperative R&D programs are typically carried out through the institutions of trade associations and research institutes. However, there is considerable flexibility in the exact institutional form of joint R&D, and many projects are carried out under the auspices of informal agreements. As Hughes [14] points out, cooperative R&D agreements effectively reduce the risks, and therefore the costs, of undertaking R&D.

The first type of risk involves uncertainty regarding anticipated consumer demand. The second type involves technological uncertainty, and the third involves the uncertainty regarding the behavior and likely success of competitors with their own R&D projects. By spreading out the risks across firms and reducing duplication costs, the overall cost of undertaking R&D can be reduced with cooperative programs. In addition, the chance of successful innovation is enhanced by the relatively wide spectrum of activities typically found in most joint R&D projects. The achievements of cooperative R&D in Japan have been thus described by Goto and Wakasugi [8]: "With the institutional arrangement of research associations it became possible to undertake R&D projects jointly that were too common, too costly, too risky and/or too difficult for a single firm to tackle alone, thus solving the under-investment problem inherent in R&D investment." In general, Japanese joint R&D programs have minimized duplicate investment and wasteful R&D, and have also facilitated the administration and monitoring of government subsidiaries.

Another important distinction between U.S. experiments with joint R&D and those in Japan is that while the U.S. federal government abstains from intervention, the MITI has gone a long way in encouraging and sponsoring cooperative R&D programs in Japan. Cooperative R&D is often undertaken under the direct auspices of the MITI. Despite being nonprofit, research associations are still subject to the Japanese Antimonopoly Law. However, the Fair Trade Commission of Japan, which is the Japanese equivalent of the Federal Trade Commission and Antitrust Division of the Justice Department in the U.S., apparently does not interpret the existence of joint R&D projects as a violation of the collusion statutes. Although such agreements could conceivably be found to be in violation of section one of the Sherman Act in the U.S., Hughes [14] notes that such flexibility is characteristic of the Japanese approach:

> The Japanese system has frequently been praised for managing to combine cooperation and competition. The prevalence of consumers has been stressed as an unimportant feature of Japanese culture as well as of its economy. By achieving consensus, Japanese firms reduce the risks facing them individually as they invest in certain technologies and industries.

Research associations are the most prevelant form of joint R&D in Japan, and are typically structured along the lines of those in the United Kingdom. Such joint R&D associations became possible in Japan in 1961 with the passage of the Act on the Mining and Manufacturing Industry Technology Research Association. However, there are some important differences between Japanese research associations and their counterparts in the United Kingdom. First, while the typical research association in Japan is established in a so-called high-technology industry, those in the United Kingdom have generally been established in heavy-manufacturing industries. That is, cooperative R&D in industries tends to be undertaken in the birth and growth stages of the product life cycle in Japan, but in the mature and declining phases of the life cycle in the United Kingdom. The second distinction is that whereas in the United Kingdom research associations tend to focus on assisting firms with technical problems, in Japan research associations are oriented towards specific R&D programs.

Research undertaken under the auspices of a Japanese research association frequently is not carried out in a joint laboratory where the members engage in cooperative research. Rather, the R&D is usually carried out in each member's own research laboratory.[3] The resulting information and scientific knowledge is subsequently exchanged in a coordinated manner directed by the research association. This effectively speeds up the process of the diffusion of technological change. Upon completion of the project, the research association is usually dissolved.

Research associations have been formed in a number of industries spanning a range of R&D projects. For example, in 1981 the Mitsui group, composed of Sumitomo Chemicals, Mitsi Toatsu, Mitsubishi Chemicals, and the Biological Research Institute, joined together to undertake cooperative R&D in biotechnology, with particular emphasis on gene recombination and utilization [9]. Similarly, the Electric Car Research Association and the Technical Research Association for Optics [15] were united explicitly to carry out joint R&D. There were 51 research associations existing in Japan as of 1985. The government subsidized half of the 65 billion yen that was spent on R&D by these research associations in 1985.

Just as the government has played a significant role in promoting sicence and technology in Japan [5], it has also intervened to encourage the development and extent of cooperative R&D programs. The guidance of R&D resources has been an important goal of government policy throughout the postwar period. While the MITI's science and technology policies were oriented towards increasing overall productivity and providing a basic productive capacity during the early postwar years, the Japanese government has more recently become involved in financing R&D in high-technology industries, especially in high-risk industries.

To foster R&D in general, and cooperative R&D programs in particular, the government has relied upon instruments such as tax incentives, grants, and preferential financing for R&D projects, along with regional development programs. Of the total expenditures on R&D by the Japanese government since the 1960s, the MITI has typically accounted for more than 12%. In 1981 alone, the Japanese government spent $6.4 billion on major technology projects [9]. Of the total 1983 MITI budget for R&D of 170 billion yen (around $708 million), 50 billion yen (around $208 million) was allocated towards energy-related projects. The remaining 120 billion yen ($500 million) went towards programs including technology development for small- and medium-sized businesses, international R&D cooperation, R&D in the electronics and machinery industries, and R&D to alleviate environmental pollution [9].

There are essentially two methods that the Japanese government employs to channel government funds for R&D. The first involves programs that are entirely funded by the government. When the government completely finances R&D, the resulting inventions and discoveries are also the property of the government. Thus, all patents resulting from the R&D belong to the government. These patents are generally licensed out for a fee. The R&D itself is usually conducted either by a National Research Laboratory or else through a private research association, as discussed above. In the former case, 16 different laboratories carry out government-funded R&D under the direction of the Agency of Industrial Science and Technology (AIST), a department within the MITI. In the latter case, the government accepts proposals from private research associations responding to announced R&D projects. Upon approval, the proposals are funded by the government through consignment, or *itakuhi* payments. The project to develop high-speed computers for scientific and technical uses is a good example of this type of funding. As with the research performed by a National Research Laboratory, patents resulting from R&D done by a private research association belong to the MITI. However, the MITI allows nondiscriminatory access to its patents, and distributes the patents to any firms willing to pay the fee [9].

The second method by which the Japanese government channels R&D funds to industries is through so-called *conditional loans* (*hojokin* loans). The essential condition of these loans is that the firm borrowing the money will not be made liable for repayment of that loan if there is no profitable activity resulting from the R&D project within a seven-year period. (The length of this period was raised from five years to seven years in 1983. Before 1983, conditional loans could finance up to one half of the R&D expenditures for any particular project.) Since 1983, conditional loans have not been allowed to finance more than 45% of the entire R&D associated with a given project. These conditions obviously enhance their attractiveness to private firms. In addition, during the seven-year period interest is not usually charged.

In contrast to the case in which R&D is completely financed by the government, the firm that receives a conditional loan retains the legal right to patent and to license the inventions resulting from the R&D program. A striking example of a project that was funded by conditional loans is the VLSI semiconductor research project [9]. Peck and Goto [6] conclude that these conditional loans have been very effective in reducing some of the risks associated with relatively long-range R&D projects.

A higher-impact method used by the Japanese Government to channel funds to private firms for R&D involves outright grants and subsidies. In the late 1970s, these grants and subsidies averaged 0.3% of R&D in pharmaceuticals, 1.4% in machinery, 0.5% in precision equipment, 18.0% in agriculture, 19.0% in mining, 28.0% in transportation, and 6.5% in computers and semiconductors. The biotechnology industry was the recipient of $35 million in direct grants and subsidies in 1983. Similarly, $15 million in direct grants and subsidies from the government went towards R&D on flexible manufacturing systems, including numerically controlled machine tools, robots, and computer-aided manufacturing; and $48 million went towards R&D in the computer and semiconductor industries [9].

The extent to which the Japanese Government intervenes in private R&D decisions should be qualified. It is perhaps a widely held belief in western countries that the MITI regulates R&D in Japan. However, the Japanese government actually accounts for a smaller share of total R&D expenditures than do its western counterparts. Not only does Japan spend less on R&D per dollar of sales than do most other developed countries [17], but also the bulk of Japanese R&D originates from private firms and not from the government. For example, in 1985 Japan spent a total of 7.5 trillion yen on R&D, while R&D expenditures in the U.S. were the equivalent of around 19.0 trillion yen. This amounted to 2.57% of national income in Japan and 2.70% of national income in the U.S. While the government accounted for about one third of all R&D expenditures in the U.S., only 27% of the Japanese R&D emanated from government sources [17].

The important role that cooperative R&D plays in Japan raises the question of whether there is some type of trade off between cooperation and competition. Freeman [18] suggests that the MITI plays a key role in balancing the forces of competition with those of cooperation. While there is a natural tension between trying to attain a consensus regarding long-range planning and market forces, he argues that the Japanese example of a middle ground may actually promote rather than hinder the competitive process.

The policy towards patents suggests that the ultimate emphasis is on disseminating scientific knowledge while still preserving competition among firms. As described above, patents that have resulted from conditonal loans must be held jointly, although firms that participate in research associations may hold individual patents. In the case where patents resulting from the R&D are held jointly, the research association generally establishes the conditions for licensing agreements and fees. In certain instances, the MITI has provided research associations with direct grants and subsidies for the R&D. In these cases the resulting patents become the property of the MITI. The general rule, then, is that where the MITI has intervened by directly financing a part of the R&D, the resulting patents will be controlled by the government. If the R&D has been undertaken only by the private participants of the research association, then the resulting patents will be controlled by the firms themselves, usually under the direction of the research association.

Although the participating firms may lose control of the patents, there are several advantages, in addition to the financial resources, of having a research association sponsored by the MITI. When the MITI effectively sponsors cooperative R&D by either providing conditional loans or consigning research, small- and medium-sized firms are eligible to receive favorable treatment in government procurement and to receive additional grants from the MITI. For example, the laboratories controlled by the MITI may make contributions to the cooperative R&D project.

Table 6–1 shows the allocation of major cooperative R&D projects that were sponsored by the Japanese Government between 1966 and 1980 across aggregated industrial sectors.[4] There has been a pronounced tendency for the MITI to channel government funds into cooperative R&D projects in industries during the early stages of the product life cycle and to avoid projects in industries during the mature and declining stages. For example, nine of the 31 projects involved office machines and computers. The total funding amounted to around 170,945 million yen. Thus, slightly more than one quarter of the resources, both in terms of number of projects and in terms of funding, occurred in this one sector. Other sectors in which there was substantial funding of cooperative R&D projects by the government include chemicals, medicinals and pharmaceuticals, electrical machinery, transportation equipment, and instruments. These are the highest R&D-intensive sectors in Japanese manufacturing. Thus, the MITI has apparently focused on enhancing the international competitiveness of these high-R&D industries.

Because the cooperative R&D programs in aircraft, computers, machine tools, robotics, and semiconductors have played an important role in the overall technological progress in these industries as well as in contributing to their ascent to leading positions in the global market, these programs

Table 6–1. Major Cooperative R&D Projects Sponsored by the Japanese Government, 1966–1980, by Industrial Sector

Sector	Number of Projects	Approximate Funding (Million Yen)	Share of Total Sponsored Projects	
			Number (%)	Funding (%)
Chemicals	4	N/A	12.90	—
Medicinal and pharmaceuticals	3	56,640	9.68	10.07
Ceramics	1	14,160	3.23	2.52
Metal products	2	N/A	6.45	—
Nonelectrical machinery	1	13,000	3.23	2.31
Electrical machinery	4	52,120	12.90	9.27
Office machines and computers	9	170,945	29.03	30.40
Aircraft	5	133,400	16.13	23.72
Instruments	1	18,040	3.23	3.21
Other	1	104,000	3.23	18.50
Total	31	562,305	100.01	100.00

Source: U.S. International Trade Commission [9].

will be examined in somewhat more detail. As Peck points out, not only is it true that "...large-scale research projects carried out jointly by profit-making corporations have become increasingly important in the computer and semiconductor industry" [13], but it is also true that the Japanese government has played a critical role in sponsoring these cooperative research projects.

In 1955 the MITI founded the Research Committee on the Computer, which included the five major electrical equipment manufacturers: Fujitsu, Hitachi, Matushita, NEC, and Toshiba. The Committee was esablished to help the Japanese companies catch up to their larger and more advanced American counterparts [19]. The electrical equipment industry then quickly became the recipient of government targeting in the form of grants and subsidized loans for R&D, special tax treatment, and protection from foreign competition. The MITI was provided with a mandate to channel special assistance to the industry and to exempt it from the Anti-Monopoly Law by passage of the 1957 Law Providing Temporary Measures for the Promotion of the Electronics Industry. In 1961 the MITI formed the Japan Electronic Computer corporation, which consisted of Fujitsu, Hitachi, Mitsubishi, Oki, Toshiba, NEC, and Matsushita. The Japan Electronic Computer Corporation was essentially a joint enterprise and received substantial funding from the Japan Development Bank. The government funds were to be used expressly for cooperative R&D projects.

After IBM established its international dominance with the introduction of the third generation of computers, the MITI responded by devloping the large-scale computer project in 1966. Consisting of the six major electronics firms, the large-scale computer project received about $33 million from the government for R&D. Similarly, in 1971 the MITI initiated a cooperative R&D project to develop a fourth-generation computer based on large-scale integration in order to compete with the IBM 370 series. Five years later, the Electrotechnical Laboratory, which is one of the laboratories operating under the MITI, organized the Very-Large-Scale Integration (VLSI) project. The VLSI project consisted of five major electronic firms, including Hitachi, Fujitsu, Mitsubishi Electric, NEC, and Toshiba. The first phase of the VLSI project lasted from 1976 to 1979. While the MITI provided $132.3 million in the form of loans, the individual firms contributed an additional $190.9 million. Thus, the MITI was responsible for 40.93% of the funds used for the project. During the second phase, which lasted from 1981 to 1985, the MITI contributed $102.3 million in loans and the individual firms provided an additional $111.4 million.

Peck [13] argues that the VLSI project was instrumental in helping Japan's semiconductor industry to ascend to a leading position in the global market. Among its other accomplishments, the VLSI project resulted in the development of the 64K RAM chip. While the explicit goal of the project was the development of the fourth-generation computer, Peck notes that the project "...served to overcome the small scale of individual company research" [13]. The five companies comprising the VLSI project subsequently proceeded to form the VLSI Semiconductor Research Association, with a budget of $325 million, including $136 million of government money. More recently, the new-function semiconductor research project includes 10 firms in an association commissioned by the MITI for the purposes of cooperative R&D [20, 21].

As table 6–2 shows, there were nine cooperative R&D projects sponsored by the government between 1966 and 1980 in the office machine and computer industries. The Supercomputer project is scheduled to last nine years, from 1981 to 1989. The goal of the project is to develop a computer

Table 6-2. Cooperative R&D Projects in the Office Machine and Computer Industries Sponsored by the Japanese Government, 1966-1980

Project	Period	Purpose	Funding (Million Yen)	Companies Involved
Computers	1972-1976	Development of basic technology for 3rd- and 5th-generation computers	8,700	Fujitsu, Hitachi, Mitsubishi Electric, NEC, Oki Toshiba
Very-large-scale project (VLSI)	1976-1979	Development of basic technology for extra large-scale integrators of 4th-generation computers	30,000	Fujitsu, Hitachi, Mitsubishi Electric, NEC, Toshiba
Development of basic software and related periphery	1979-1983	Development of software for the 4th-generation computers, particularly operating system software	47,000	Fujitsu, Hitachi, Matsushita Electric, Mitsubishi Electric, NEC, Oki, Sharp, Toshiba
Pattern information processing system (PIPS)	1971-1980	Development of technology for an information processing system capable of understanding patterns of words, colors, voice, and sounds	22,073	Hitachi, Fujitsu, Matsushita, Mitsubishi, NEC, Oki, Sanyo, Toshiba, Hoya Glass
High-speed scientific computer	1981-1989	Development of technology for an information processing system	22,073	Fujitsu, Toshiba, NEC, Mitsubishi Electric, Sanyo, Matsushita, Konishiroku, Hoya Glass

Table 6-2. *(continued)*

Project	Period	Purpose	Funding (Million Yen)	Companies Involved
Flexible manufacturing system using lasers	1977–1982	Development of a complex production system that can produce various kinds of machinery components and parts in small batches	13,000	N/A
Software automation	1976–1981	Develop capability for computers to write own software automatically	6,600	Over 100 software firms
Development of 5th-generation computers	1979–1991	Development of 1990s computers	11,375	Fujitsu, Hitachi, Mitsbuishi, NEC, Oki, Toshiba
Development of super-high-speed performance computers, large scale	1966–1971	Development of the newest, most powerful computer. All combine high-performance software to create the largest model computer system	10,124	Fujitsu, Hitachi, Mitsubishi, NEC, Toshiba, Oki

Source: U.S. International Trade Commission [9].

114

with extremely high-speed calculating capabilities and with particular applications for science and defense. The research is being carried out at the Electrotechnical Laboratory, which operates under the auspices of the MITI, as well as in each of the participating firms' laboratories. The fifth-generation computer project is a 12-year project that lasts until 1991. The goal of the project is to develop computers that possess some degree of artificial intelligence and that have the ability to evalutate knowledge independently rather than just to process date mechanically. In addition, the MITI has also sponsored a number of joint R&D programs that are attempting to develop advanced computer software. As part of the Next-Generation Computer Project,[5] a software-development program is being funded to develop standard operating systems and new program languages. The total funding for the project is about $192 million, with about one half of the funds coming from the government [9].

The cooperative R&D projects that were established between 1966 and 1980 in the aircraft and electrical machinery industries are listed in table 6-3. As with computers, and more recently semiconductors, the civil aircraft industry has been the recipient of considerable targeting by the Japanese government. What is perhaps most striking is that, despite the preferential loans and direct grants and subsidies from the government, the industry has not performed well in the global market. The MITI has been heavily involved in funding joint R&D associations in the industry through the Agency for Industrial Science and Technology (AIST). In a project designed to develop fan-jet aircraft engines, the AIST contributed to a consortium of Japanese firms, including Kawasaki, IHI, and Mitsubishi, slightly more than 20 billion yen in consignment payments between 1971 and 1982. The Japanese firms worked in conjunction with Rolls-Royce to develop the FJR-710 engine [22].

The goal of the STOL project was to develop a civil-aircraft engine. The project has been supported by the Science and Technology Agency of the Prime Minister's Office and by the MITI's National Aerospace Laboratory. With a goal of developing a 767 aircraft in cooperation with Boeing, the Civil Transport Development Corporation (CTDC) was formed in 1973. CTDC consisted of Mitsubishi, Kawasaki, and Fuji Heavy Industries and was operated under the auspices of the MITI—in other words, the budget, financial statements, and planned activities were first approved by the MITI. The MITI accounted for nearly half of the costs of the project. Most of the funds were channeled to the CTDC through success-conditional loans [22].

Cooperative R&D projects have played a similarly important role in the machine-tool industry. Several large joint projects have been recently es-

Table 6-3. Cooperative R&D Projects in the Aircraft and Electrical Machinery Industries Sponsored by the Japanese Government, 1966–1980

Project	Period	Purpose	Funding (Million Yen)	Companies Involved
Aircraft	1978–1982	International joint development of 200-seat aircraft resulting in the Boeing 767	16,000	Kawasaki, Fuji, Mitsubishi
Development of civil-aircraft engine RJ-500	1980–1987	International joint development of an engine for a 150-seat jet with Rolls Royce Ltd.	47,000	IHI, Kawasaki, Mitsubishi
Development of next-generation civil aircraft	1981–1987	International joint development of 150-seat jet	25,000	N/A
FJR-170 experimental engine	1971–1981	Develop civil-aircraft engine	20,400	IHI, Kawasaki, Mitsubishi
STOL aircraft	1978–1990	To develop a commercial short take-off and landing aircraft	25,000	Kawasaki, others
New function elements-integrated circuits		Develop technologies basic to industries of the 1990s	27,120	N/A
Supergrid components (ICs)	1981–1990	Develop technologies basic to industries of the 1990s	8,000	Fujitsu, Hitachi, Sumitomo Denko
Three-dimensional components (ICs)	1981–1990	Develop technologies basic to industries of the 1990s	9,000	Nippon Electric Corp. (NEC), Oki, Toshiba, Mitsubishi Electric, Sanyo Electric, Matsushita Electric, Sharp
Elements with increased resistance to the environment	1981–1988	Develop technologies basic to industries of the 1990s	8,000	Toshiba, Hitachi, Mitsubishi Electric

Source: U.S. International Trade Commission [9].

116

tablished. In 1977, for example, 20 firms joined a cooperative project for developing complex manufacturing systems that use lasers. Also in 1977, another joint project with the goal of developing flexible manufacturing systems was established. As with computers, semiconductors, and aircraft, the government has played an active role in promoting these cooperative R&D projects. Recently, the government has been channeling between 10 and 15 billion yen annually into the machine-tool industry in the form of direct grants for R&D. However, the smaller firms tend to be the beneficiaries of government-sponsored R&D programs. It may be that the larger firms feel they have more to lose if they share their accumulated knowledge with smaller firms. [23].

Another embryonic industry in Japan, robotics, has also been targeted for government support for cooperative R&D programs. The Japan Industrial Robot Association was the recipient of 770.0 million yen to support a joint R&D project to develop the utilization of industrial robots and 100.0 million yen for a project to develop safety and automation technologies for deburring cast-iron applications. The Japan Industrial Robot Assocation is essentially a trade assocation representing the major producers in the industry [9].

Table 6-4 lists the cooperative R&D projects in the medical and pharmaceutical and chemical industries sponsored by the Japanese government between 1966 and 1980. Like most of the other cooperative R&D projects supported by the government, those in the chemical and drug industries typically involve new products and technologies.

3. The Effectiveness of Japanese R&D Policies

Most evaluations of cooperative R&D in Japan, or in any country for that matter, have been quite subjective. For example, the U.S. International Trade Commission [9], in its evaluation of cooperative R&D undertaken in Japan, concluded, "Cooperative research and development projects that are jointly financed by the government and private industry frequently have been used to make Japanese firms more competitive in targeted industries." Because cooperative R&D and government policy are so highly interrelated, it is virtually impossible to separate cooperative R&D from R&D in general and from the targeting policies of the government. As the Director General of the Planning Bureau of the Science and Technology Agency of Japan acknowledges, "Generally speaking, the development of technology requires large amounts of expenditures and long periods between investments and profit returns. In most cases it is too risky for the

Table 6–4. Cooperative R&D Projects in the Medicinals and Pharmaceuticals and Chemicals Industries Sponsored by the Japanese Government, 1966–1980

Project	Period	Purpose	Funding (Million Yen)	Companies Involved
Technology for large-scale cultivation and utilization for biotechnology	1981–1990	Develop technologies basic to industries of the 1990s	28,320	Asahi Chemicals, Ajinonmoto, Kyowa Fermentation, Takeda Pharmaceutics, Toyo
Bio reactor	1981–1990	Develop technologies basic to industries of the 1990s	28,320	Kao Soap, Daiseru Chemicals, Electro-Chemistry, Mitsui Petro-chemicals, Mitsubishi Gas, Mitsubishi Chemicals
Gene recombination and utilization	1981–1990	Develop technologies basic to industries of the 1990s	N/A	Sumitomo Chemicals, Mitsui Toatsu, Mitsubishi Chemicals, Biological Research Inst.
High-efficiency separation film	1981–1990	Develop technologies basic to industries of the 1990s	N/A	Toray, Teijin, Asahi Chemicals, Kuraray, Toyobo
Conductive macromolecule	1981–1990	Develop technologies basic to industries of the 1990s	N/A	Suminoto Denko, Daiseru Chemicals Asahi Glass, Mitsubishi Chemicals
High-crystalline macromolecule	1981–1990	Develop technologies basic to industries of the 1990s	N/A	Toray, Teijin, Asahi Chemicals, Sumitomo, Denko, Sumitomo Chemicals
High-molecular-composite materials	1981–1990	Develop technologies basic to industries of the 1990s	N/A	Toray, Teijin, Mitsubishi Chemicals, Nippon Carbon

Source: U.S. International Trade Commission [9].

private sector alone to carry it out. Consquently, it is the government that plays a leading role in promoting R&D" [23]. That is, just as cooperative R&D cannot be separated from the entirety of R&D and technology policies in Japan, it also cannot be separated from the industrial policies implemented by the government.

Thus, in this section we relate the shifts in R&D intensity over time to the specific industries that have received support from the Japanese government to undertake cooperative R&D. In addition, we relate the performance of Japanese exports to the R&D policy to evaluate the success of Japanese R&D. Of course, since cooperative R&D is a vital component of the overall R&D policy, any inferences about the success of R&D policy presumably reflect upon the viability of cooperative R&D.

Table 6–5 provides two measures of R&D intensity in Japanese manufacturing industries—R&D expenditures-per-sales and the percentage of scientists in the labor force, both for 1969 and 1979. With respect to the industries in which most of the major cooperative R&D projects sponsored by the Japanese government took place, there are two important trends. The first is that industries in which R&D intensity is not only relatively high, but also increasing between 1969 and 1979, also tend to be industries in which there was a substantial amount of cooperative R&D. The medicinals and pharmaceuticals, electrical machinery, computers, transportation equipment, and instruments industries all experienced 1) high levels of R&D intensity, 2) an increase in R&D intensity during the decade of the 1970s, and 3) substantial cooperative R&D activity funded by the government. The second trend is that industries in which R&D intensity is not only relatively low, but also decreasing between 1969 and 1979, also tend to be industries in which there was no or very little cooperative R&D. The textiles, paper, and ceramics industries all experienced 1) low levels of R&D intensity 2) a decrease in R&D intensity during the decade of the 1970s, and 3) no significant cooperative R&D activity funded by the government.

The only major exceptions to these patterns occurred in the rubber and plastics industry, where there was an increase in R&D over this period but no major cooperative R&D projects sponsored by the government, and in the nonelectrical machinery sector, where there was a marked decrease in R&D intensity but substantial cooperative R&D activity still took place. In general, however, it is apparent that the government has tended to place priority in targeting for cooperative R&D projects industries that are high in R&D and becoming even more so. That is, the government appears to believe that promoting cooperative R&D in the so-called high-tech industries will yield a greater return than in mature and declining industries.

Table 6−5.   Japanese Export Performance and R&D by Industrial Sector,
1962−1984

Industry	Japanese Mean Export Share[a]		R&D/Sales (%)		Percentage of Scientists in Labor Force	
	1962–1974	1975–1984	1969	1979	1969	1979
Food and beverages	0.0989	0.0689	0.27	0.51	0.45	1.45
Textiles	0.4053	0.2899	1.67	0.82	4.02	1.12
Paper	0.2030	0.1887	2.30	0.42	2.49	1.51
Chemicals	0.1516	0.1408	3.17	2.54	4.50	5.80
Medicinals and pharmaceuticals	0.0780	0.0915	1.67	5.53	1.16	6.22
Rubber and plastic	0.1953	0.3517	0.71	2.44	2.50	2.84
Ceramics	0.7471	0.2623	1.99	1.27	2.33	1.66
Iron and steel	0.3751	0.5025	0.58	1.04	1.60	2.22
Metal products	0.4023	0.5162	0.31	1.28	2.26	1.77
Nonelectrical machinery	0.0955	0.4850	5.43	1.85	4.54	2.60
Electrical machinery	0.3826	0.6065	1.31	3.55	2.81	6.17
Office machines and computers	0.1002	0.3810	1.82	3.91	1.76	6.81
Transportation equipment	0.4414	0.2848	1.68	2.37	2.45	2.51
Instruments	0.3312	0.4685	1.59	2.94	1.53	3.94

[a] Defined as the share of exports in the market comprised solely by the EC, Japan, and the U.S.

Source: The export data are from the OECD and the R&D measures are from Japan, Bureau of Statistics, Office of the Prime Minister, Report on the Survey of Research and Development in Japan (annual).

One way to measure the success of Japan's R&D policy is to compare Japan's trade performance in these high-R&D industries, where virtually all of the cooperative R&D projects occur, with low-R&D industries, where there is a marked absence of such projects. The measure of trade performance used in table 6–5 is the Japanese mean share of exports in the market composed of the U.S., EC countries, and Japan. The market is limited to these three regions,[6] since the U.S. and EC countries clearly represent the greatest rivals for high-R&D products.

The OECD trade statistics enable analysis of the Japanese mean export share among these three regions to be undertaken at a farily disaggregated level.[7] The consideration of export patterns over a relatively long period, 1962–1984, enables 165 industries to be included in the data sample.[8] To maintain consistency over time, only the six original member countries in the region constituting the EC are included.[9] The Japanese export share (JXS_{it}) in industry j and period t is defined as the exports from Japan to the EC and U.S. (JX_{it}), divided by the total amount of exports from each of the three regions to the remaining two:

$$JXS_{it}^{j} = JX_{it}^{j} \bigg/ \sum_{i=1}^{3} X_{it}^{j},$$

where X_{it} is defined as the exports of a given region to the other two regions.

The advantage of this export-share measure is that it reflects the relative competitiveness of Japan vis-a-vis the EC and the U.S. One important qualification is that this measure does not at all indicate the performance of exports in markets outside these countries. For certain products, export competition in third-party markets may be, in fact, more significant that in the markets of these major trading partners. An additional qualification is that the extent of foreign direct investment is not incorporated in the export-share measure. Because foreign direct investment can be a substitute for exporting, this omission is likely to distort, at least somewhat, inferences regarding industries such as transportation equipment and chemicals.

The Japanese mean export share is compared between two subperiods, 1962–1974 and 1975–1984. For example, the mean export share of Japan in the 30 disaggregated industries comprising the broader food and beverages industry was 9.89% in the early period and 6.89% in the recent period. There are three important trends that can be identified between the change in the Japanese export performance over these two periods and R&D intensity, which, as explained above, generally coincides with the intensity to which the government supports cooperative R&D projects. The first trend is that in industries in which the Japanese mean export share decreased between the two periods, R&D intensity also decreased. Industries such as textiles, paper, and ceramics fit into this category. These are industries in which there has been virtually no government support for cooperative R&D.

The second trend is that in industries in which Japan's export performance improved over the two periods, R&D intensity also increased. Industries such as electrical machinery, computers, instruments, metal products, and iron and steel fit into this category. Many of these industries were targeted for government support of cooperative R&D programs. Finally, in several industries, such as chemicals, there was no appreciable change in either export performance or R&D intensity. Thus, there appears to be at least some evidence that the Japanese export performance tended to be stronger in industries in which government R&D policy, including the support of cooperative R&D programs, played a major role. However, whether this observed statistical tendency implies that the MITI's policies were actually responsible for the strong Japanese export performance cannot be unequivocally ascertained. For example, it is conceivable that the MITI, in fact, had a policy of targeting industries that were relatively strong and likely to succeed in the world market.[10]

4. Conclusions

The rich tradition emphasizing individual enterprise in the U.S. has caused Fusfeld and Haklisch [24] to observe "An element of contradiction is implicit in the phrase 'collaborative research'." While such an inherent contradiction surely exists in the U.S., it is less apparent in Japan. Just as the U.S. has relied upon individual units competing with each other to ensure markets with a maximum amount of technological progress, Japan has emphasized cooperation. That is, there is a long tradition in Japan of directing resources by the government towards their most productive use. Thus, cooperative R&D policies in Japan cannot be analyzed independent of the entirety of R&D and technology policies in Japan. Joint R&D can only be analyzed in the context of how successful the entire Japanese R&D policy was.

In this chapter the role of the government in directing cooperative R&D resources in Japan has been examined. While it would be virtually impossible, due to the reasons discussed above, to provide a general quantitative test of the success of Japanese joint R&D and the government's specific support of such programs, several simple empirical patterns do emerge. First, the government has tended to target support in high-tech and high-information industries rather than in industries in the mature and declining stages of the product life cycle. The targeted industries are generally industries that are both R&D-intensive and becoming increasingly so. Second, the trade performance of Japanese industries in these industries vis-à-vis their American and European counterparts has generally been improving rather than deteriorating. This leads to the conclusion that the empirical evidence is consistent with the hypothesis that those Japanese industries that have been targeted by the government for support to carry out joint R&D programs have consistently exhibited a superior trade performance.

Nelson [25] argues that the boundaries of cooperative R&D programs will become increasingly transnational in the future: "Companies do need broad-gauged competence to compete in complex, connected, fast-moving fields. Companies in such fields are increasingly multinational. And joint ventures of a relatively broad and long-lived nature will become increasingly important, further blurring national lines." However, Yamamura [26] doubts whether the old industrial policies implemented by the MITI will be flexible and effective under such a transnational scenario. Similarly, Imai and Itami [27] suggest that, as innovation becomes relatively more important and imitation relatively less important in Japan, the government policies that served to promote imitation may not be the appropriate ones conducive to innovation. Thus, whether the government's active support of cooperative R&D programs in Japan continues to be successful in the future remains an open question.

Notes

1. For example, see the prepared testimonies of F. M. Scherer, and of Zoltan J. Acs and David B. Audretsch on "R&D and Small Firms" before the Subcommittee on Monopolies and Commercial Law, Committee on the Judiciary, U.S. House of Representatives, February 24, 1988.

2. These controls were ended by the late 1960s.

3. In fact, the only research associations that have their own laboratories are the Very Large Scale Project (VLSI) Research Association, which is devoted to developing the basic technology for extra-large-scale integrators for the fourth-generation computers, and the Opt-Electronics Research Association [8].

4. Several of these projects did not actually begin until 1981.

5. Because the Next-Generation Computer Project was scheduled for 1982–1985, it is not included in table 6–2.

6. Since the EC constitutes a region and not a country, the standard of referring to the EC, Japan, and U.S. as regions is adapted here.

7. The export data are from the annual reports of the Organization for Economic Cooperation and Development (OECD), *Trade by Commodities (Market Summaries: Exports)*, Paris.

8. A list of these industries is available upon request from the author.

9. The original EC countries included are Belgium, France, Germany, Italy, Luxembourg,

and the Netherlands.

10. However, even in the context of multiple regression analysis, where the major factors determining trade flows have been controlled for, Japanese industrial policy and R&D policy are still found to have a positive influence on the Japanese trade advantage [10, 12].

References

1. Link, A.N., and Bauer, L.L. "An Economic Analysis of Cooperative Research." *Technovation* 6 (1984): 247–260.
2. Pugel, T.A. "Industrial Policy in Japan: Implications for Technological Catch-Up in Leadership." In: T.A. Pugel (ed.), *Fragile Interdependence: Economic Issues in U.S.–Japanese Trade and Investment*. Lexington, MA: D.C. Heath, 1986, pp. 209–227.
3. Ueno, H. "The Conception and Evaluation of Japanese Industrial Policy." In: K. Sato (ed.), *Industry and Business in Japan*. White Plains, NY: 1980.
4. Krause, L.B., and Sekiguchi, S. "Japan and the World Economy." In: H. Patrick and H. Rosovsky (eds), *Asia's New Giant: How the Japanese Economy Works*. Washington, DC: The Brookings Institution, 1976, pp. 383–458.
5. Audretsch, D.B. *The Market and the State*. Brighton: Wheatsheaf, 1989.
6. Pugel, T.A. "Japan's Industrial Policy: Instruments Trends, and Effects." *Journal of Comparative Economics* 8 (1984): 420–435.
7. Peck, M.J., and Tamura, S. "Technology." In: H. Patrick and H. Rosovsky (eds.), *Asia's new Giant: How the Japanese Economy Works*. Washington, DC: The Brookings Institution, 1976, pp. 525–586.
8. Goto, A., and Wakasugi, R. "Technology Policy in Japan: A Short Review." *Technovation* 5 (1987): 269–279.
9. United States International Trade Commission. *Foreign Industrial Targeting and Its Effects on U.S. Industries, Phase I: Japan*. USITC publication 1437, Washington, DC, 1983.
10. Audretsch, D.B., and Yamawaki, H. "R&D Rivalry, Industrial Policy, and U.S.–Japanese Trade." *Review of Economics and Statistics*, 70 (1988): 438–447.
11. Odagiri, H., and Iwata, H. "The Impact of R&D on Productivity Increase in Japanese Manufacturing Companies." *Research Policy* 15 (1986): 13–19.
12. Yamawaki, H., and Audretsch, D.B. "Import Share under International Oligopoly with Differentiated Products: Japanese Imports in U.S. Manufacturing." *Review of Economics and Statistics*, 70 (1988): 569–579.
13. Peck, M.J. "Joint R&D: The Case of Microelectronics and the Computer Technology Corporation." *Research Policy* 15 (1986): 219–231.
14. Hughes, K.S. "The Changing Dynamics of International Technological Competition." In: D.B. Audretsch, L. Sleuwaegen, and H. Yamawaki (eds.), *The Convergence of International and Domestic Markets*. Amsterdam: North-Holland, 1989.

15. Saxonhouse, G. R., "Evolving Comparative Advantage and Japan's Import of Manufactures." In: K. Yamamura (ed.), *Policy and Trade Issues of the Japanese Economy*. Seattle: University of Washington Press, 1982.

16. Peck, M. J., and Goto, A. "Technology and Economic Growth: The Case of Japan." *Research Policy* 10 (1981): 222–243.

17. National Science Board. *Science Indicators*. Washington, DC: National Science Foundation, 1985.

18. Freeman, C. *Technology Policy and Economic Performance*. London: Pinter, 1987.

19. Peck, M. J. "Government Coordination of R&D in the Japanese Electronic Industry." Yale University Economics Dept. Working Paper, 1983.

20. Wheeler, J. W.; Janow, M. E.; and Pepper, T. *Japanese Industrial Development Policies in the 1980s: Implications for U.S. Trade and Investment*. Croton-on-the-Hudson, NY: Hudson Institute, 1980.

21. United States General Accounting Office. *Industrial Policy: Case Studies in the Japanese Experience*. Washington, DC: U.S. Government Printing Office, 1982.

22. United States General Accounting Office. *Industrial Policy: Japan's flexible Approach*. Washington, DC: U.S. Government Printing Office, 1983.

23. Sonoyama, S. "Japanese Innovation Policy." In: *Organization for Economic Co-operation and Development, Innovation policy: Trends and Perspectives*. Paris: 1982, pp. 51–55.

24. Fusfeld, H. I., and Haklisch, C. S. "Collaborative Industrial Research in the U.S." *Technovation* 5 (1987): 305–315.

25. Nelson, R. "The Role of Knowledge in R&D Efficiency." *Quarterly Journal of Economics* 97 (1982): 453–470.

26. Yamamura, K. "Caveat Empor: the Industrial Policy of Japan." In: P. Krugman (ed.), *Strategic Trade Policy and the New Industrial Economics*. Cambridge, MA: MIT Press, 1986.

27. Imai, K. I., and Itami, H. "Interpenetration of Organisation and Market." *International Journal of Industrial Organisation* 2 (1984): 285–310.

7 COOPERATIVE RESEARCH AND INTERNATIONAL RIVALRY

L. Fernando Ruiz-Mier

1. Introduction

The competitive position of the U.S. in the international economy has been eroding in recent years. This erosion has been attributed to a number of complex factors. Among the factors frequently mentioned is the practice of industrial targeting, or more generally industrial policy on the part of the U.S. trading partners. It has been argued that an activist industrial policy on the part of foreign governments may confer upon foreign firms an unfair comparative advantage.[1] Demands for a U.S. industrial policy and for retaliatory trade practices are based, in part, on the notion that strategic moves by foreign firms with the support of their governments are placing U.S. firms under considerable pressures.

One area that has attracted special attention is that of policies aimed at stimulating research and development (R&D). The case of industrial policies aimed at R&D is particularly interesting because it is believed that R&D policy is central to any discussion of the international trade position of the U.S. in high-technology industries [2]. A report released by the President's Commission on Industrial Competitiveness in January 1985 emphasized that the chief comparative advantage of the U.S. is its technological superiority. The commission suggested that the U.S. industry's competitive potential can be released only if this advantage is strengthened and promoted. Furthermore, there is some support for the view that R&D has been successfully employed by Japanese firms as a strategic instrument to enhance market share.[2]

Policies aimed at stimulating research and development have, for the most part, consisted of tax credits and/or subsidies. The role of cooperative research or research joint ventures (RJVs) as a means of stimulating R&D, however, has received considerable attention recently. It is believed that allowing firms to engage in cooperative research could lead to increased levels of R&D.[3]

Although the rationale for policies aimed at increasing R&D is couched in terms of the effect of increased R&D on the overall competitive position of the U.S., the theoretical discussion of cooperative research has been done in the context of closed economy models. Polices aimed at increasing the R&D level of domestic firms are not considered to be trade policies in the traditional sense. However, by promoting such policies, which alter the environment in which domestic firms operate, the government may indirectly affect the competitive position of these firms in international markets. Thus, a government may be able to influence the institutional environment so as to confer upon its national firms a competitive edge. This is a form of *endogenous comparative advantage* and has been referred to as strategic trade policy or industrial policy in the trade literature.

The recent trade literature suggests that strategic trade policy can, under certain conditions, improve a country's welfare relative to free trade. One way in which policies can improve a country's position is by enhancing the ability of domestic firms to secure a larger share of world markets in which rents are present. It should be noted that this argument presumes that the industry in question is imperfectly competitive.

This chapter considers the trade-related effects of cooperative research ventures among domestic firms. The formation of research joint ventures may require a relaxation of antitrust restrictions. Thus the government's policy would be one of altering the institutional environment so as to facilitate cooperative research by domestic firms. We investigate the effects of an RJV on domestic R&D levels as well as on the competitiveness of domestic firms in an international market.

2. The Setting

To study the effects of allowing domestic firms to engage in joint research ventures, a simple, yet illustrative structure based on the previous work of

Ruiz-Mier and Link [5] and Ruiz-Mier [6] is employed. The focus is on the case of two domestic firms competing against one foreign firm. The three firms produce the same product for the same international market.[4] Once the two domestic firms choose to participate in a cooperative research agreement, the model can be viewed as a two-stage game. The first stage consists of firms choosing the optimal levels of R&D so as to maximize profits. The second stage consists of each firm choosing the profit-maximizing level of output, given the production costs associated with the R&D performed in the previous stage.

The focus is on a Cournot–Nash equilibrium concept. That is, as firms choose R&D and output levels in the first and second stages, respectively, they take the levels of their competitors as given. The establishment of a research joint venture will, by altering the incentives of domestic firms, lead to a different outcome in the first, and consequently the second, stages. It is assumed, however, that once the research agreement is established, the two domestic firms choose their R&D levels independently so as to maximize profits. The discussion focuses, for simplicity, on the symmetric case. Furthermore, to focus attention on the effects of RJVs it is assumed that the two countries differ only in that an RJV is established in one country.

The analysis is linked to the strategic trade literature. The general idea is that in certain markets, domestic firms are players in an international market game and that certain policies, by altering the environment in which domestic firms operate, can confer upon firms a comparative advantage. When the domestic firms operate in markets in which rents are being made, it may be in a country's best interest to adopt policies so as to place its firms in a favorable position, thus enabling them to capture a greater share of the rents. Various writers have illustrated the possibility that subsidies or other policies can increase a country's rent share, thereby increasing its welfare at the expense of other countries.[5] In markets where rents exist, a trade subsidy provides firms with a credible strategy that allows them to expand output. Rival firms respond by contracting their output, thereby increasing the price, and hence the profits that the expanding firms can obtain. This adjustment is referred to as the *strategic* effect.

3. The Nature of R&D and Research Agreements

In order to describe the problem and introduce some notation, let us consider one firm's choice of a level of R&D. Let r_i denote the ith firm's expenditure on R&D. The effective level of R&D available to firm i, denoted $t^i(\cdot)$, is given by

$$t^i(r^1,\ldots,r^n) = r^i + \phi\Sigma r^j \qquad i, j = 1,\ldots,n \quad i \neq j \qquad 0 \leq \phi \leq 1. \quad (7.1)$$

Equation (7.1) illustrates the fact that a firm could capture, in part, the knowledge resulting from other firms' R&D activities. The degree to which the output of other firms' R&D activities spills over to firm i is quantified by the parameter ϕ. We assume, for simplicity, that there are no spillovers unless a RJV is established.[6] In such a case, ϕ captures the extent to which one member benefits from R&D undertaken by other member firms, and n is the number of firms that have joined the RJV.

The result of both direct and indirect R&D efforts is the lowering of production costs (R&D is process-improving). Abstracting from risk considerations, the relationship between R&D and costs is presumed to the deterministic and given by

$$c^i = c\,(t^i). \qquad (7.2)$$

Assume that $c' < 0$, $c'' > 0$, $c'(t) \to -\infty$ as $t \to 0$ and $c'(t) \to 0$ as $t \to \infty$. Further assume that unit production costs are independent of output levels.

A research agreement has to specify rules for sharing both costs and the results of R&D as well as the particular way in which R&D will be performed. In general, the sharing rules that characterize a research joint venture will be chosen optimally by member firms. For the purpose of simplicity, the choice of rules is not modeled. Thus when evaluating the RJV option, firms consider only one type of agreement.[7]

This description of cooperative research is a modified version of that of Katz [9]. Each of the firms engaged in cooperative research has an R&D department. Once firms agree on how to share the costs and results of R&D, each chooses the level of R&D to be undertaken in its R&D department. Firms share the cost of R&D and the result of R&D efforts according to the following rules.

3.1. Cost Sharing

The RJV will be characterized by linear cost-sharing rules. Total expenditures on R&D for the ith firm engaged in an RJV is given by

$$\lambda r^i + (1 - \lambda)\, r^j \qquad i \neq j \qquad 0 \leq \lambda \leq 1, \qquad (7.3)$$

where λ is the share of the costs of its own R&D that a firm must bear and $(1 - \lambda)$ is the share of another member's R&D costs that each firm must bear. When firms do not enter RJV agreements, $\lambda = 1$, and the firms must bear the full cost of their R&D activities.

3.2. R&D Sharing

When an RJV is formed, member firms share the results of each other's R&D activities. A firm's effective level of R&D is thus a function of its own R&D efforts as well as those of other member firms. The specific form in which R&D results are shared is captured by equation (7.1). When the RJV consists of only two firms, the ith firm's effective R&D level can be written as

$$t^i\,(r^i,\,r^j) = r^i + \phi r^j \qquad i \neq j \qquad 0 \leqslant \phi \leqslant 1. \tag{7.4}$$

As noted above, the parameter ϕ captures the extent to which the results of one firm's R&D can be passed on to another member firm. In general, ϕ can be viewed as a choice parameter that might be constrained by technological and/or policy considerations.

4. The Effect of Cooperative Research Agreements

Our consideration of equilibrium in the presence of a cooperative research agreement is limited to the case of a symmetric outcome. In such a case, both member firms will have identical levels of effective R&D. Letting superscripts 1 and 2 denote the two domestic firms and superscript 3 denote the foreign firm, the profit functions can be written as

$$\Pi^i\,(x;\,t^i\,(r^1,\,r^2)) = R^i\,(x^1,\,x^2,\,x^3) - c^i\,(t^i)x^i - \lambda r^i$$
$$- (1 - \lambda)\,r^j \qquad i,\,j = 1,\,2 \quad i \neq j \tag{7.5}$$

for the domestic firms and

$$\Pi^3\,(x;\,t^3\,(r^3)) = R^3\,(x^1,\,x^2,\,x^3) - c^3\,(t^3)\,x^3 - r^3 \tag{7.6}$$

for the foreign firm. Output levels are denoted by x^i, and $R(\cdot)$ denotes the revenue function. It is assumed that $R^i_j < 0$ and $R^i_{ij} < 0 \; (i \neq j)$.

In the output stage, firms will choose their profit-maximizing levels of output taking R&D levels as given. The optimal output levels will depend on the effective R&D levels and can be written as

$$x^i = q^i\,(t^1\,(r^1,\,r^2),\,t^2\,(r^1,\,r^2),\,t^3\,(r^3)) \qquad i = 1,\,2,\,3. \tag{7.7}$$

The resolution of the R&D stage determines the optimal levels of R&D for each of the three firms. In the absence of an RJV ($\lambda = 1$, $\phi = 0$), the three firms will choose the same level of R&D expenditures. Denoting this cost by r^o,

$$r^o = r^1 = r^2 = r^3,$$

implying that the level of R&D, say t^o, is also identical across firms:

$$t^o = t^1 = t^2 = t^3.$$

The equality of R&D levels across firms will, in turn, lead to equal output levels, and hence market shares. It should be noted that, given the nature of the Nash equilibrium, firms have no incentives to depart from their choices of R&D levels.

It can be seen, from equations (7.5) and (7.6) that the establishment of a research joint venture ($\lambda < 1$, $\phi > 0$) alters the position of the domestic firms relative to the foreign firm. How this agreement affects industry equilibrium can be shown to depend on the nature of the research agreement as well as on the relevant demand conditions. Industry equilibrium, or the resolution of the output stage, depends on the R&D levels that obtain in the first stage. More specifically, it can be shown that $x_i^i > 0$, $x_i^j \gtrless 0$ and $x_i^3 < 0$, where the subscript i denotes the derivative with respect to the ith firm's level of R&D.[8] This implies that, as the R&D level chosen by domestic firms increases relative to the foreign firm's R&D level, the market share of domestic firms will also increase. Keeping this is mind, attention is given to how the particular type of the agreement will affect the level of R&D. When doing this, it is useful to focus on each of the parameters characterizing the RJV agreement separately.

On the one hand, sharing the costs of R&D increases the firms' incentives to conduct R&D and thereby leads to a higher level of R&D. That is, a decrease in λ, by lowering a firm's own cost of R&D, induces the firm to choose a higher level of R&D. On the other hand, R&D output sharing lowers the incentives to conduct R&D but raises the efficiency of R&D. Thus, an increase in ϕ, by providing the other member firm with a higher level of R&D and thereby causing it to expand output, affects the firm's revenues negatively and induces it to choose a lower level of R&D.[9] At the same time, however, a higher degree of R&D sharing will, by reducing duplicative efforts, result in a more efficient provision of R&D.

The net effect of a research agreement on R&D levels will depend on the magnitude of λ relative to ϕ. The relationship between these two parameters and effective R&D levels is illustrated in figure 7–1. The upper left-hand corner of the box diagram, labeled N, corresponds to the value

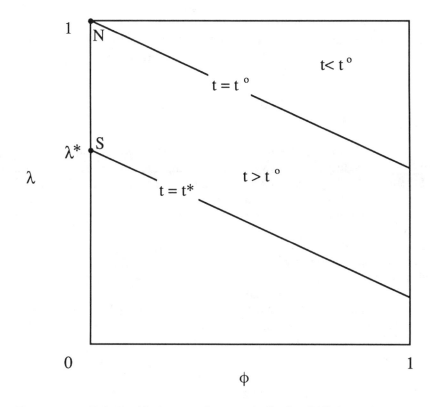

Figure 7-1. Relationship between λ, ϕ, and effective R&D levels.

the two parameters take when there is no joint research agreement ($\lambda = 1$, $\phi = 0$). The effective level of R&D in this case is given by t^o. The downward sloping line is an iso-effective R&D curve. It represents the combinations of λ and ϕ (or types of RJV agreements) that yield the same level of effective R&D as the case of no agreement. Note that, for all the points along this iso-effective R&D curve, the incentive to increase R&D levels due to a lower λ is just neutralized by the lowering of these incentives as ϕ increases. The exact shape and slope of the iso-effective R&D curve depends on the particular type of demand faced by the firms, since some of these effects work through the firms' revenue functions.

As indicated on the figure, any agreement above and to the right of the depicted iso-effective R&D curve is associated with a lower level of effective R&D for the member firms. Conversely, agreements below and to the left are associated with higher levels of effective R&D. In general, the level of effective R&D will increase as we move southwest on the agreement space. This will allow domestic firms to capture a larger share of the market.

5. Comparison of Cooperative Research Agreements with Subsidies

Spencer and Brander [10] have shown that an R&D subsidy will lead a firm to choose a higher level of R&D, thus enabling it to capture a larger share of the market. This result occurs because a government can alter the strategic environment in which firms are making choices. In the case of a subsidy, the government provides a *credible threat* that affects rival firms' behavior in a way that a self-subsidy on the part of the firm cannot. In a framework similar to the one employed here, Spencer and Brander [10] show that R&D subsidies can be welfare-improving and that the optimal subsidy is positive. This optimal subsidy is associated with a given level of R&D, say t^*, and the corresponding market share.

It seems plausible that an R&D subsidy, by inducing firms to increase their R&D levels, leads them to capture a larger share of profitable markets. There is, however, some disagreement among trade theorists about the desirability of an activist trade policy [11, 12]. If an activist trade policy is to be successful, policymakers need to be provided with information of sufficient detail and quality so as to allow them to pick the industries that should be targeted. The difficulties involved in gathering the necessary information, together with the incentives to manipulate information in an attempt to seek rents on the part of special interest groups, suggests that caution be exercised when considering industries as potential candidates for targeting.

Given that the major criticism to a subsidy lies in the fact that the relevant information may not be available and/or reliable, it is desirable to determine whether there is an alternative way in which the government can alter the strategic environment, thereby conferring an advantage upon domestic firms. Ideally, such an alternative would require less information and a lesser degree of government intervention.

The comparison of cooperative research agreements will R&D subsidies is aimed at answering two questions. First, given that cost sharing allows firms to subsidize each other, can research joint ventures replicate the outcome that would obtain when the government chooses the optimal R&D subsidy, and if so under what conditions? Second, can it be determined in what respects subsidies and joint research ventures differ?

It can be shown that the outcome achieved by an optimal subsidy can be replicated by an RJV.[10] In fact, there is a set of RJV agreements that yields, the same effective R&D levels as that obtained under an optimal subsidy. This set is illustrated in figure 7–1, and consists of all the agreements on the iso-effective R&D curve that goes through the point S ($\lambda = \lambda^*$, $\phi = 0$). The special case of an agreement characterized by $\lambda = \lambda^*$ and $\phi = 0$ is a useful benchmark. This agreement has the same effect of an optimal subsidy, say s^*, when $\lambda^* = (1 - s^*)$—that is, when the fraction of a firm's R&D expenditures paid for by the other member firm is the same as the optimal subsidy (given as a fraction of expenditures on R&D). The reason for this is that when firms choose their R&D levels they take into account only their share of expenditures on their R&D (the choice variable). Whether the share of expenditures not paid by the firm is covered by the government in the form of a subsidy, or by another firm in the form of cost sharing, is not relevant to the firm's problem.

A cost-sharing scheme characterized by λ^* will, in the absence of R&D sharing, result in a level of effective R&D equal to t^*. This level of R&D leads domestic firms to capture the optimal share of the market, as measured by the rents that domestic firms appropriate. Note that $t^* > t^o$, since the iso-effective R&D curve associated with t^* lies below and to the right of that associated with t^o. Also note that a number of research agreements that yield a level of effective R&D greater than t^* are possible. However, for any given degree of R&D sharing, those agreements are less profitable than the one which yields t^*. The reason for this is that a higher level of effective R&D allows domestic firms to capture a larger share of the market by expanding output. This expanded output causes the market price to drop. The rival firm responds by contracting its output, thereby increasing price. This results in a smaller decrease in price than would otherwise have been the case. At first, the above adjustments increase profits of the expanding firms; the gains from an increased market share more than make up for the lower price. Beyond a certain point, however, this will cease to be true, and the negative effect of a lower price on a firm's profits will dominate the positive effect of expanded sales. The optimal subsidy induces firms to select the level of R&D that will allow them to capture the market share associated with the maximum profits.

The previous discussion suggests that firms entering a cooperative research agreement should choose an agreement that yields an effective level of R&D of t^*. It can be seen, however, that there are many agreements that induce that level of R&D. Which agreement should firms choose? This question can be easily answered by noting that, as we move southeast along the iso-effective R&D curve, the level of effective R&D remains at t^* but the expenditures associated with obtaining this level of R&D decrease. This is because an increased sharing of R&D lowers the duplication of research efforts and thereby raises their efficiency. Ideally, in order to maximize profits, firms in an RJV should choose an agreement such as that described by point A.

The above discussion can be neatly summarized by making use of the concept of iso-profit curves. For the case of an RJV, iso-profit curves over the agreement space can be defined. An iso-profit curve consists of the set of agreements (λ, ϕ) that yield the same aggregate profit for the two firms in the research venture. Iso-profit curves are represented in figure 7–2 by the c-shaped curves. In order to understand the shape of these curves,

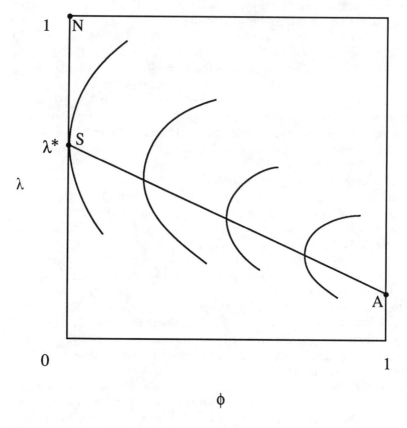

Figure 7–2.   Iso-profit curves for the use of an RJV.

consider for a moment the iso-profit curve going through point S. Note that an increase in λ will, by reducing the level of effective R&D, lead to lower profits. If profits are to remain constant, ϕ will have to increase, thereby reducing R&D costs and increasing profits, so as to neutralize the decrease in profits due to a higher λ. In a similar way, as λ decreases (thus increasing the effective level of R&D), profits will be driven down since the price effect dominates. Here again, in order for profits to remain constant, ϕ will have to increase. Finally, it can be readily determined from our earlier discussion that profits increase as we move southeast from one iso-profit curve to another.

How firms perform under an RJV relative to the case of no RJVs and R&D subsidies can be readily illustrated with the use of iso-profit contours. The fact that subsidies and/or an RJV can increase profits of the domestic firms can be determined by pointing out that point N lies on a lower iso-profit curve than does S or most agreements. It is possible for an agreement consisting only of cost sharing to replicate the outcome of an optimal subsidy. In fact a number of possible RVJ agreements can result in domestic industry profits identical to those obtained under the optimal subsidy. These agreements are represented by all the combinations (λ, ϕ) on the iso-profit curve that goes through S. The fact that RJVs may incorporate R&D sharing makes cooperative research ventures attractive, since it allows for profits greater than those obtained under the optimal subsidy. The agreement that maximizes profits of the domestic firms is the one that allows for full R&D sharing and a level of cost sharing that, given $\phi = 1$, will result in the optimal effective level of R&D and hence market share. This agreement was labeled A in figure 7–2.

6. Some Policy Implications

The model discussed allows for general policy implications to be drawn. It may seem that, by regulating the type of agreements that can be established, the government can manipulate the outcome. In the context of our model, this would consist of the government imposing restrictions on the parameters λ and ϕ. It can be readily seen that there is no role for government action in the situation we have described, since the domestic firms will choose the agreement that leads to the optimal outcome on their own.

It is worth noting that, when firms consider R&D agreements, they may face a parameter space that is a subset of the one we have discussed. This could be because of numerous reasons, such as technological or administrative limitations. It is possible that under such conditions government action could be welfare-improving. One such possibility is illustrated in figure 7–3. Suppose that the possible RJV agreements are limited to those described by the shaded area. In such a case, firms forming an RJV would maximize profits by choosing the agreement $\lambda = \lambda^F$, $\phi = \phi^F$ described by point F. The outcome that obtains under this agreement could be improved upon if the government provides an R&D subsidy inducing firms to increase their R&D levels. The optimal R&D subsidy in this case is that which, given the RJV agreement, reduces a firm's own R&D costs to a fraction $\lambda = \lambda^G$. Such a subsidy would result in an outcome equivalent to that obtained with an RJV agreement described by point G. The reader will notice that, if the agreement space is restricted in a different manner, an

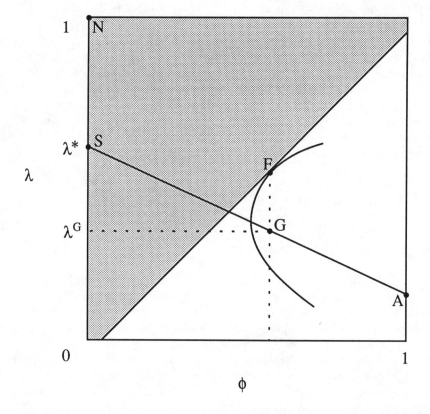

Figure 7–3.   An example of a possible RJV outcome in which government action could be welfare-improving.

example can be constructed in which the optimal policy is for government to impose an R&D tax.

It should be kept in mind that we have considered only one type of agreement structure, namely that consisting of linear sharing rules and firms having separate R&D departments. The ability of firms to share R&D and also the incentives facing firms, are likely to be sensitive to the agreement structure. Various possibilities including nonlinear sharing rules and centralized R&D centers are worth considering. Further research to determine whether a class of agreements has more desirable properties would be beneficial. If such is the case, the role for the government might be that of inducing firms to adopt the agreement structure with the desired characteristics.

7. Conclusions

Following the strategic trade literature, this chapter has focused on an international market in which, because of the imperfectly competitive nature of the market, firms enjoy rents in the form of profits. We address the question of whether allowing for cooperative research agreements in high-technology industries would, by altering the strategic environment in which domestic firms operate, enable them to capture a larger share of international markets. It was shown that, under certain conditions, co-operative research agreements could improve the strategic position of domestic firms vis-a-vis foreign competitors.

Allowing for an RJV to be formed leads to an outcome similar to that obtained under government subsidies of R&D. Thus RJVs could provide an alternative to government subsidies as a means of strengthening the competitive position of domestic firms. The attractiveness of RJVs lies in the fact that government plays a passive role. The decision concerning the desirability as well as the level of subsidies is left to the participating firms, which presumably have better information available than policymakers.

Finally, it was shown that RJVs introduce an additional source of gains. This is associated with the decreased duplication of R&D efforts. For any given market share, this means that profits are higher the greater the extent of R&D sharing.

Notes

1. Two case studies of this, in the semiconductor and optoelectronics industries, are discussed in Link and Tassey [1].

2. Audretsch and Yamawaki [3] provide some empirical evidence.

3. See Link and Bauer [4] for a review of federal initiatives related to cooperative research and for a theoretical analysis per se.

4. Although the number of firms is different, these assumptions are the same as those in Brander and Spencer [7]. The assumption that the industry's output is sold outside the domestic market allows for a simple measure of the industry's contribution to domestic welfare, namely industry profits.

5. See for example Brander and Spencer [7]. Grossman and Richardson [8] provide an excellent survey of the strategic trade literature.

6. The absence of an RJV, the case of $\phi > 0$, could capture the public-good nature of technical knowledge that sometimes results in firms choosing a level of R&D lower than the socially optimal one. When this is the case, n refers the number of firms in the industry.

7. Restrictions on the particular types of agreements that firms may adopt could reflect government requlations.

8. The derivation of this result assumes that the matrix of second-order terms associated with the system of first-order conditions for profit maximization is negative definite. This assumption requires that $\Pi_{ii}^i < 0$ and that a firm's own marginal effects on profits exceed cross-effects $\Pi_{ii}^i < \Pi_{ij}^i < 0$.

9. This argument is closely related to that of underprovision of a public good.

10. See Ruiz-Mier and Link [5] for technical details.

References

1. Link, A.N., and Tassey, G. *Strategies for Technology-based Competition: Meeting the New Global Challenge*. Lexington, MA: Lexington Books, 1987.

2. Branson, W.H., and Klevorick, A.K. "Strategic Behavior and Trade Policy." In: P.R. Krugman (ed.), *Strategic Trade Policy and the New International Economics*. Cambridge, MA: MIT Press, 1986.

3. Audretsch, D.B., and Yamawaki, H. "R&D Rivalry, Industrial Policy, and U.S.–Japanese Trade." In: D.B. Audretsch and M. Claudon (eds.), *The Internationalization of U.S. Markets*. Cambridge, MA: Ballinger Press, Forthcoming.

4. Link, A.N., and Bauer, L.L. *Cooperative Research in U.S. Manufacturing: An Assessment of Policy Initiatives and Corporate Strategies*. Lexington, MA: Lexington Books, 1989.

5. Ruiz-Mier, L.F., and Link, A.N. "R&D Policy and Trade Advantage." In: "The Internationalization of U.S. Markets." In D.B. Audretsch and M. Claudon (eds.), *The Internationalization of U.S. Markets*. New York, NY: New York University Press, forthcoming.

6. Ruiz-Mier, L.F. "Cooperative Research Agreements and International Competitiveness." Mimeo, 1988.

7. Brander, J.A., and Spencer, B.J. "Export Subsidies and International Market Share Rivalry." *Journal of International Economics* 18 (1/2) (1984): 83–100.

8. Grossman, G.M., and Richardson, J.D. "Strategic Trade Policy: A Survey of

Issues and Early Analysis." Princeton *Special Papers in International Economics*, No. 15, April, 1986.

9. Katz, M. L. "An Analysis of Cooperative Research and Development." *Rand Journal of Economics* 17 (4) (1986): 527–543.

10. Spencer, B. J., and Brander, J. A. "International R&D Rivalry and Industrial Strategy." *Review of Economic Studies* 50 (1983): 707–722.

11. Grossman, G. M. "Strategic Export Promotion: A Critique." In: P.R. Krugman (ed.), *Strategic Trade Policy and the New International Economics*. Cambridge, MA: MIT Press, 1986.

12. Krugman, P. R. "Targeted Industrial Policies: Theory and Evidence." In: D. Salvatore (ed.) *The New Protectionist Threat to World Welfare*. Amsterdam: North-Holland, 1987.

III IMPACTS ON INDUSTRIAL STRATEGIES

8 COLLABORATIVE RESEARCH AND HIGH-TEMPERATURE SUPERCONDUCTIVITY

David C. Mowery*

1. Introduction

The discovery in 1986 and 1987 of the possibilities for achieving super-conductivity at relatively high temperatures has focused attention on the commercial exploitation of high-temperature superconductivity (HTS). The commercial possibilities for this technology are profound if superconductivity can be achieved with materials that are producible in commercial quantities.

Within the United States, this commercial potential has led to a number of proposals for public policies to accelerate the exploitation of HTS and to prevent U.S. firms from falling behind foreign enterprises in this commercial competition. One such mechanism is collaboration in research

* This chapter draws on a report prepared for the Office of Technology Assessment [1]. The analysis benefited from the comments of John Alic, Clare Delmar, and Dorothy Robyn of OTA. Neither these individuals nor the Office of Technology Assessment are responsible for conclusions, errors, or omissions in this chapter.

between firms or between universities and industry, which raises at least two questions:

1. What role should government play in encouraging, discouraging, or funding collaboration in HTS research and development?
2. Is collaboration between U.S. and foreign firms in HTS research, product development, or manufacture desirable for national competitiveness and technological prowess?

This chapter considers the role of collaborative research in developing commercial applications of HTS. In order to evaluate the possibilities for collaborative research and the influence of public policy on such research, the following two sections present an overview of domestic and international collaborative research. The final section evaluates the role of collaborative research in the commercial exploitation of high-temperature superconductivity.

2. Collaborative Research: Pros and Cons

Collaboration involving the research or financial resources of U.S. firms is but one of a number of forms of interfirm collaboration that have developed during the 1980s. Other types of domestic collaboration include cooperative research agreements involving one or more domestic firms and a university, and collaboration between one or more firms and a public (generally federal) research laboratory. International collaborations between U.S. and foreign firms in R&D, production, and marketing also have sprung up in industries ranging from steel to semiconductors and biotechnology [2, 3].

2.1. Advantages of Research Collaboration

Many of the perceived advantages of collaborative research are grounded in the economic analysis of market failure in R&D investment. The arguments of Arrow [4] and Nelson [5] that markets did not provide optimal incentives for investment led to recommendations for public funding of research capable of yielding results that could not be easily appropriated by the discoverer. Collaboration among firms in R&D provides a complementary means to address this market failure (see [6]). If research collaboration among firms lowers the costs to individual firms of R&D, and if the results of such research are made available to all participants, cooperative research can reduce the effects of the disincentives for investment in R&D that result from the limited appropriability of research results. Since the profits from basic research are particularly difficult to appropriate, cooperation among firms in basic research should be especially effective.

Access to research results at lower cost has been an important motive for the establishment of a number of cooperative research programs and university–industry cooperative research programs in recent years. These programs allow participants to monitor developments in specific technologies or scientific areas at lower cost than the development of an independent in-house research capability. The importance of such a monitoring capability has increased in recent years, as the costs of research and development have grown [7]. Technological convergence, which has made new technologies in many industries central to the competitive future of firms in these industries, also has made this monitoring function more important. Computer technologies now are important to the development of telecommunications, robotics, and machine-tool technologies; biotechnologies are of growing importance in pharmaceuticals, food processing, and agriculture; and materials technologies are critical to competitiveness in a wide range of manufacturing industries. Firms in these industries are faced with the need to develop expertise quickly in "foreign" technologies, and as a result have pursued research collaborations with other firms and universities or public laboratories (see [8]).

Another argument in favor of cooperative R&D concerns its greater efficiency. Duplication among the research activities of competitor firms [9] can be reduced by collaboration in research. Moreover, if the research process is characterized by economies of scale, collaboration can lower the costs per unit of R&D. By spreading the costs of R&D among firms, cooperative R&D also lowers the costs to any single firm of the failure of a research program, reducing another disincentive to invest in R&D.

Interfirm collaboration in product development, manufacture, or marketing also allows firms to exchange and realize profit from technological and nontechnological assets. Weak protection of intellectual property rights, among other factors, means that firms may be unable to realize the profits, through licensing or sale in the market, of firm-specific assets based on technology, marketing, or production expertise [2, 10]. Teaming allows firms to pool their assets in a specific product line without either the high transactions costs of licensing or the complexities of a merger between two independent enterprises. Such collaborative ventures typically center on the development of a specific product or process and less frequently incorporate basic research.

Much recent interfirm collaboration, especially where it extends downstream into product development, manufacture, or marketing, involves the teaming of U.S. and foreign firms. Changes in the supply of inputs and in the nature of product demand have increased U.S. firms' demand for foreign partners in R&D and other activities. The enhanced technological capabilities of many foreign firms make them more attractive partners in joint ventures with U.S. firms. Simultaneously, product demand in the world market for many high-technology and other goods has become more homogeneous, and the U.S. share of world demand for many high-technology products has declined. This shift in the profile of world demand has made penetration of foreign markets by U.S. firms essential to commercial success in many industries. Collaboration in research, production, or marketing with foreign firms offers a lower-risk and lower-cost alternative to direct foreign investment, and allows more rapid foreign market access than the export of finished products. European and Japanese firms also collaborate with U.S. firms to penetrate the vast U.S. market.

Even as the commercial importance of foreign markets to U.S. firms has grown, however, access to many of these markets has been restricted by the industrial and trade policies of foreign governments. Purchase decisions of foreign governments play a major role in the export markets for a number of goods and frequently are influenced by the availability of offsets, the production (or development and production) of components for a product by domestic firms in the purchaser nation.[1] Restrictions on foreign access to the U.S. market in such industries as automobiles, steel, and semiconductors also have resulted in collaboration between U.S. firms and foreign firms wishing to export to the United States.

Foreign governments also frequently provide development funding and risk capital to domestic firms as part of their industrial development strategies. Combined with restrictions on access to foreign markets and high and rapidly increasing product development costs in many U.S. industries, the availability of capital from public sources for foreign firms has enhanced their attractiveness as partners in product-development ventures.

Technological factors also have influenced recent collaborative ventures between U.S. firms and other domestic or foreign firms. In a number of industries (e.g., microelectronics or automobiles), product cycles are becoming shorter—the period of time during which a product design dominates its market is shorter than in previous decades. In such a situation, rapid market penetration at low cost is essential, and may be facilitated through collaboration with a firm with an established marketing network or production capacity. Technological progress in telecommunications and in computer-aided manufacturing and design technologies also has made international collaboration in research and other activities more efficient and effective.

2.2. Disadvantages of Collaborative Research

The benefits of collaborative research discussed above rest on a number of assumptions. Critical evaluation of these assumptions suggests that cooperative research ventures are not a panacea and will not be equally useful in all industries. In addition, research collaboration may be a necessary condition for the rapid commercialization or development of many technologies, but collaboration alone is insufficient for commercial success or the realization of an economic payoff. Other factors also must be present and must be incorporated into policies aimed at rapid commercialization or technological development.

The first limitation of cooperative research stems from the nature of scientific and technological knowledge and the factors necessary to transform such knowledge into innovations. The fruits of research do not consist solely of information that can be utilized for commercial purposes at minimal cost. The output of cooperative research must be absorbed by the participant firms and transformed into commercially relevant knowledge. This transformation typically requires considerable intrafirm expertise [11, 12].

Cooperative research is not a substitute for, but a complement to, in-house research. Government policies of support for cooperative research programs in industries in which firms pursue little or no internal R&D have yielded disappointing results [11]. In order to exploit external research, whether this research is performed in a multifirm consortium, a federal laboratory, or a university, participant firms must have some in-house expertise.[2] Some duplication of the in-house research investments of firms thus is inevitable even when these firms participate in a collaborative research program. Moreover, to the extent that basic research requires a larger investment in this in-house absorptive capacity, participants in cooperative research may react to the high costs of exploiting collaborative basic research by shifting the collaborative research agenda away from basic research. These pressures appear to have led such well-known cooperative research institutions as the Electric Power Research Institute and the Microelectronics and Computer Technology Corporation to reduce their basic research commitment.[3]

Other factors, in addition to the incentives of the participants, may reduce basic research within collaborative research programs, especially when these programs are publicly funded. Cohen and Noll [13] argue that the short time horizons of the political supporters of U.S. public nondefense research programs create a strong bias in favor of funding development work rather than basic research. Similar tensions are now apparent in the politically salient British Alvey program of publicly funded research in information technologies, which has been criticized for not producing applications of new information technologies quickly.[4] Impatience over applications also has characterized recent discussions about the next phase of the European Community's ESPRIT (European Strategic Program of Research in Information Technologies) program [14].

A central characteristic of publicly funded Japanese cooperative research programs, many of which appear to have used small investments of public funds to enhance the competitiveness of Japanese firms, is the stability and duration of the national government's commitment to these programs [15–17]. Particularly in the U.S. political environment, low political visibility may improve the performance of public cooperative research programs. An enduring commitment to a modest, incrementalist program of research may be more effective than a high-visibility, flagship program, such as the synthetic fuels initiative of the late 1970s.

Nonetheless, publicly funded research must be combined with other policies to yield the greatest national economic impact. Support for the adoption of the results of publicly funded research is an essential complement to publicly funded, precommercial collaborative, or other programs of R&D. This requirement creates some obvious dilemmas—policymakers designing adoption incentives that target specific applications must make assumptions about the course of technological and commercial evolution, a task that they historically have performed poorly. In addition, policies intended to support technology development (e.g., stronger patent protection) may impede the rapid diffusion of new technologies within an economy.

The structure of cooperative research programs also may undercut the productivity of research. Nelson [18] has argued that diversity in research projects provides an important hedge against the possibility that any single research project will prove to be fruitless. Yet if all or most firms in an industry participate in a cooperative research scheme, the number of independent lines of inquiry in specific problem areas may decline. If reliance on cooperative research reduces the diversity of research projects in a sector or technology (an outcome that is not a necessary result of cooperative research), the productivity of the larger research effort may be reduced.[5] Scott's analysis [19] of preliminary evidence suggests that the National Cooperative Research Act (NCRA) may have had this effect.

The research economies of scale that are widely cited as a source of efficiency gains through research collaboration also are not well supported by empirical evidence. Large specialized research facilities, such as wind tunnels, clearly display declining average costs as a function of increased use by different firms. No strong evidence exists, however, to suggest that all industrial R&D exhibits significant economies of scale [20], nor can one identify those industries or technologies characterized by R&D scale economies.

Cooperative research that focuses exclusively on basic research offers relatively few opportunities for collusion among competitors in the marketplace, but other forms of research may create the potential for anticompetitive behavior. There is little evidence that recent cooperative research programs have resulted in such collusion in research, development, or other dimensions of competition (e.g., pricing or output decisions), nor is collusion among U.S. firms likely to produce significant market power in an open economy. Nevertheless, such collusion could restrict the diffusion of a technology in the early stages of its development or prevent the development of a diversified portfolio of technologies. Collaboration among U.S. automobile companies during the 1960s in applied research on antipollution technologies was the target of an antitrust suit by the U.S. Department of Justice that was based in part on these concerns [15, 16, 21]. The potential for such abuses is greater in domestic and international ventures that involve applied research, product development, or manufacturing.

The effects of international collaboration on the long-term competitive strength of U.S. firms have been the subject of extensive debate. Arguments against collaboration [22] suggest that the technological crown jewels developed by U.S. firms are given away within these ventures by myopic U.S. managers who do not appreciate the true value of such assets and who have little incentive to invest in the long-term development of these technologies. International collaborative ventures to which U.S. firms provide only technological assets may result in the loss by these firms of the manufacturing and marketing skills that are necessary to realize commercial returns from R&D [10]. International collaborative research ventures thus may impose significant costs on U.S. firms and workers.

3. An Evaluation

Different forms of collaborative research appear to work best for different types of research. Domestic consortia of private firms (e.g., MCC,

SEMATECH) tend to focus on applied, rather than basic, research. Research collaborations between universities and industry, however, appear to conduct research of a more fundamental character. International collaborations typically extend well beyond research alone to subsume product development, manufacturing, and marketing.[6] The opportunities for one or another form of collaborative research are conditioned heavily by the state of the underlying science or technology—in the early stages of the development of a technology, university–industry collaboration may be more effective and stable than domestic or international collaboration among firms.

The characteristics of the market also influence the structure of collaborative research within an industry. The contrasting development of the biotechnology and semiconductor industries highlights the significant role of government procurement in supporting the development of new firms. The dominance of the military market during the early years of the semiconductor industry lowered marketing barriers to entry and allowed a large number of relatively small, new firms to enter the industry. By contrast, the products of biotechnology firms are sold primarily in heavily regulated civilian markets, making these marketing entry barriers much higher. Collaboration among firms (often, between an established firm and a start-up; see [23]) that focuses on the development and marketing of applications of new technologies is widespread in this industry.

The U.S. government has influenced the growth of other industries, of course, by funding research that often involved substantial interfirm collaboration. The operation and effects of such programs as the National Advisory Committee on Aeronautics and the aeronautics R&D program of NASA [24, 25] suggest that publicly funded research can assist the technological development of an industry without picking winners, i.e., committing public funds to the commercial development of specific applications. Although it typically focused on precommercial research in generic technologies, the NASA program extended beyond basic research, supporting design and proof-of-concept work. When support for research or adoption of new technologies targets specific commercial applications, however, the risks of failure increase dramatically, as in the SST program, a major failure in U.S. civilian aeronautics R&D [26].

Another key factor in the success of federally funded research in the commercial aircraft industry, of course, was the inadvertent and nontargeted support for the adoption of new technologies provided by federal regulation of interstate air transportation until 1978. Similar support for technology adoption, including the JECC program for lease-purchase of computers and the analogous JAROL program for robots, has been a key component of many Japanese programs for technological development [27, 28].

There is little evidence to single out international collaboration as disadvantageous to the technological capabilities or longer-term competitiveness of U.S. firms. Technology transfer within international collaborative ventures is more modest in scope and less uniformly outward bound from the United States than some assessments [22] assume. Just as U.S. industries vary in their trade balances in goods, the net inflows or outflows of technology through international collaboration vary across industries. Requiring balance in technology transfer on an industry-by-industry basis makes no more sense than does a requirement for such balance in goods trade. Moreover, efforts to restrict international collaboration overlook the fact that in a number of industries, such collaboration can improve the international competitiveness of U.S. firms (see the studies in [3]).

4. Collaborative Research and Superconductivity

The design of public policies for the support of collaborative and other forms of precommercial research must be based on an understanding of the characteristics of the technology and structure of the relevant industries. It is important, therefore, to consider some salient characteristics of HTS science and technology before discussing the scope for collaborative research initiatives.

4.1. The Current State of HTS Knowledge and Technology

The most salient characteristic of HTS is the embryonic state of theoretical and technological knowledge about this phenomenon. As recent reports from the Committee on Science, Engineering, and Public Policy [29][7] and other groups have noted, HTS poses a fundamental challenge to current theories of superconductivity. Although scientific knowledge is likely to grow in tandem with, rather than in advance of, engineering knowledge in superconductivity, the modest level of current scientific understanding of HTS inhibits confident prediction of applications in areas beyond current uses of low-temperature superconductivity (LTS). Applications of HTS require significant advances in the technologies for producing and form-the materials in which HTS thus far has been observed. As a result, large-scale application of HTS technologies in areas beyond current low-temperature superconductivity applications is likely to be at least one decade away. Development of these applications will require substantial precommercial research in basic science and in materials engineering. The high levels of uncertainty mean that a diverse portfolio of research projects is needed in the near term.

Although discussions of HTS applications are speculative, one can distinguish between two classes of applications—those that are likely at existing "high" temperatures and those that would be feasible if much higher temperatures (room temperature) were achieved. The recent advances create a potential for applications described in the COSEPUP report as "not revolutionary" [29] but significant, since liquid helium refrigeration can be replaced with liquid nitrogen, and the costs and complexity of refrigeration can be reduced. The incremental character of recent research advances has several implications. Superconductivity at these temperatures will in the near term be applied in areas currently utilizing low-temperature superconductivity. Firms active in low-temperature superconductivity applications are more likely to utilize current high-temperature superconducting technologies. These firms may well have the internal research capabilities and expertise necessary to utilize external sources of research effectively.

If superconductivity at significantly higher temperatures is achieved in the laboratory, potential applications expand considerably and uncertainty over areas of future application increases. At the same time, firms previously unfamiliar with HTS or other forms of superconductivity will have to develop expertise in HTS applications. Many of these firms lack the internal capacity to utilize the results of external research. Collaborative research in applications alone may not suffice to develop the broad knowledge base necessary for these firms to commercialize HTS.

Much of the research necessary to accelerate the development of HTS is basic research, the results of which are widely disseminated within the scientific community. The basic character of much of HTS research means that universities, where the majority of U.S. basic research is carried out, will play a central role in developing scientific and technical knowledge with potential commercial applications. In this respect, HTS resembles biotechnology. Since much HTS research initially will not focus on applications, international collaborative ventures, which generally focus on joint product development, manufacture, or marketing, are not likely to be significant in HTS in the near term. Domestic consortia that focus heavily on applications also are of limited utility at this point in the development of HTS.

4.2. Industry Structure and International Collaboration

The commercialization of HTS also will be affected by the characteristics of the U.S. firms investing in its development, the nature of the market for applications, and international competition in the development and application of HTS. Although no reliable data exist on the structure of an emerging HTS industry, most accounts suggest that many of the U.S. firms that are active in the development of low-temperature superconductivity are relatively small—indeed, a number of firms recently have been established to exploit HTS. Will this industry's development resemble that of the U.S. biotechnology and semiconductor industries, in which small, entrepreneurial firms played a major role? Does such a pattern of development pose unusual problems or risks for the commercial exploitation of HTS by U.S. firms?

The characteristics of markets for HTS applications have significant implications for the structure of the industry that will develop to serve these applications. If the primary market for HTS applications initially is a military market, the marketing-related barriers to entry into HTS applications will be low, and the HTS industry may develop a large population of small, specialized producers. If the primary markets for HTS applications are commercial ones, however, the costs of market penetration will be higher. Especially in applications outside of LTS markets, small firms established to commercialize HTS applications are likely to find it necessary to team with established firms. The need for such teaming will be even greater for foreign markets.

Recent intense HTS-related activity in the venture capital industry [30] suggests that large amounts of investment capital have been attracted to this technology. Nevertheless, the needs of start-up firms for capital provide an additional motive for the establishment of collaborative ventures between foreign firms interested in gaining access to HTS research and small U.S. firms, just as in the biotechnology industry. Although some small U.S. firms have already been approached by foreign (frequently, Japanese) firms, international collaborative ventures in HTS are likely to be significant only when scientific understanding of HTS and of the production requirements of HTS materials is sufficient to make commercial applications a reality, rather than a very uncertain possibility.

The arguments against international collaboration in HTS applications, as was noted above, are not compelling. International collaborative ventures in other industries thus far have not resulted in large-scale technology transfer and have not themselves been responsible for intensified foreign competition [3]. Where foreign firms are providing capital for U.S. firms' development of technologies, as is generally the case in collaborative ventures between large foreign firms and new U.S. firms, the U.S. economy reaps important benefits that can aid the domestic diffusion of the technology. These spillover benefits are realized through several channels, including the turnover of employees within the U.S. partner in the venture—individuals act as effective agents for the transfer of technology. Scientific papers based on such research that are published in English and presented at U.S. meetings, as well as the financial support that such ventures often provide for training of U.S. scientists and engineers, also diffuse the technology from the joint venture within this nation.

An additional argument against restrictions on international collaboration in HTS stems from the fact that the design and enforcement of such restrictions on the development of HTS and other technologies would be a policy nightmare. The far narrower web of national security controls on exports and transfer of key dual-use technologies have been limited in their effectiveness and appear to have impeded U.S. exports of high-technology goods [31]. Similar restrictions on international collaboration in commercial HTS technologies would be far broader, would require a vast investment in enforcement, and would place impossible demands on public officials to make difficult judgments about the commercial prospects of new technologies.

Two areas that affect international collaboration in the development of civilian technologies are appropriate points for public intervention. Restrictions on access by U.S. firms to foreign markets provide a major incentive for collaboration between U.S. and foreign firms, one that is reinforced by restrictions on foreign firms' access to U.S. markets. Trade policy can improve access by U.S. firms to foreign markets, limit the power of foreign governments to restrict public procurement choices, and thereby reduce a serious source of distortion in international markets for technological assets. Stronger international intellectual property protection also will lessen the dangers of foreign exploitation of U.S. firms' technological assets through collaborative ventures. Stronger protection for intellectual property rights can strengthen the bargaining position of U.S. firms in establishing international collaborative ventures or can remove the necessity for collaboration altogether, since such protection facilitates the licensing of technological assets and thereby reduces the need for collaborative ventures. Moreover, if stronger international protection for intellectual property imposes on U.S. trading partners the standards of protection already present in the U.S. domestic market, domestic diffusion of HTS applications and other innovations need not be impeded.

The argument raised in Reich and Mankin [22] or Nelson [32] that U.S.

antitrust policy is an important factor in the decisions of American firms to collaborate with foreign enterprises receives little support from a comparison of international collaboration in a cross section of U.S. industries [3]. In most instances, international collaborative ventures are not partial substitutes for the collaboration among U.S. firms that might develop in the absence of antitrust restrictions.[8] This argument applies to potential HTS collaborations as well, which will be motivated primarily by the desire to gain access to new markets and the need of new U.S. firms for capital.

4.3. Implications for Policy

Where can collaborative research contribute to the development and application of HTS? The initial 5–10 years of a significant research initiative in HTS would as a matter of necessity focus on basic science and engineering, rather than specific applications. The case for public support (e.g., through matching grants) of university–industry research collaborations in HTS seems strong. Rather than targeting specific applications, however, public policy should attempt to broaden and enrich the R&D network and the knowledge base on which individual firms can draw in developing HTS applications.

University–industry collaboration would allow even firms currently active in low-temperature superconductivity to maintain a window on the development of HTS, something that is particularly important during theoretical and experimental research on this phenomenon. University–industry research collaboration in HTS could make two other contributions. HTS research requires personnel, theory, and methods from a number of disciplines, including physics, electrical engineering, materials science, and mechanical engineering, that are not easily brought together in a research or teaching capacity within most U.S. universities. External financial support of interdisciplinary university research will provide a powerful impetus for the assembly of these research teams. In addition, research and the development by industry of HTS applications will require trained personnel. The establishment or strengthening of interdisciplinary programs in HTS could expand the training of technical personnel and make it easier for firms to screen and hire graduates.

Diversity is an important element of any program for collaborative research in HTS. Rather than a single center of excellence in HTS research, a number of independent programs should be supported, increasing the number and variety of approaches to HTS research. Public funding of HTS research should support university–industry collaboration in engineering as well as in scientific research. Collaboration between firms and the federal laboratories also is desirable, since a considerable share of U.S. research expertise in HTS is located within these facilities. Either direct links between firms and national laboratories or the development of joint programs between graduate schools and national laboratories could tap the expertise of these institutions.

Current U.S. strategies for the development of superconductivity are a mixed bag. The Reagan administration's Superconductivity Competitiveness Act, introduced in 1988, contains three components, one of which will be of little or no help in the near term, one of which is likely to prove harmful to the development of a strong U.S. HTS knowledge base, and one of which may be useful. Although it is portrayed as an initiative supporting HTS development, the Act's provisions in fact would affect the organization of R&D and international scientific cooperation in a great many U.S. industries.

The Act proposes an amendment to the National Cooperative Research Act of 1984 that would allow explicitly for joint production ventures. This proposal is unlikely to aid HTS commercialization, for several reasons. One of the most valuable forms of proprietary knowledge in future applications of HTS is fabrication and production methods. Firms are unlikely to cooperate to share such commercially valuable knowledge. In addition, current understanding of the basic scientific principles underlying HTS is so limited that research on production technologies appears to be somewhat premature. The proposal to allow production collaboration also assumes that joint research on process technologies either is insufficient or is handicapped by the terms of the NCRA and remaining antitrust restrictions. There is little or no evidence, however, to support either of these assumptions. The effects of this proposal on HTS development are likely to be modest, since HTS will be applied in many areas, each of which will have unique production technologies and requirements. Although HTS applications eventually may be concentrated in a specific manufacturing area or product, predicting these sectors at this point in the development of HTS is impossible. Moreover, joint research on applications and production processes for a new technology over which firms may exercise considerable market power (e.g., through patents), even in the face of foreign competition, could (in the absence of strong licensing requirements) restrict the domestic diffusion of HTS applications.

Another provision of the Act restricts the rights of foreign nationals to gain access under the Freedom of Information Act to the results of publicly funded U.S. research. This proposal could impede the development and commercialization of HTS by U.S. firms. Advanced research in HTS currently is being carried out throughout the industrial world, with significant advances made in Japan, Western Europe, and the United States. The United States, no less than other industrial nations, has a major stake in the free flow of basic research results in HTS and increasingly demands equal access to foreign programs of public funded research. Actions to restrict the international flow of scientific knowledge of HTS are detrimental to the interests of U.S. scientists, entrepreneurs, and citizens. Rather than excluding foreign scientists, engineers, and firms, U.S. policymakers should ensure that reciprocity and a free international flow of information are maintained. Much of the responsibility for exploiting foreign sources of HTS research is properly that of U.S. firms, which have been slow to do so. The Japanese government recently announced a program of HTS research that is open to U.S. firms upon payment of a membership fee, but thus far U.S. firms have been slow to express interest in participating [33].

The final major provision of the Act strengthens patent protection for process technologies. This provision is no more closely related to the development of HTS than are the revisions proposed for the NCRA or the Freedom of Information Act, nor is this provision likely to affect HTS development substantially in the near term. Strengthened process patent protection may be useful in other industrial sectors or other technologies, but the cost of stronger protection for this form of intellectual property is slower domestic adoption of new process technologies. Whether the impediments to adoption are outweighed by the benefits of increased incentives to invest in process R&D is an empirical question. Unfortunately, little reliable evidence on such questions is available.

The Reagan administration also has sought increased funding for HTS research. A total of nearly $95 million for HTS research was appropriated by Congress for fiscal 1988.[9] Of this amount, $45 million was drawn from the Department of Defense and roughly $27 million came from the Department of Energy's programs in military and civilian technological development. As much as 50%–70% of current public funding for HTS research thus may draw on military sources. If HTS is applied in weapons systems, this proportion could increase substantially.

Military dominance of research funding and procurement demand for applications has costs and benefits for the HTS industry. The importance of diverse sources of funding for HTS research and development means that reliance on the Defense Department for such funding is unwise. Although military applications of HTS technologies will yield some civilian spin-offs, the current regime of controls on the export of dual-use technologies means that export of products embodying these civilian applications will be difficult. Moreover, the classified nature of much defense research may restrict the diffusion of scientific and engineering knowledge from this research within the U.S. economy, further limiting the payoff from such research investments. Nevertheless, military markets are likely to prove easier for small U.S. firms to enter, especially if military procurement of weapons systems utilizing HTS is limited to US sources by Congressional edict (as in "Buy American" language in appropriations bills).

As scientific understanding of HTS grows, research will focus increasingly on engineering and applications. Publicly funded collaborative research can play an important role in this phase, especially in the provision of a research infrastructure, e.g., design and testing facilities that are similar to those provided by NASA for the U.S. aeronautics industry. The national laboratories are excellent sites for such facilities and could subsidize use of their facilities by U.S. firms. Support for university–industry research collaboration should continue during this phase, since this will support the essential upstream research and training of personnel for the exploitation of HTS technology.

The difficulties encountered by previous flagship programs for the development of civilian technologies, such as the SST and the synthetic fuels program, suggest that this strategy for the commercialization of HTS technology is unwise. Although a flagship strategy will ensure high political visibility and may result in substantial funding, these programs rarely have produced commercially successful innovations. Flagship programs often require that public policymakers in the Executive branch and Congress make commercial judgments about technologies and market demand that are difficult at best. They are particularly prone to failure in the environment of incentives and information that characterizes these programs. The example of synthetic fuels suggests that an unsuccessful flagship program can harm future funding of research for major new technologies.

Once sufficient basic scientific and engineering knowledge is developed, research in HTS applications will be pursued by private domestic collaborative ventures for development, production, or marketing. The experience of other industries suggests that domestic collaborative ventures focused on applications will be of limited significance, although this assertion does not provide a basis for their prohibition. International collaborative ventures, based as they are on a slightly different set of motives, may well develop and prove to be more durable. Since little evidence indicates that these joint ventures, focused on product development or marketing, result in serious competitive harm for U.S. firms as long as the trade-distorting policies that motivate many of them are contained, international collaborative ventures in HTS should not be discouraged.

5. Conclusions

The U.S. R&D system that developed in the aftermath of World War II is undergoing substantial change, as firms and other institutions explore new ways of organizing technological innovation. One manifestation of this change, which traces its causes to a large number of factors, is increased interest in collaborative research for the accelerated development of commercial applications of significant scientific discoveries, such as HTS. Although collaborative research can convey significant benefits and has been employed creatively by the governments of other industrial nations and the U.S. government in some areas, collaborative research alone will not suffice to increase the commercial benefits realized by U.S. firms from scientific advances. Other policies, most notably policies to encourage the domestic adoption of innovations, must be in place as well.

Policies to encourage the development of applications, such as relaxation of antitrust restrictions on collaboration, should not restrict the domestic adoption of innovations; nor should these policies restrict international cooperation in basic research. The realities of international competition and collaboration in high-technology industries mean that many of the key technologies of the twenty-first century will not be developed by any single nation or firm, but will result from the collaboration of scientists, engineers, and managers from many industrial nations. Although intervention against trade-distorting policies is justified, restrictions on international cooperation or information flows are likely to cause more economic harm than good.

Notes

1. Recent efforts by a number of European governments to sell off publicly owned enterprises may prefigure a significant change in the character of major foreign markets in some industries. This trend, however, is a very modest ripple at present, and will not dissolve the informal ties and sources of financial pressure and support that enable governments to exert considerable influence on the purchase decisions of private corporations.

2. Okimoto [28] makes a similar argument in stating that "...the most important R&D in Japan takes place outside the framework of national projects...At most the work done for national projects supplements what individual companies are doing."

3. The Electric Power Research Institute serves electric utilities, firms that historically have maintained modest in-house research budgets. EPRI member firms also are not direct competitors, serving different geographic areas. EPRI originally was charged with focusing on "...a small number of large, long-range projects. This was in part due to the industry's concern that EPRI not duplicate or compete with the product development work of the commercial

vendors, for fear of undermining their incentives to pursue R&D. The intention was to complement the work of others..." [34] Since its foundation, however, EPRI's research agenda appears to have adopted a shorter time horizon. In 1976, short-, medium-, and long-term research respectively accounted for 45%, 45%, and 10% of total R&D expenditures. By 1981, short-term R&D had risen to 50% of the total and the share of medium-term research had been cut to 40%. In 1982, short-term research accounted for 69% of the total EPRI research budget, long-term research absorbed 3%, and medium-term research accounted for 28% of the total budget.

MCC is experiencing a similar shift in research priorities. A recent article on the new chairman of MCC, Grant Dove, noted his concern with developing applications more rapidly for members: "To carry out Dove's directive, MCC is restructuring its largest program—Advanced Computer Architecture—to enable its members to focus resources on areas that promise immediate paybacks" [35].

4. Georghiu et al. [36] note in their interim evaluation of the Alvey program that "... equivocation about the role of collaborative R&D ventures apropos of the balance between short-term and long-term R&D is counterproductive. There are heavy administrative pressures and costs which are deleterious to a balanced technological profile and overall technical progress. In this respect, it has to be noted that the Alvey Programme has not been free from such pressures. In particular, political and media pressures to equate programme success with commercially exploitable deliverables has led to a distorted set of expectations for a programme of comparatively limited scale." Fagan's description of the criticism of the recent evaluation of the British Alvey program [14] reveals the demands on this research program to pick technological winners for the development of applications:

> Fairclough [John Fairclough, chief scientific adviser to the Cabinet Office] said that the evaluation gave no analysis of what Britain's strengths in science and technology are, nor of which areas could have greatest potential for industry and for the economy. It did not show, he said, which R&D areas in Alvey deserved more support and money and which should be discontinued so that money could be given to others.

5. Flamm [37, 38] argues that federal funding of R&D in computer science and technology during the postwar period was particularly effective because it supported a number of diverse approaches: "We would be much poorer technologically, today, if some single funding authority had been granted an exclusive franchise on deciding research priorities" [38].

6. Recent efforts by U.S. firms to develop offshore technology windows have utilized wholly owned R&D facilities, rather than international joint ventures or other forms of collaboration (see [39]). This tendency is contrary to the one that would be expected if international collaboration focused mainly on precommercial research.

7. "Given the wealth of puzzling experimental features in a variety of different materials, it may take a considerable effort, with a diverse theoretical program, to unravel fully the secrets of these compounds" [26].

8. See [3, 40]. Langlois [41] notes that the U.S. microelectronics firms that are most active in international collaborative ventures are also among the firms most actively pursuing domestic collaboration, quite opposite the result if international and domestic collaboration were substitutes.

9. See [42]. How do these figures compare with HTS research expenditures by the Japanese government? The major source of Japanese government support for superconductivity research through 1986 was the Education Ministry, which provided a total of $2.6 million during 1984–1986. A more ambitious program of research was announced by the Science and Technology Agency in 1987; it called for total expenditures of $133 million during the next three to

four years, or roughly 30%–40% of the U.S. government research budget in HTS (see [43]).

References

1. Mowery, D. C. "Collaborative Research: An Assessment of Its Potential Role in the Development of High Temperature Superconductivity." Prepared for the Office of Technology Assessment, U.S. Congress, January, 1988.
2. Mowery, D. C., "Collaborative Ventures Between U.S. and Foreign Manufacturing Firms." *Research Policy*, 1989, forthcoming.
3. Mowery, D. C. (ed.), *International Collaborative Ventures in U.S. Manufacturing*. Cambridge, MA: Ballinger Publishing Company, 1988.
4. Arrow, K. J. "Economic Welfare and the Allocation of Resources for Invention." In: *The Rate and Direction of Inventive Activity*. Princeton, NJ: Princeton University Press, 1962.
5. Nelson, R. R. "The Simple Economics of Basic Scientific Research." *Journal of Political Economy* 67 (1959): 297–306.
6. Bozeman, B.; Link, A.; and Zardkoohi, A. "An Economic Analysis of R&D Joint Ventures." *Managerial and Decision Economics* 7 (1986): 263–266.
7. Rosenberg, N. "Science, Technology, and Economic Growth." Presented at the meetings of the American Association for the Advancement of Science, Chicago, Illinois, February 14, 1987.
8. Link, A. N. and Tassey, G. *Strategies for Technology-Based Competition*. Lexington, MA: D. C. Heath, 1987.
9. Hirshleifer, J. "The Private and Social Value of Information and the Reward to Innovation." *American Economic Review* 61 (1971): 561–574.
10. Teece, D. J. "Profiting from Technological Innovation: Implications for Integration, Collaboration, Licensing, and Public Policy." *Research Policy* 15 (1986): 285–305.
11. Mowery, D. C. "Economic Theory and Government Technology Policy." *Policy Sciences* 16 (1983): 27–43.
12. Cohen, W. M., and Levinthal, D. A. "Learning to Learn–An Economic Model of Firms' Investment in the Capacity to Learn." Unpublished manuscript, Carnegie-Mellon University, 1987.
13. Cohen, L., and Noll, R. "The Technology Pork Barrel." Unpublished manuscript, Brookings Institution, 1987.
14. Fagan, M. "Esprit Sprints to the Next Phase." *New Scientist* (October 8, 1987): 24–25.
15. Alic, J. A. "Cooperation in R&D: When Does It Work?" Presented at the Colloquium on International Marketing Cooperation Between Rival Trading Nations, San Miniato, Italy, May 29–31, 1986.
16. Office of Technology Assessment, U.S. Congress. *U.S. International Competitiveness: A Comparison of Steel, Electronics, and Automobiles*. Washington,

DC: U.S. Government Printing Office, 1981.

17. Office of Technology Assessment, U.S. Congress. *International Competitiveness in Electronics*. Washington, DC: U.S. Government Printing Office, 1983.

18. Nelson, R. R. "Uncertainty, Learning, and the Economics of Parallel Research and Development Efforts." *Review of Economics and Statistics* 43 (1961): 351–364.

19. Scott, J. T. "Diversification versus Cooperation in R&D Investment." *Managerial and Decision Economics*, (9) 1988: 173–186.

20. Fisher, F. M., and Temin, P. "Returns to Scale in Research and Development: What Does the Schumpeterian Hypothesis Imply?" *Journal of Political Economy* 81 (1973): 56–70.

21. Brodley, J. "Joint Ventures and Antitrust Policy." *Harvard Law Review* 95 (1982): 1523–1590.

22. Reich, R. B., and Mankin, E. D. "Joint Ventures with Japan Give Away Our Future." *Harvard Business Review* (March/April, 1986): 79–86.

23. Pisano, G. P.; Shan, W.; and Teece, D. J. "Joint Ventures and Collaboration in the Biotechnology Industry." In: D. C. Mowery (ed.), *International Collaborative Ventures in U.S. Manufacturing*. Cambridge, MA: Ballinger Publishing Company, 1988.

24. Mowery, D. C., and Rosenberg, N. "Commercial Aircraft: Cooperation and Competition Between the U.S. and Japan." *California Management Review* 27, (1985): 70–92.

25. Mowery, D. C. "Federal Funding of Research and Development in Transportation: The Case of Aviation." Presented at the Symposium on the Returns to Federal R&D Funding, National Academy of Sciences, Washington, DC, November 20, 1985.

26. Committee on Science, Engineering, and Public Policy, NAS/NAE/IOM. *Research Briefings 1987: Report of the Panel on High-Temperature Superconductivity*. Washington, DC: National Academy Press, 1987.

27. Eads, G., and Nelson, R. R. "Government Support of Advanced Civilian Technology: A Power Reactors and the Supersonic Transport." *Public Policy* 3 (1971): 405–427.

28. Okimoto, D. I. "Regime Characteristics of Japanese Industrial Policy." In: H. Patrick (ed.), *Japan's High Technology Industries* Seattle: University of Washington, 1986.

29. Ergas, H. "Does Technology Policy Matter?" In: B. Guile and H. Brooks (eds.), *A Technology and Global Industry*. Washington, DC: National Academy Press, 1987.

30. "Putting Superconductors to Work—Superfast." *Business Week* (May 18, 1987): 124–126.

31. Panel on National Security Export Controls and Global Economic Competition, Committee on Science, Engineering, and Public Policy. *Balancing the National Interest*. Washington, DC: National Academy Press, 1987.

32. Nelson, R. R. *High-Technology Policies: A Five Nation Comparison*. American Enterprise Institute, 1984.

33. Yoder, S. K. "Americans Spurn Japan's Research Offer." *Wall Street Journal* (December 30, 1987):
34. Barker, B. "Decade of Change: EPRI and the Climate for Research." *EPRI Journal* 8 (January/February, 1983): 5–13.
35. Lineback, J. R. "It's Time for MCC to Fish or Cut Bait." *Electronics* (June 25, 1987): 32–33.
36. Georghiu, L.; Guy, K.; Cameron, H.; Ray, T.; Hobday, M.; and Duncombe, R. "Evaluation of the Alvey Programme: Draft Interim Report." Science Policy Research Unit, University of Sussex, 1987.
37. Flamm, K. *Creating the Computer.* Washington, DC: Brookings Institution, 1988.
38. Flamm, K. "Government's Role in Computers and Superconductors." Prepared for the Office of Technology Assessment, March, 1988.
39. Yoder, S. K. "Western Research Labs Sprout in Japan as U.S. Firms are Lured by High-Tech Boom." *Wall Street Journal* (November 12, 1987): 33.
40. Mowery, D. C. *Alliance Politics and Economics: Multinational Joint Ventures in Commercial Aircraft.* Cambridge, MA: Ballinger Publishing Company, 1987.
41. Langlois, R. N. *Microelectronics: An Industry in Transition.* Center for Science and Technology Policy, Rensselaer Polytechnic Institute, 1987.
42. Office of Technology Assessment, U.S. Congress. *Commercializing High-Temperature Superconductivity.* Washington, DC: U.S. Government Printing Office, 1988.
43. National Science Foundation, Tokyo Office. "Science and Technology Agency to Propose New Initiative for R&D on New Superconductors." Report Memorandum #129, July 30, 1987.

9 COOPERATIVE RESEARCH IN THE AUTOMOBILE INDUSTRY: A MULTINATIONAL PERSPECTIVE

Gerhard Rosegger

1. Introduction

The global activities and effects of multinational enterprises (MNE) in manufacturing have been examined in an extensive literature. Although many aspects of these activities remain controversial on theoretical as well as on political grounds, there seems to exist agreement on one point: MNE are the most effective organization form yet invented for the accumulation of technical and market information. Indeed, the desire to exploit the advantages of firm-specific knowledge without reliance on the "tyranny of the market" has been accepted as one of the main reasons for the growth of direct foreign investment over the last three decades.

To the extent that such internalization motivated the vertical and horizontal integration of activities without regard to national boundaries, the growth of MNE could be explained entirely within the theoretical framework originally proposed by Coase [1], and later extended by Williamson [2] and others. Application of this framework, adumbrated by the contributions of many scholars, resulted in a body of work dealing with the dominant phenomena of the 1960s and 1970s: one-way and two-way direct foreign investment in different industries. A recent collection of studies [3]

167

investigated the implications of yet another significant development, the rapid expansion of intraindustry direct foreign investment. These various forms of globalization resulted in increased rates of international technology transfer, as reflected in statistics on payments of fees and royalties. Quite in keeping with theoretical expectations, most of these flows were between parents and affiliates, or between affiliates of the same MNE.

Meanwhile, however, there has been an upsurge in arrangements whose consequences, for technology transfer as well as for other MNE activities, go well beyond what was explained by the original theories: *interfirm cooperative agreements* to research, develop, engineer, and exploit product and process innovations. Vickery [4] observes that such agreements appear to be most prevalent in the so-called high-technology industries, but he adds that there is little in the way of hard evidence on their full magnitude and impact. In a pioneering study, Mariti and Smiley [5] did provide such evidence on some 70 cooperative agreements among enterprises in a range of European industries. They concluded that firms entered into these agreements mainly in a quest for economies of scale in the acquisition and utilization of technical as well as market information. In addition, they hypothesized that cooperation permitted the continued existence of a larger number of firms in a market than would be predicted by the received, industrial organization view.

In a comprehensive survey, Teece [6] interpreted alternative arrangements for "capturing value from technological innovation." These range from classical internalization to what he calls *strategic partnering* (i.e., more or less formal types of coopreation). He goes further than Mariti and Smiley by claiming that cooperation not only helps to maintain the competitive *status quo*, but also that "coalitions ought to be seen not as attempts to stifle competition, but as mechanisms for *lowering entry requirements* [emphasis added] for innovators." Doz [7] extended the argument by pointing to growing economics of scale in R&D on the one hand, and to new manufacturing techniques that reduce minimum efficient scales on the other, as explanations for globalization.

In this chapter, an attempt is made to explore these issues for the case of the automobile industry, where worldwide, interfirm cooperation has grown at an accelerating rate. It is argued that the unique character of product innovation and of manufacturing technology in the industry requires that research, development, design, and engineering (RDD&E) be seen as one unified activity and furthermore that the motives for cooperation in RDD&E must be interpreted in terms of corporate strategies that extend to supplier relations and vehicle assembly, as well as to marketing and distribution.

In the next section, evidence is presented on the extent to which the world's major motor vehicle manufacturers have became involved in various forms of cooperation, with special attention to the position of America's Big Three (GM, Ford, and Chrysler). In the subsequent section, a taxonomy of firm strategies is proposed along with more specific explanation of the factors that determine whether a firm will undertake stand-alone or cooperative efforts in RDD&E. These efforts are also placed into the framework of variegated motives for the setting up of alliances. The implications of these developments for competition in the U.S. market are examined in the concluding section.

2. Patterns of Interfirm Cooperation

Interfirm cooperation can take many different shapes, ranging from quite informal agreements regarding the exchange of information, goods, or services, to such definitive forms as the acquisition of an equity position by one partner in another, or the setting up of a joint venture. Agreements may be bilateral or they may involve several parties. There exists no authoritative definition for these arrangements, and no attempt at one will be made here. A few examples may, however, illustrate the delineations used in collecting the data presented subsequently.

Arm's-length, spot transactions among firms, no matter how often they are repeated, do not imply an agreement to cooperate; on the other hand, a one-time contract to develop and manufacture a new product does. The practice of Japanese car manufacturers to select a few parts suppliers on a long-term basis and to work with them in designing parts specifications [9] constitutes an agreement to cooperate; the traditional American practice of selecting suppliers annually does not. The taking of a patent license is not a form of cooperation, even if royalty payments extend over a period of years; the sharing of patents and know-how does imply an agreement.

Defining the ultimate object of cooperation, the automobile as a final product, would seem to be unnecessary; however, as soon as one recognizes that in recent years van and light truck sales have made up one of the fastest-growing segments of the personal-transportation market, the matter becomes less straightforward. Cooperative agreements entered into by a number of firms were triggered by the desire of one of the partners to get a foothold in these segments.

There exists no single source documenting cooperative arrangements. As Vickery [4] points out, the few available statistics greatly understate the range and significance of these ventures. Therefore, the following information is based mainly on reports in the general business press and in automotive-industry trade publications.[3] Given the fact that these sources are likely to cover only activities of major actors or particularly important activities of minor players, this survey is neither all-inclusive, nor based on a random sample.

2.1. Cooperation Among the World's Major Producers

Figure 9–1 summarizes the most significant cooperative arrangements among the 20 largest motor vehicle manufacturers.

The upper half of the matrix shows all cooperative arrangements among the major firms. Of the 49 agreements, 22 cover multiple activities, ranging from RDD&E to marketing. Another 17 involve the exchange of parts and

	GENERAL MOTORS	FORD	CHRYSLER	TOYOTA	NISSAN	VW-AUDI	RENAULT	PEUGEOT	FIAT	HONDA	MAZDA	MITSUBISHI	SUZUKI	DAIMLER-BENZ	ISUZU	SUBARU	DAIHATSU	B.L.	VOLVO	BMW
GEN. MOTORS			•				1					1	•		•					
FORD							1	1	1	•		1								1
CHRYSLER				1	•	•	•	•	•			•								
TOYOTA	J					•	3													
NISSAN		J				4					•				1					
VW-AUDI		J					3	3	1					•		3	2			
RENAULT								•	1							2	•			
PEUGEOT									•	1	•			•		1		•	•	
FIAT																	1	•		
HONDA														•			•			
MAZDA	E, J											1								
MITSUBISHI		E, J												•			4			
SUZUKI	E, J													•						
DAIMLER-B.																				
ISUZU	E																			
SUBARU					E									J						
DAIHATSU				E																
B. L.																				
VOLVO									E											
BMW																				

E = Equity position
J = Joint venture

1 = Component sharing
2 = Marketing
3 = RDD & E
4 = Production or assembly
• = Multiple relationships

Figure 9–1. Cooperative Arrangements Among the Largest Producers. E = Equity position, J = Joint Venture, 1 = Component sharing, 2 = Marketing, 3 = RDD&E, 4 = Production or assembly, = Multiple relationships.

components; but of course this also implies a degree of coordination in product design and engineering. For reasons to be discussed in the next section, agreements among major firms that focus purely on cooperation in RDD&E are least numerous. Those of the above agreements that are institutionalized in joint ventures or in the acquisition of equity positions by partners are shown also in the lower half of the matrix.

It is important to stress that each of the major partners in these equity and joint-venture arrangments brings to them, in turn, its own network of relationships that connect it with other firms in various countries. One example may serve as an illustration: Chrysler Canada intends to import Mitsubishi Colt cars built by Mitsubishi's joint-venture partner in Thailand, MMC Sittipol. These cars are assembled from locally manufactured components as well as from parts supplied by Mitsubishi and its Korean joint-venture partner, Hyundai.

2.2. Cooperative Networks of America's Big Three

Historically, American automobile manufacturers have been reluctant to establish permanent, cooperative relationships with other firms, domestic or foreign. In their home market, they were no doubt sensitive to the antitrust implications of any kind of formal cooperation among themselves, even in research and development at the basic end of the spectrum. In fact, Fusfeld [10] attributes the failure of the Carter administration's Cooperative Automotive Research Program (CARP) to this sensitivity. In foreign markets, the manufacturers relied largely on their own subsidiaries.[4] There seemed to be little point in impairing the decision-making autonomy of these operating divisions of large, seemingly self-sufficient MNE by establishing long-term relationships with foreign partners [11].

For reasons to be traced in the next section, these attitudes changed radically since the 1970s, and each of the Big Three began to develop networks of cooperative arrangements with foreign manufacturers, the most important of which were sealed through the acquisition of equity in the partners, or through the establishment of joint ventures.

Chrysler pioneered the new trend with the purchase, in 1971, of a 15% share in Mitsubishi. The now-defunct alliance between Renault and AMC followed in 1978. In 1979, Ford acquired its interest in Toyo Kogyo (Mazda). In 1980, General Motors began discussions with Toyota that led to the 1983 formation of a joint venture for production, the New United Motor Manufacturing Inc. (NUMMI), in California. Further linkages with European and Far Eastern manufacturers were established in rapid succession.

Figure 9–2 shows the main relationships between the American Big Three and foreign manufacturers. Several of the joint ventures are located in third countries, such as the Ford–VW production facilities in Brazil, and the Ford–Nissan venture in Australia. It seems clear that, in terms of equity holdings and joint ventures, distinct groupings are beginning to emerge. Some of these are reinforced by one of the partner's

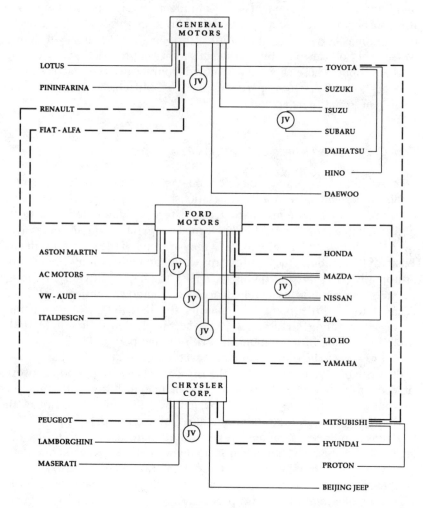

Figure 9–2. Major Cooperative Relationships of U.S. Producers. JV = Joint venture, solid line = Equity holding, dotted line = Other cooperative agreement.

interests in yet other firms, such as Mitsubishi's 15% equity share in Hyundai, and the many interests of other Japanese producers in the newly industralizing countries.

Not shown are the numerous linkages among European producers. Also, it would be next to impossible to trace the complex networks of manufacturer–supplier connections that have been built up around the core groups, both in the United States and abroad. Thus, for example, the welding robots used in the Korean Daewoo plant for the assembly of the Pontiac Le Mans were produced by a joint venture between General Motors and the Japanese firm, Fanuc. In the United States, a joint venture between General Motors and NHK Spring and a similar venture between a GM subsidiary, Delco Moraine, and Akebono Brake Industries supply components to Japanese DFI and to American plants. Other ventures, such as that between Pittsburgh Plate Glass (PPG) and Asahi Glass (Japan) were set up in Korea to provide safety glass for the car industry there. In yet a different arrangement, Mazda, Ford, and Matsushita have formed a new California company to develop and produce automotive heating and air-conditioning units, with the intent of supplying Mazda's Hiroshima plant.

Anecdotal evidence of this type cannot establish the dimensions of the evolving networks, but it suggests something of the contours along which globalization of the automobile industry is proceeding.

3. Cooperation: Strategies and Motives

Many observers have stressed the fact that American auto producers' cooperative strategies have been mainly *technology-driven*, reflecting an effort to catch up with the more advanced RDD&E and manufacturing capabilities of their foreign rivals. Although this contention appears unexceptional, it also raises two questions:

1) Would the achievement of parity in product and process technology guarantee the return of the industry to international competitiveness? Gold [12] has argued persuasively that it would not, but that many other strategic factors impinge upon competitive performance. In the case of the motor vehicle industry, his argument is buttressed by the fact that the position of any one firm is affected by a complex mix of strategies concerning product design, styling, and engineering; the supply of parts and components; final assembly operations; and marketing, distribution, and after-sales service. Decisions to cooperate in RDD&E must be evaluated within this broader strategic framework (discussed below).

2) *If* technological advantages were tilted entirely in favor of foreign firms (an arguable proposition), then what were the motives of these firms in developing strategic alliances with American producers? As will be argued, cooperation in RDD&E must be explained by the *nature* of the advances sought and not just by one partner's desire to acquire technical information from another. Furthermore, the opportunities for mutual gains from cooperation necessarily extend beyond the boundaries of technology, and therefore an exclusive focusing on RDD&E as the strategic arena would present an inaccurate picutre.

3.1. A Taxonomy of Strategies

At any given time, an established manufacturing firm has a base of technology-specific physical assets,[5] of vertical and horizontal market linkages, and of what Nelson and Winter [14] have called "organizational capabilities." Its goal then is to find a mix of strategies through which it gains maximum leverage from this base. The point is worth making only because too often critics of industry seem to be making the assumption that, given a shift in technological or market conditions, firms can initiate appropriate strategies de novo (i.e., as though their past simply could be written off).

In the case of the automative industry, it is useful to identify four major concerns of strategy: 1) technology, 2) the acquisition of parts and components, 3) the actual manufacturing or assembly of vehicles, and 4) marketing and distribution. In each of these four areas, firms have a choice of strategies that, although constrained in individual cases by the historical factors referred to above, range from a stand-alone effort to a full integration of activities with those of a partner or partners.

Table 9–1 presents a synoptic taxonomy of possibilities. Needless to say, these are not mutually exclusive, nor is the table meant to imply that firms actually pursue only one type of strategy at a time. The mix of strategies and the weight accorded to each area of strategy depend on the current condition of a firm as well as on the potentials for technological advance.

Consider, for example, the degree of vertical integration as a determinant of strategies. While General Motors has traditionally produced some 70% of required parts and components in its own facilities, Toyota obtains roughly the same percentage from outside suppliers. Although American firms are in the process of transforming their production systems along Japanese lines, in the meantime the difference in integration acts a powerful constraint on strategy choice.

Advances in the organization and management of product innovation

Table 9−1.   Classification of Manufactures' Strategies

Research, Development, Design, Engineering	Acquisition of Parts and Components	Manufacturing and Assembly	Marketing and Distribution
Stand-alone RDD&E	Vertical integration	Production in and for home market	Sales under own name, through own dealers
Arm's-length acquisition of technology (licensing)	Spot transactions with outside suppliers	Production in home country, exporting	Sales of partner's products through own dealer network
Long-term agreements for interfirm exchanges of technical information	Long-term contractual relations with suppliers	Stand-alone DFI in country of sale or third country	Sale under own name of partner's products, through own dealers
Joint support, with other manufacturers, of third-party RDD&E	Acquisition of equity interest in suppliers	Joint ventures for production, in home country or third country	Joint distribution system with partner
Joint ventures in RDD&E, joint projects for development of models	Joint supply ventures with other manufacturers Exchange of components with partners	Merger with domestic of foreign manufacturer	Merger of existing distribution systems

have led to a closer coordination of decision-making in the various stages of product development, thus avoiding the risks of suboptimization. Outstanding among these advances has been the early involvement of suppliers and manufacturing divisions in RDD&E. According to one insider [15], the main result of the integration of the traditionally separate and sequential inputs of designers, product engineers, and manufacturing engineers has been that between 50% and 70% of a car's production costs are determined when the layout of the car (i.e., the first complete cross section) is completed.

Finally, we must recognize that major manufacturers typically sell as range of models, for each of which a different mix of strategies may be appropriate, depending in large measure on the firms's past experience, production capabilities, and market share. Thus, the sale of another manufacturer's model under the firm's own nameplate can be seen as a quick method for rounding out its range of offerings. The original 1971 alliance between Chrysler and Mitsubishi is an example of this type of strategy. The case also demonstrates how the scope of such alliances can evolve over time to include the entire spectrum of activities.

This taxonomy does not cover an additional element of strategy, namely, decisions about the location of various types of activity. In the past, these decisions of American manufacturers were closely tied to their marketing strategies.[6] The rapid, worldwide diffusion of all phases of motor-vehicle production has broken this linkage, adding further complexity to strategy formulation [16]. As Hannay [17] points out, how one interprets this development depends on whether one sees automotive technology as being in the mature stage of the life cycle or whether recent advances are regarded as harbingers of a renewed take-off.

3.2. Motives for Cooperation in RDD&E

What explains the growth of international cooperative arrangements in RDD&E? In trying to answer this question, we must first reemphasize an earlier point: if one of the partners comes to such an arrangement motivated solely by the desire to catch up in technology, the other partner obviously must expect to gain in another area of strategy. It may well be that the majority of strategic alliances involve the expectation of gains across a range of activities. This is an issue discussed below; here we want to isolate the reasons why partners might expect to derive benefits from the joint development of products and processes.

Table 9–2 summarizes the considerations that will influence whether a firm chooses cooperation or a stand-alone effort in RDD&E. A distinction is made between *generic* technology and *specific* technology. The former concerns the development of new information that is applicable across a range of products, regardless of the make or model of a vehicle; the latter consists of information that is directly applicable only to particular products or producers.

In the case of generic technology, the expected appropriability of the information will play a major role in firms' decisions to seek an alliance or to pursue RDD&E on their own. Cooperation is most likely to be the strategy of choice in situations involving government-mandated new tech-

Table 9–2.   Strategic Motives in RDD&E

	Cooperative Efforts	Stand-Alone Effort
Generic technology	*Low expected appropriability* [Basic research, electronics, new materials, gov't.-mandated innovation]	*High expected appropriability* [First-comer advantages, required capacity in place]
Specific technology	*Technological complementarities* [Merging of existing capabilities] *Scale economies in new-product development* [Common engines, platforms, etc.]	*Differentiation of final product* [Body design and engineering, etc.] *Enhancement of existing products and facilities* [Niche-filling]

nology and in work tending toward the basic end of the applied-research spectrum [18], such as investigations into vehicle electronics or into the use of new materials. Stand-alone efforts tend to be encouraged in situations where a firm thinks it has the capability to gain a head start over competitors, who might then license the generic technology. Emphasis has to be placed on the term *expected* appropriability, because decision-makers may of course turn out to have been wrong in their assessments. Thus, for example, Honda, Toyota, Nissan, and Mazda have been engaged in patent litigation over their respective four-wheel steering systems, which appeared on the market at about the same time. Each firm apparently misestimated its first-comer advantages.

The prospect of exploiting technological complementarities (both in the product lines and in the existing stock of information each firm brings into a partnership) is one motive for cooperation in the development of specific technology. While the notion of synergy in RDD&E may be somewhat vague, it nevertheless seems clear that there are many cases in which producers expect to gain substantially from pooling their knowledge in cooperative efforts, at least by reducing the amount of time required for the completion of projects.

The single most important factor leading to cooperation in the specific-technology area, however, has been a shifting in the locus of scale economies, from assembly and component manufacture to RDD&E [19]. Historically, integrated plant complexes in the United States were estimated to achieve sharp reductions in unit costs up to annual capacities of 300,000 vehicles, with further improvements in cost efficiency likely up to 600,000-unit capacities [20]. By contrast, current manufacturing techniques justify plant capacities of 150,000 to 200,000 units per year, and the development of multiple-model assembly lines has further reduced the cost penalties of small runs [21].

At the same time, competition and changes in buyer preferences have forced firms to offer an increasing array of models as well as an increasing number of model variants. Therefore, the traditional strategies for the exploitation of scale economies—concentration on a narrow range of standard body configurations and infrequent basic-model changes—have become obsolete. While some firms managed to shift to the luxury end of the market, most major manufacturers of necessity instituted programs for supplying their dealers with a wider variety of vehicles, from entry-level to luxury models.[7] Pace setters for this trend were the Japanese. As of 1988, Toyota offered 35 different models, followed by Subaru with 30 models, Nissan with 25, and Mazda with 22. Altogether, importers accounted for 337 different models, for an average of 8.5 per make, while domestic producers (including DFI plants) provided a choice of 251 models, for an average of 15 per make [22].

While basic technical characteristics (horsepower, dimensions, weight) of American-made and imported cars have tended to converge, differences among the models sold by any one manufacturer have increased. As figure 9–3 shows, over the past decade this has resulted in a remarkable widening of the price ranges for all major competitors in the American market. Annual sales volumes for individual models have declined as the market has become increasingly segmented. Consumer reaction to fluctuating fuel prices, in the form of rapidly shifting preferences for large versus small cars, added a further element of uncertainty to the formulation of firm strategies.

These developments set the stage for strategic alliances in RDD&E. Given the fact that introduction of an entirely new vehicle may involve total project costs as high as $3 billion and may take three to four years from concept formation to production start-up, the attractiveness of cooperation is evident. To the extent that partners can rely on jointly designed and developed major components, such as engines, transmissions, and suspension systems, they will achieve reductions in unit costs that only a few of them could obtain in a stand-alone effort, and only for a few of their models.[8] The setting of joint specifications for parts and modules purchased from outside suppliers provides further opportunities for cost reduction.

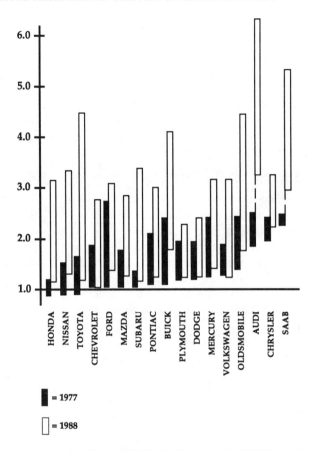

Source: Automotive News, 1977 Market Data Book, 1987 Market Data Book.

Figure 9–3.   Price Ranges for Models of Major Sellers in U.S. Market, as Multiples of Lowest-Priced U.S.-Made Model, 1977 and 1987. Dark bars = 1977, Light bars = 1987.

3.3. Cooperative Strategies: A Broader View

Although the arguments for cooperation in RDD&E are persuasive per se, many other strategic goals enter into firms' decisions to form alliances. In fact, as the Chrysler–Mitsubishi case demonstrates, a full partnership may evolve from such modest beginnings as the sale of one producer's model through the dealer system of another. Whatever the initial motives, in order for a cooperative arrangement to succeed, each partner must contribute some specific strengths in product mix, product engineering capabilities, established relationships with suppliers, manufacturing technology, managerial know-how, or marketing networks. The failure of the American Motors–Renault partnership may well be ascribed to the fact that it lacked such complementary strengths. A joint venture between Nissan and Alfa Romeo to produce a car for the Italian market fell apart for the same reasons, although it was dissolved in a face-saving fashion when Fiat acquired Alfa Romeo in 1986.

While a detailed examination of each of the major manufacturer's motives in forming strategic alliances would go well beyond the scope of this survey, it is possible to identify typical patterns and to relate these, at least in the form of examples, to the interests of the participants:[9]

1) Given the observations made above, it is clear that one of the main considerations leading to partnerships is the need to round out product offerings in growing markets. For American firms, this has meant mostly acquiring entry-level, inexpensive cars and selling these under their own model names. To the extent that these firms brought unique market knowledge to such deals, it was inevitable that they would begin to have an influence on engineering and design characteristics of the vehicles sold. Producers abroad have followed the same path, as evidenced by the agreements between Daimler–Benz and Mitsubishi, and between Volkswagen and Toyota, under which the German companies will market Japanese light trucks in Western Europe.

2) Such partnerships provide low-cost opportunities for firms to enter markets. While it would be difficult to generalize about the minimum efficient size of a dealer network in a given market, especially one as large as the American market, there can be no doubt that the establishment of such a distribution system requires a substantial up-front investment. That it is also risky is illustrated by the case of Fiat, one of the largest European producers, which never managed to gain a firm foothold in the United States and finally withdrew altogether. Formation of an alliance as an entry strategy may be followed by the gradual establishment of a parallel, independent marketing network. Mitsubishi and Isuzu, partners of Chrysler and General Motors, respectively, have taken this step.

3) Firms in the newly industrializing countries are interested in partnerships with established manufacturers primarily as a means of acquiring product and process technology, offering in exchange low costs of production. Only in the case of the emerging Chinese industry is the output

intended for the home market. More typical is South Korea's Kia Motor Company, in which Ford and Mazda hold equity shares, and which is producing the entry-level Ford Festiva for sale in the United States.

4) The desire to acquire organizational and managerial know-how, in addition to technology, has motivated the formation of joint ventures between American and European manufacturers on the one hand, and Japanese firms on the other. The Chevrolet Nova, produced jointly by Toyota and General Motors, is the product of such a venture; the British Rover Sterling, based on cooperation with Honda, is another.

5) The sharing of economic and political risks in unstable markets has produced some partnerships between major companies. Thus, Volkswagen and Ford Motors have merged their RDD&E, manufacturing, and distribution facilities in South America. In a different vein, pressures from host governments may lead to cooperation among DFI firms. An outstanding example is Australia, where the government has strongly encouraged a rationalization of production through alliances among the country's major producers, General Motors, Ford, Toyota, and Nissan.

6) Their prestigious history and their ability to move rapidly in the development and implementation of leading-edge technology have made a number of small European producers attractive partners for the major automotive manufacturers. Even where the formation of partnerships was sealed by outright acquisition, as in the cases of Fiat–Ferrari, General Motors–Lotus, or Ford–Aston Martin, the acquiring firms were careful to retain the separate identities of their counterparts. These and other alliances, such as General Motors–Pininfarina and Chrysler–Maserati, also provided the mass producers with representation at the luxury and high-performance end of the market.

7) In addition to these technical and economic reasons for the growth of cooperative arrangements, the desire to forestall or mitigate the impact of protectionist government policies has no doubt played a role in firms' decisions to form strategic partnerships. Wherever such measures as import quotas and local-content requirements threaten to restrict or close a market, foreign producers have an incentive to undertake a stand-alone direct investment or to form a venture with a local partner. While the former has the advantage of preserving full decision-making autonomy, the latter is attractive because local partners have experience in government relations and other political matters.

This brief enumeration suggests a great diversity of reasons why firms may enter into cooperative arrangements on a global scale; nevertheless one may surmise that, no matter what combination of factors motivated the formation of particular alliances, they are likely to have direct or indirect repercussions in the technological sphere. In the most obvious cases, cooperation is based on the expectation of mutual gains in research, development, design, and engineering; but even where other considerations triggered the establishment of joint activities, a number of plausible scenarios could show how these evolve into a common concern with product characteristics, make-or-buy decisions, and maufacturing techniques.

4. The Persistence of Rivalry: A U.S. Perspective

Since World War II, the position of the United States as the world's leading producer of motor vehicles has been steadily eroded. In 1985, Japan's output (in units) surpassed that of America of the first time, as did the combined output of the European Community. During most of the period, this process was accompanied by a concentration of production among fewer and fewer firms. In the United States, consolidation had essentially run its course by the 1940s, and the standard American car had become an increasingly homogeneous product [26]. In Western Europe, the late 1950s and the 1960s saw a merger movement, combined with exit of many unsuccessful competitors. In the meantime, Japan's industry had begun its rapid ascendancy as a factor in international competition; and in the 1980s, producers in the newly industrializing countries added yet another dimension to globalization.

None of these developments has altered the fact that the United States continues to be the world's largest market for motor vehicles. It accounts for approximately one third of all vehicle exports from other producing countries. Even though it is also the country with the highest car density, and the bulk of all demand is for replacement, total annual sales of 10 to 12 million units are expected to continue into the foreseeable future. It is not surprising, therefore, that the interplay between the forces of competition and cooperation have manifested themselves most obviously in the American market.

For reasons that have been widely discussed and amply documented [27], the large U.S. firms had fallen behind in product and process technology and consequently had lost market shares to imports as well as to expanding DFI production. For them, entering into strategic alliances, together with massive programs for investment in up-to-date capacity, provided a means of recovery from difficulties that had been accentuated, though not caused, by the oil shocks of the 1970s.

On the whole, U.S. government policy has been supportive of these effort. The program to salvage Chrysler [28], the arrangement with Japan for the imposition of "voluntary" export quotas, and the tough stand taken in negotiations on U.S.–Japan auto parts trade [9] are testimony to this policy stance. Recurrent protectionist rumblings in the Congress served as further warnings to foreign producers.

Despite some ambivalence about the role of domestic joint ventures with foreign manufacturers, especially with respect to their effects on American parts suppliers, reaction to the growing involvement of American automotive producers in global cooperative arrangements has been muted. There seems to have been little in the way of suspicion that the formation of strategic groups in the automobile industry may lead to the kind of "...restricting of production, withholding new products, and fencing in and blocking off new developments" [29] for which the international manufacturers' cartels of the pre-World War II era had been indicted. Nor, for obvious reasons, have there been any worries that cooperation might lead to exports of technology that could be detrimental to the country's long-term interests.

Developments in the American automobile market certainly justify this apparent lack of public or official concern. Coalitions have made it easier for new competitiors to enter the market and for existing competitors to expand their offerings. Therefore, consumers presently can choose among a wider array of products with more variegated technical characteristics than ever before. And while prices have been affected by the "voluntary" quota system and by exchange-rate fluctuations, competitive pressures continue to force producers into offering effective price reductions via discounts, rebates, and low-interest loans. To the extent that the expansion of DFI will lead to substantial excess capacity in the domestic industry, these pressures can be expected to persist. Industry spokesmen have even expressed fears of a price war in the next few years, as more of the foreign-owned plants come on-stream [30].

The ultimate driving force behind cooperation continues to be the struggle for market share. In this struggle, advanced technology, quality, service, and cost are the main determinants of success. In order to survive, firms have to find the proper strategic mix among integration of activities, arm's-length contracting, and cooperation. National boundaries and narrow definitions of the national interest are likely to become increasingly irrelevant as the members of strategic alliances draw upon information, physical assets, and production infrastructures that are spread across the globe.

Acknowledgments

I thank my colleagues at Case Western Reserve University, Marvin Barloon, Asim Erdilek, and Nguyen Quan, who commented on an earlier draft of this chapter. Some of the material contained herein was presented at a colloquium, *International Marketing Cooperation between Rival Trading Nations*, held in May 1986 at San Miniato, Italy. Discussions with participants helped to clear up a number of issues, especially from the European perspective. In October 1987 I read a preliminary version of the chapter at a seminar at Lehigh University, where I also received valuable comments. Thanks go to Professor Nicholas Balabkins for making the necessary arrangements.

Last but not least, I must record my appreciation of the stimulating and congenial working environment I enjoyed during my stay as visiting professor at the Graduate Center for the Management of Advanced Technology and Innovation, in the College of Business Administration, University of Cincinnati.

Notes

1. The setting of industry-wide technical standards is an historically important, if often overlooked, form of interfirm cooperation. For a detailed discussion, see [8].

2. While Japanese firms were the leaders in developing light trucks, Chrysler pioneered in what arguably is one of the most significant product innovations of the last decade, the compact van.

3. In addition to the daily press, especially *The Wall Street Journal*, the most important sources consulted were the weekly *Automotive News*, as well as the monthly publications, *Automotive Engineering, Automotive Industries, Car and Driver, Motor Trend*, and *Road & Track*.

4. In 1987, General Motors produced or assembled vehicles in 17 countries, Ford in 16 countries. Even Chrysler, which had essentially withdrawn from global production during its crisis years, maintained operations in four foreign countries.

5. On the role of technological specificity in firms' evaluations of innovations, see [13].

6. Marketing strategies were influenced, in turn, by foreign-government policies concerning local content and export incentives.

7. Each of the major Japanese manufacturers is engaged in producing and marketing at least one luxury model, aimed at competing directly with such European producers as BMW, SAAB, and Volvo.

8. In 1987, the best-selling product of a domestic manufacturer was the Ford Escort, with sales of 392,000 units, in five different versions. (Three similar versions were sold as Mercury Lynx.) The best-selling import of a major foreign producer was the Toyota Camry, with 187,000 units, in six versions. The largest volume among imports was recorded by the entry-level Hyundai Excel, which sold 264,000 units.

9. In addition to the newspapers and trade publications referred to note 3 above, this compilation relied on material in [11, 23, 24, 25].

References

1. Coase, R. "The Nature of the Firm." *Economica* 4 (16) (1937): 386–405.
2. Williamson, O.E. "The Modern Corporation: Origins, Evolution, Attributes." *Journal of Economic Literature* 19 (1981): 1537–1569.
3. Erdilek, A. (ed.). *Multinationals as Mutual Invaders: Intra-Industry Direct Foreign Investment.* London: Croom-Helms, 1985.
4. Vickery, G. "International Flows of Technology—Recent Trends and Developments." *STI Review* 1 (1986): 47–84.
5. Mariti, P., and Smiley R H. "Cooperative Agreements and the Organization of Industry." *Journal of Industrial Economics* 31 (4) (1983): 437–451.
6. Teece, D.C. "Capturing Value from Technological Innovation: Integration, Strategic Partnering, and Licensing Decisions." In: B.R. Guile and H. Brooks (eds.), *Technology and Global Industry: Companies and Nations in the World Economy.* Washington, DC: National Academy Press, 1987, pp. 65–95.
7. Doz, Y. "International Industries: Fragmentation versus Globalization." In: B.R. Guile and H. Brooks (eds.), *Technology and Global Industry: Companies and Nations in the World Economy.* Washington, DC: National Academy Press, 1987.
8. Thompson, G.V. "Intercompany Technical Standardization in the Early American Automobile Industry." *Journal of Economic History* 14 (1) (1954): 1–20.
9. Higashi, C., and Lauter, G.P. *The Internationalization of the Japanese Economy.* Boston, MA: Kluwer Academic Publishers, 1987.
10. Fusfeld, H.I. *The Technical Enterprise: Present and Future Patterns.* Cambridge, MA: Ballinger, 1986.
11. Harrigan, K.R. *Strategies for Joint Ventures.* Lexington, MA: Lexington Books–D.C. Heath, 1985.
12. Gold, B. "Technological and Other Determinants of the International Competitiveness of U.S. Industries." *IEEE Transactions on Engineering Management* E–M 30/2 (1983): 53–59.
13. Rosegger, G. "Diffusion Research in the Industrial Setting: Some Conceptual Clarifications." *Technological Forecasting and Social Change* 9 (1976): 401–410.
14. Nelson, R.R., and Winter, S.G. *An Evolutionary Theory of Economic Change.* Cambridge, MA: Belknap Press of Harvard University Press, 1982.
15. Eaton, R.J. "Product Planning in a Rapidly Changing World." *International Journal of Technology Management* 2 (2) (1987): 183–89.

16. Jurgen, R. K. "Survival strategy: go global." *IEEE Spectrum* 24 (10) (1987): 34–38.
17. Hannay, N. B. "Technology and Trade: A Study of U.S. Competitiveness in Seven Industries." In R. Landau and N. Rosenberg (eds.), *The Positive Sum Strategy*. Washington, DC: National Academy Press, 1986.
18. Link, A. N., and Bauer, L. L. *Cooperative Research in U.S. Manufacturing: Assessing Policy Initiatives and Corporate Strategies*. Lexington, MA: D. C. Heath, 1989.
19. Link, A. N., and Tassey, G. *Strategies for Technology-based Competition: Meeting the New Global Challenge*. Lexington, MA: D. C. Heath, 1987.
20. Bain, J. S. *Barriers to Competition*. Cambridge, MA: Harvard University Press, 1956.
21. Altshuler, A., et al. *The Future of the Automobile*. Cambridge, MA: MIT Press, 1984.
22. Teahen, J. K. Jr. "Imports on the Rise." *Automotive News* (March 14, 1988).
23. Buss, D. D., and Ingrassia, P. "While Trying to Curb Imports, Auto Makers Set More Foreign Ties." *Wall Street Journal* (October 28, 1985):
24. Corcoran, E. "Cooperating to Compete." *IEEE Spectrum* (October, 1987): 53–56.
25. McElroy, J. "Building an American Empire." *Automotive Industries* (March, 1985): 26–30.
26. Rosegger, G., and Baird, R. N. "Entry and Exit of Makes in the Automobile Industry, 1895–1960: An International Comparison." *Omega* 15 (2) (1987): 93–102.
27. Subcommittee on Trade, Committee on Ways and Means, U.S. House of Representatives. *Auto Situation: 1980*. Washington, DC: U.S. Government Printing Office, 1980.
29. Berge, W. *Cartels: Challenge to a Free World*. Washington, DC: Public Affairs Press, 1944.
30. "Will Auto Glut Choke Detroit?" *Business Week* (March 7, 1988): 54–62.

10 COALITIONS, COOPERATIVE RESEARCH, AND TECHNOLOGY DEVELOPMENT IN THE GLOBALIZATION OF THE SEMICONDUCTOR INDUSTRY

Asim Erdilek

1. Introduction

The emergence of microelectronics, based on solid-state physics, a few years after World War II has brought about the Second Industrial (or the Information) Revolution. The invention of the point-contact transistor at AT&T's Bell Laboratories in 1947, followed by the invention of the integrated circuit a decade later, has radically transformed modern industry and society. An entirely new, rapidly (albeit erratically) growing and changing industry, the semiconductor industry, spearheaded this transformation[1–4].

Semiconductors are materials whose electrical characteristics are in between a conductor and an insulator. A transistor is a semiconductor device that can, using a semiconducting material such as silicon, either amplify (as linear devices) or switch (as digital devices) electrical current. Transistors are divided into bipolar and field-effect (or unipolar) transistors. Metal-oxide semiconductor (MOS) devices are the most common type of field-effect transistors. In MOS devices, electricity flows between two negative (n) or positive (p) regions instead of through an n,p,n or p,n,p sequence of regions. They are superior to bipolar devices in terms of

187

their lower power consumption and fewer processing steps. The development of MOS technology in the 1960s led to the four-bit microprocessor and the 1K (1000 bits) DRAM (dynamic random access memory) integrated circuit (IC) during 1970–1971. The monolithic IC has dominated since then the discrete devices that had replaced the electron tubes and were the only semiconductors produced in the 1950s [4].

An integrated circuit (IC) is a semiconductor device, often referred to as a *chip*, that incorporates many transistors or other elements such as diodes or passive components on a single piece of semiconductor material. ICs have three distinct stages of production: 1) circuit design and mask making, 2) fabrication of the circuit on a silicon chip, and 3) testing and assembly of the circuit [3]. These stages can and often do take place in different locations, leading to intrafirm international vertical integration. The density or scale of integration of transistors has increased steadily and significantly since the invention of the IC [4]. As intermediate inputs or core components, ICs play the same crucial role once played by steel in the manufacture of both producer and consumer goods. They have been called the "industrial rice" or the "crude oil" of the 1980s [5].

Initially, all ICs were bipolar. The MOS IC appeared in 1962. MOS ICs are of three types: 1) nMOS, in which negatively charged channels dominate; 2) pMOS, in which positively charged channels dominate; and 3) CMOS, complementary MOS, in which n-channel and p-channel transistors are combined. MOS ICs are more advantageous than bipolar ICs in terms of lower power consumption, greater density, and higher production yields, all of which result in lower cost per components. Bipolar ICs are more advantageous in terms of higher processing speed [2].

ICs are also distinguished on the basis of their scale of integration: 1) small-scale integration (SSI), with fewer than 100 components (active elements); 2) medium-scale integration (MSI), with between 100 and 999 components; 3) large-scale integration (LSI), with between 1000 and 99,999 components; and 4) very-large-scale integration (VLSI), with between 100,000 and 999,999 components [4].

In terms of their functions, digital ICs can be divided into 1) memory devices, and 2) microprocessors, microcontrollers, and logic devices. The former store and the latter process data. The storage capacity of a memory device is measured in 1000-bit units, i.e., kilobits or K. Microprocessors are classified in terms of the number of bits that they can process simultaneously. Memory chips are basically commodities, homogeneous and interchangeable. Microprocessors, however, are differentiated by special design and can run only software written specifically for their circuits.

The United States, with critical support channeled through the Department of Defense, created the chip industry after World War II [3, 6]. It dominated both segments of this highly innovative industry until the late 1970s when Japan challenged its leadership in memory chips. Japan may have owed its recent dominance to its successful application of industrial targeting and strategic trade policy. This claim by the U.S. chip industry formed the basis of U.S. government actions, such as the negotiation of the 1986 Semiconductor Trade Agreement (STA) with Japan, in responding to the Japanese challenge.

This chapter focuses on private coalitions or strategic alliances in the chip industry both within and outside the United States as a counterforce to public strategic industrial and trade policies, which are neomercantilistic. It chronicles several recent cooperative research agreements and production joint ventures among U.S. and non-U.S. chip firms. They support the thesis of this chapter that both segments of the chip industry have become increasingly globalized through two-way international trade as well as two-way direct foreign investment [4, 7]. U.S. as well as non-U.S. firms have found it essential to combine cooperative and competitive strategies both at home and abroad. This has been partly due to the specific technological characteristics and requirements of the industry and partly due to the attempts of national governments to create and maintain domestic production capabilities via strategic trade policy. Coalitions, especially in the form of technology sharing and cooperative research agreements, are argued to be critical to the continued rapid innovation and increasing productive efficiency of the global chip industry.

Section 2 examines the different reasons for and types of coalitions in the semiconductor industry in terms of globalization. Section 3 focuses on several recent coalitions, emphasizing the theme of horizontal diversification through technology exchange. Section 4 contains the basic conclusions of the chapter.

2. Globalization and Coalitions in the Semiconductor Industry

The semiconductor industry is a global (as opposed to a multidomestic) industry, in which a firm's competitive positions in different countries are interdependent. This requires a semiconductor firm to integrate its worldwide activities through a global strategy in order to capture the international linkages and strengthen its competitive advantage [4, 8–10].

One of the significant implications of globalization for a firm is the role played by coalitions in its global strategy. Coalitions are long-term interfirm arrangements that include joint ventures, licensing, technology sharing, marketing, supply agreements, and other types of linkages, but do not result in mergers, In a coalition, a firm performs one or more activities jointly with another independent firm as a means of configuration (i.e., in determining where and in how many places the activities are located). Coalitions arise when they are more efficient and effective than internal development, merger, or arm's-length transactions in configuring activities [11].

According to case studies, coalitions are often formed to pool R&D resources [12]. Recently, the U.S. semiconductor industry has been one of the most R&D-intensive industries [2]. In 1986, the industry spent 12.2% of its sales on R&D [13]. Access to technology, besides capital requirements, has been an absolute cost barrier in the industry. Although patent control over IC technology has lacked potency, possession of or access to unpatented technical know-how has been absolutely critical to success in the industry. Most new U.S. semiconductor firms have been established by defectors from existing firms, who have presumably taken with them critical technical know-how [3]. In the innovation-driven semiconductor industry, a firm's technology strategy is very likely the most crucial component of its competitive strategy, whether it emphasizes low-cost or product differentiation [2, 4].

The legal forms and the business purposes of coalitions need not have simple relationships. Coalitions often result from the same forces that bring about globalization. Firms team up with others when they confront obstacles to forming their own global strategies. These obstacles relate to risk reduction, economies of scale, R&D, learning curves, and market access [8, 10, 11].

Coalitions may have four types of benefits. First, coalition partners may gain economies of scale or learning by having one of the partners perform the activity for all the partners. Second, a coalition may benefit partners with asymmetric advantages when access to knowledge or ability to perform an activity is acquired, pooled, or sold. Such coalitions for access reduce the cost or time required to master an activity. Third, coalitions can spread and reduce the risk of the jointly performed activity. Fourth, coalitions can shape competition by influencing the identity of the competitors and the nature of the competition [11].

Coalitions may have three types of costs: coordination costs, loss of competitive advantage, and weaker bargaining position. These costs are likely to change during a coalition's life. Coalitions may have either general or partner-specific learning effects, which will reduce the costs and enhance the benefits of future coalitions [11].

Coalitions can take different forms depending on the motivations of partners. They may include activities in operations and logistics; marketing, sales, and services; or technology development. They may cover a single activity (country) or multiple activities (countries). In technology-development coalitions—perhaps the most important type for the semiconductor industry—the large, fixed costs of R&D may motivate partners to achieve learning or economies of scale. Those costs may also lead to coalitions in order to gain access to technology or innovation when one partner is far ahead of the others. Since R&D is inherently risky, risk reduction is often a primary motivation for technology-development coalitions. Such coalitions may also serve as a means for shaping competition, especially in diffusing and standardizing technology, and creating second sources for buyers.

Technology-development coalitions are often preferred to arm's-length transactions for three reasons. First, effective technology exchanges may require stable, long-term interfirm relationships. Second, coalitions may help keep technologies off the open market and maintain barriers to entry and mobility. Third, coalitions may alleviate the contractual difficulties inherent in arm's-length technology transactions [11]. The importance of technology-development coalitions was recognized by U.S. Congress in 1984 when it passed the National Cooperative Research Act [14].

During the last decade, the R&D and capital intensities of the semiconductor industry have increased. Economies of scale and the benefits associated with vertical integration have also become more significant [3, 4]. The minimum efficient plant scale for commodity chips has increased, too. As design and development costs have grown, firms have had to tie themselves to specific chip architectures for longer periods. These two developments have in combination led to a rise in precommitment costs. With each new generation of chip architecture, R&D and equipment costs—and hence, the investment risks—have risen. The rapid pace of innovation has exacerbated the derivative cyclical volatility of demand for semiconductors. Consequently, coalitions have acquired greater strategic importance [4, 13, 15].

The transition in the early 1980s to VLSI (very-large-scale integration) technology has been the industry's technological watershed. Submicron-channel-width semiconductor devices, microprocessors with 32 (or more) bits, and 256 (or more) K DRAMs characterize the VLSI period [1, 2]. The complexity as well as the high design and production costs of the VLSI devices have favored large and integrated firms at the expense of the smaller merchant firms. (The *merchants* are independent firms whose primary business is the manufacture and sale of semiconductors. The *captives*, on the other hand, are large vertically integrated electronics or computer firms that produce semiconductors for internal use and seldom sell them in the open or merchant market [13].) The VLSI period is witnessing higher concentration, further vertical integration, and greater globalization of the semiconductor industry.

The major technological changes introduced by VLSI involve the chip design and packaging technologies more than the manufacturing processes. The complexity of VLSI chips has intensified the industry's efforts to automate chip design. The transformation of the industry from a commodity-oriented industry to a value-added, engineering service industry is expedited by design automation [15].

Even for the large and integrated firms, technological self-sufficiency has become impossible with the advent of VLSI. Interfirm technological alliances have acquired strategic importance for international competitiveness. Most such alliances involve exchanges or sharing of developed technologies, as opposed to joint research. Joint R&D efforts have been based on research corporations and university-centered consortia under national programs, as opposed to interfirm agreements. Japanese semiconductor firms have engaged in much closer direct R&D collaboration and joint technology development among themselves, even outside the government-sponsored projects, than their U.S. counterparts [16].

U.S. and Japanese firms account for the bulk of the international interfirm agreements. Although the technical areas of cooperation cover a broad range, they cluster in microprocessors, memories, and gate arrays (and other nonstandard ICs), all which involve CMOS technology. In microprocessors, which are highly proprietary devices, U.S. firms have possessed a strong advantage in design, whereas Japanese firms have excelled in CMOS-fabrication technology. Most U.S.–Japanese technical alliances have reflected these bilateral strengths. Second-sourcing has been a prominent feature of the microprocessor-centered agreements [4]. Second-sourcing provides customers with the security of alternative suppliers and manufacturers with a larger customer base and greater standardization based on their particular microprocessor designs.

In memory chips, in contrast to microprocessors, design has been relatively less important than process technology. Learning-by-doing effects are crucial in manufacturing successively more design-intensive memories. Older generations of memory chips can serve as technology drivers for the newer generations. Japanese firms have been dominant recently in this area, with the flow of technology more unidirectional—from Japan to the United States and Europe—than in other areas.

3. Recent Coalitions in the Semiconductor Industry

3.1. Siemens–Philips Mega Project

The Siemens–Philips Mega Project, which involves joint R&D on DRAM and static RAM (SRAM) technologies during the period 1984–1989, is by far the most ambitious coalition in memory devices. It is also the largest of the very rare international joint R&D agreements in the global chip industry. The Mega Project, co-financed by the two private firms and the West German and Dutch governments, is aimed at developing the submicron CMOS technology.

According to the terms of the Mega Project, Philips and Siemens have been focusing on the one-megabit SRAM and the four-megabit DRAM, respectively. Philips and Siemens had been major chip producers until they began to lose international competitiveness along with other European firms in the 1960s [2].

3.2. Motorola–Toshiba

In November 1986, Motorola agreed to form a coalition with Toshiba. The expected benefits for Motorola were the expansion of its presence in Japan, which is the largest chip market in the world, and direct access to Toshiba's state-of-the-art memory-chip-making processes. For Toshiba, the major expected benefit was the access to Motorola's microprocessor technology. Each firm was weak in the other firm's area of strength. In fact, Motorola had recently terminated its presence in memory chips as a result of overwhelming Japanese rivalry. The agreement would enable it to reestablish itself globally in that market segment. This technology exchange for horizontal diversification has been the dominant theme of most semiconductor coalitions [17, 18].

Toshiba, whose chip sales ranked third in Japan, after NEC and Hitachi, and fifth worldwide, was not a dominant producer in any segment of the semiconductor industry. Focused on ICs for consumer goods, it wished to increase its presence in industrial ICs [19].

Under the agreement, one of the most ambitious and elaborate strategic alliances between a U.S. and a Japanese company, Motorola and Toshiba would form a joint venture and build a plant in Izumi, Japan. The plant would manufacture MOS DRAMs up to four-megabit density, SRAMs up to one-megabit using Toshiba's designs and technology, and eight-bit, 16-bit, and eventually 32-bit HCMOS (high performance, complementary MOS) microprocessors using Motorola's designs and technology. Motorola would transfer additional technology to the joint venture as it gained greater access to the Japanese chip market.

The equally owned plant was scheduled to begin production in the second half of 1988. Its output would be shared equally between the two partners. Motorola would be able to sell its share of the output globally. Motorola, which already had a wholly owned plant in Aizu Wakamatsu, Japan, producing MOS ICs, planned to build another one soon. It also had an ASIC (application-specific IC) design unit at the Nippon Motorola facility in Tokyo. In other words, Motorola's presence in Japan had not been and would not be limited by its joint venture with Toshiba.

Motorola acquired the unconditional right to use Toshiba's product designs and process technologies for both DRAMs and SRAMs at all of its plants. It would have immediate access to Toshiba's currently most advanced one-megabit DRAMs and to Toshiba's four-megabit DRAMs when they were developed. Toshiba, on the other hand, would be able buy immediately Motorola's eight-bit and 16-bit microprocessors. Its phased access to the more advanced 32-bit chips, however, would be contingent on Motorola's increasing presence in Japan during 1987–1991. Motorola commanded 57% of the world market for the 32-bit chip at the time of the agreement. Intel and National Semiconductor had 30% and 10% of the market, respectively.

Until this agreement, Motorola had not concluded any technology-sharing agreements on its 32-bit microprocessor. Earlier in 1986, it had refused to license its 32-bit technology to Hitachi, which had a license to produce Motorola's eight-bit and 16-bit microprocessors. In 1981, Motorola had received access to Hitachi's high-performance CMOS process technology in exchange for the design of its 68,000 microprocessor.

The agreement was seen to mark the beginning of a trend toward more strategic alliances between U.S. and Japanese chip makers. (In an earlier agreement, reached in August 1986, Motorola had acquired the right to distribute certain Toshiba memory chips in the United States under its own name.) The Semiconductor Trade Agreement (STA) between the United States and Japan, concluded in July 1986, increased the attractiveness of such alliances by stipulating that U.S. firms should be allowed greater access to the Japanese chip market. It also motivated Japanese firms to co-operate with U.S. firms in order to ease the frictions between Japan and the United States in semiconductor trade.

Motorola, the second largest chip maker (after IBM) in the United States, is known for its cautious, prudent expansion strategy. It stresses diversification across several product categories and avoids heavy dependence on any single end-user. It has a broad product mix in semiconductors, communications, information systems, government electronics, general systems, and automotive/industrial electronics. In semiconductors, it is not heavily dependent on the computer end-users. It is the largest maker of discrete devices in the world. Its chip product mix extends across bipolar and linear devices that reduce the exposure to the computer industry.

This strategy enabled Motorola to weather the 1985–1986 semiconductor depression with less damage than its less diversified U.S. competitors. At the first sign of the chip crash that followed the collapse of the personal computer market, Motorola stopped producing DRAMs whose prices had dropped sharply below cost.

In 1987, Motorola reentered into the memory market and began to produce one-megabit DRAMs, using initially dice from Toshiba. It planned, however, to launch the wafer fabrication of those memory chips in the latter half of 1988. It also added 256K, 64K, and 16K devices to its SRAM portfolio.

Motorola's main technological rival in microprocessors has been Intel, the supplier to IBM's personal computers. Motorola launched its first 32-bit product, the 68020, ahead of Intel, in 1984. Intel brought out its competing 80386 chip early in 1987. Late in 1987, Motorola launched an enhanced 32-bit chip, the 68030, which was fully compatible with the 68020. Motorola also announced that it had begun work on an even more powerful, third-generation 32-bit device, designated 68040, and on a RISC (reduced-instruction-set computing) processor. In March 1988, Motorola unveiled its latest microprocessor family, the 88000 line, based on RISC technology [20–22].

In early 1988, Intel's microprocessors dominated the overall office-equipment market, with Motorola's chips strongly established in more specialized areas such as industrial automation equipment, robots, and telecommunications. Competition in this most advanced segment of the microprocessor market is expected to increase sharply along with the demand. Prices are likely to drop from $188 per unit in 1987 to $28 by 1991, with the demand rising from 100,000 units to 11.2 million per annum. The 32-bit processor would then become a standard component in office products, especially technical workstations.

The recent advent of the RISC technology, however, might alter the global microprocessor market drastically and throw it wide open again. RISC theory is based on research conducted at IBM in the 1970s. Representing a back-to-basics approach, it is a radical departure from the conventional microprocessor design theory that has shaped the development of six generations of increasingly powerful chips. Those chips, based on CISC (complex-instruction-set computing) theory, have used miniature programs called microcodes to decode special functions and varied commands into simple steps.

RISC eliminates the microcode decoder, restricts the number of instructions (basic commands that define the computer functions), and keeps all instructions at equally short length. It relocates many of the infrequently used complex functions, designed into CISC microprocessors, to memory chips. Therefore, it is claimed to not only simplify microprocessor design but also improve performance (i.e., increase processing speed in terms of millions of instructions processed per second (MIPs)). According to RISC advocates, whose claims remain controversial, RISC chips capable of 100 MIPs, one hundred times faster than the existing CISC chips, are possible by the early 1990s. In that case, lower-cost and higher-performance RISC microprocessors would mark another major turning point in the chip and thereby the computer industries. RISC critics argue that even if RISC chips are simpler in design and faster in speed, they are harder to program because they "speak" a more primitive language. These critics also note that RISC architecture necessitates the creation of a huge memory pool, or cache, in computer language, next to the microprocessor, to constantly provide instructions to the central chip [20, 22].

Several small as well as large companies have entered into the RISC market. Thanks to the increasing sophistication of automatic chip design, newcomers to microprocessors, such as Sun Microsystems, MIPS Computer Systems, and VLSI Technology, have been able to challenge the established industry leaders. Motorola, however, is the largest, most recent, and most aggressive entrant. Its 88100 chip performs 14–17 MIPs, five times faster than any competing RISC chip. Intel, on the other hand, has been reluctant to embrace RISC. Its new 80960 chips incorporate elements of RISC design but are not real RISC chips.

The emergence of RISC as the mainstream microprocessor architecture depends on the outcome of AT&T's efforts to establish Unix, its computer operating system, as an industry-wide standard. AT&T, Motorola, Sun Microsystems, and MIPS Computer Systems have concluded interfirm agreements toward that objective. Then computers could be built around RISC chips with a ready-made base of essential applications software.

For Toshiba, the technology-sharing coalition with Motorola was crucial to its efforts to strengthen its electronics division. It had started out in 1875 as a manufacturer of telegraph equipment. After World War II, it concentrated in heavy electrical machinery. In the early 1980s, it began to shift toward microelectronics and information processing. It needed strong chip-making capabilities against its Japanese archrivals, such as NEC and Hitachi, that were already well established in computers and telecommunications.

In the 1970s, Toshiba concentrated on ICs for consumer goods. When is later wished to diversify into memory chips for computers, it found itself at a competitive disadvantage vis-a-vis NEC and Hitachi. As a result of heavy investment in its electronics division, however, Toshiba was able to leap-frog into the front lines in memory chips. It succeeded in being the first firm to market the one-megabit memory chip. In the 1980s, Toshiba established semiconductor design, fabrication, and assembly facilities in the United States, focusing on DRAMs, SRAMs, and other memory ICs.

The agreement reached with Motorola was one of several such agreements Toshiba concluded in order to strengthen its global presence in the semiconductor industry. In 1982, it reached a cross-licensing agreement with Zilog, according to which Zilog received CMOS technology and the CMOS (versus bipolar) versions of its designs in exchange for licensing those designs to Toshiba. The two firms later second-sourced each other's version. In 1985, Toshiba agreed with LSI Logic Corp. of the United States to develop and distribute gate arrays. It also agreed to transfer to Siemens of West Germany its one-megabit memory-chip process technology. In return, it would receive money and product designs from Siemens. Furthermore, it agreed to send one of its top electronics engineers to Hewlett-Packard Co. to manage the U.S. firm's chip division for three years. Finally, in August 1986, Toshiba agreed with General Electric Co. of the United States and Siemens AG of West Germany to develop cell libraries jointly. Cells are circuit patterns that are etched onto a chip.

3.3. Hitachi–Fujitsu

In October 1986, Hitachi, which had failed to obtain a license to manufacture Motorola's 32-bit microprocessor, and Fujitsu announced that they had joined forces to develop a 32-bit microprocessor technology. This announcement came only three days after Fujitsu revealed its later aborted plans to take over Fairchild Semiconductor. Under an earlier licensing agreement, Hitachi had manufactured Motorola's eight-bit and 16-bit microprocessors [23].

The two companies had evidently decided to break the U.S. hold on the global market for microprocessors. This decision must have been prompted by the refusal of both Motorola and Intel to license their 32-bit processors to these two Japanese companies. Both Hitachi and Fujitsu still wished to produce the U.S. 32-bit designs, but they hoped that their jointly produced chip would help wean them from U.S. technology for the latest designs.

Hitachi and Fujitsu claimed that their 32-bit chip would be completely Japanese and would run faster than the existing U.S. designs. It would be based on a circuit created by a Japanese research team at the University of Tokyo, backed by Japan's major computer makers. This team had created a chip design and operating system, collectively called Tron. Hitachi and Fujitsu hoped that their 32-bit chip would help make Tron a global standard.

The design of the Tron system was aimed at running Japanese-language programs more efficiently as well as at performing the functions of existing chips. The major objective of the Tron system, however, was to free Japanese companies from dependence on U.S. chip designs and software. It was offered to all takers who wished to develop uses for it. Its designers hoped to develop eventually an even faster 64-bit chip.

3.4. National Semiconductor – NMB Semiconductor

In September 1986, National Semiconductor Corporation (NSC), which acquired Fairchild Semiconductor in October 1986, signed a long-term agreement with NMB Semiconductor of Japan to design, produce, and distribute CMOS-technology-based SRAM chips in Japan. NSC would provide design and marketing know-how to NMB, which operated a highly automated chip plant [24].

NMB, which also made ball bearings, was strictly a foundry with no marketing or product development. It had similar agreements with other semiconductor companies. Although NSC stated that the agreement with NMB had been negotiated over two years and therefore was not directly related to the U.S.–Japan STA, industry analysts expected similar agreements to be stimulated by the STA.

3.5. National Semiconductor – Mitsubishi Electric

In November 1987, National Semiconductor (NSC) signed a distribution agreement with Mitsubishi Electric. According to the five-year agreement, Mitsubishi acquired the right to import NSC's 32,000 series 32-bit microprocessors and related software. Until this agreement, U.S. chip producers had resisted forming distribution arrangements with major Japanese electronics companies. By breaking ranks, NSC hoped to improve its penetration of the 32-bit microprocessor market in Japan, which was dominated by Motorola [25].

3.6. Advanced Micro Devices – Sony

Advanced Micro Devices (AMD), which had acquired Monolithic Memories in August 1986, announced in May 1987 an agreement with Sony of Japan to develop SRAMs, using CMOS technology. The global market for SRAMs, used primarily in devices, such as field-combat equipment and portable computers that run on limited power supplies, had amounted to about $800 million in 1986 and was expected to double by 1991 [26].

This three-year agreement was presented as the first of several joint ventures the two companies were planning to pursue for horizontal diversification. Sony, primarily a captive producer of chips for its electronics goods, was highly regarded for its semiconductor-process technology. AMD, which held about 6% of the SRAM market, was stronger in the lower-end products, whereas Sony, like several other Japanese chip companies, had excelled in the introduction of more sophisticated SRAM designs. The AMD–Sony venture would concentrate on high-end 64K and 256K SRAMs, using a 1.2 micron CMOS process. AMD was already the largest U.S. distributor of NEC's memory chips.

3.7. Intel – Mitsubishi Electric

Intel, along with NSC and AMD, initiated legal action in 1986 against several Japanese competitors accused of unfair trade practices (A. Erdilek, unpublished). In July 1987, Intel reached a subcontracting agreement with Mitsubishi Electric. The Japanese firm, which had excess capacity, would manufacture EPROM (erasable programmable read-only memory) chips, based on Intel's designs, which Intel would distribute in Japan under its own label. Intel regarded these EPROMs as relatively unsophisticated and did not wish to invest in additional productive capacity that would soon become technologically obsolete. The subcontracting arrangement also enabled it to meet rapidly the growing Japanese demand for its EPROMs [27].

In March 1988, Intel, which had not produced memory chips since 1985, announced that it would market DRAMs made by Micron Technology. According to the three-year agreement, Intel would distribute Micron Technology's 256K DRAMs stamped with Intel's trademark [28].

3.8. Sematech

In the debate on the competitiveness of the U.S. memory-chip industry, the national security argument has been prominent. After the U.S. industry lost more than $1 billion in 1986 as a result of depressed demand and Japanese price-slashing, fears arose that the United States might be losing a mainstay of its military power. Heeding these fears, the U.S. government began to consider whether and how it should subsidize the domestic industry more heavily and directly [29]. It already subsidized the Semiconductor Research Corporation (SRC), the industry's cooperative venture that funded R&D at U.S. universities [30].

In September 1986, the Defense Science Board (DSB) was set up to advise the Department of Defense (DOD) on chips. A separate group at the National Security Council (NSC) also took up the matter. Soon after, U.S. firms asked the DSB to consider a proposal to form a consortium, with government financing, for developing and producing advanced DRAMs.

In December 1986, the draft report of the DSB's Task Force on Semiconductor Dependency was issued. It called for a government subsidy to the domestic industry of $1.7 billion over five years to end U.S. national defense dependence on Japanese memory chips. U.S. firms would be asked to form a consortium for designing and manufacturing advanced DRAMs.

The DSB's final report on semiconductors was issued in February 1987. It called for a subsidy of $1 billion over five years as well as special antitrust exemptions for U.S. chip makers to form a consortium. The consortium would consist of chip makers, producers of chip-making equipment, and computer companies. Another $1 billion would be channeled into laboratory research on chips. The Semiconductor Industry Association (SIA), which liked the report, named the consortium the SEMATECH (semiconductor manufacturing technology) initiative.

The goal of SEMATECH would be to develop new manufacturing processes and a prototype production line for advanced high-volume memory chips. It would not mass-produce the chips itself. This was a compromise between the current leaders in manufacturing such as IBM that wanted SEMATECH to be a prototype for research only and those weaker firms that wished SEMATECH to demonstrate high-volume manufacturing. It was also initially unclear as to how closely the members of SEMATECH would cooperate. For example, Texas Instruments stated that it would have to decide project by project what to reveal about its manufacturing processes [31].

Another issue in the deliberations on SEMATECH was who would be allowed to participate. Several Japanese companies had U.S.-based semiconductor operations. Most of the U.S.-owned chip companies opposed the participation of Japanese companies with U.S.-based operations.

In May 1987, the SIA decided to fund SEMATECH, with 20 to 30 expected members, at $250 million per annum for up to six years. The U.S. government, however, would have to provide half of the total cost.

SEMATECH would be the U.S. industry's response to Japanese government's targeting of the semiconductor industry for global domination. It would help internalize the public-good externalities in terms of 1) nonrivalry in use of new or improved manufacturing technologies, 2) nonappropriability of essential but leaky technologies, 3) wasteful duplication of R&D, and 4) large risk and short time horizon of individual projects [16].

However, the SEMATECH proposal was regarded by some chip-industry experts as inadequate by itself. Unless it were made part of a comprehensive Japanese-style national industrial policy by the U.S. government, it would fail to overcome the strong advantages possessed by the Japanese chip industry. Lower cost of capital, better educated and harder-working work force, more efficient manufacturing, less impatient shareholders, and closer ties to customers were the purported Japanese advantages [32].

Initially, the Japanese chip industry was nurtured by a national industrial policy. In the mid-1970s, the Ministry of International Trade and Industry (MITI) guided several of Japan's large electronics companies into producing DRAMs. The government supported the industry's early efforts with research grants, procurement contracts, and a protected domestic market [6]. At the corporate level, Japanese firms cooperated with each other in government-sponsored research but also competed vigorously against one another for market share. This combination of cooperative research and cutthroat competition drove down Japanese production costs. These costs fell far and fast enough to turn predatory pricing into profit-making. Therefore, the expansionist market-share strategy eventually paid off.

In this aggressive strategy, Japanese chip makers were helped by being part of huge, strong conglomerates that could afford to take early losses in return for long-term profits. The conglomerates themselves were aided by close-knit groups of institutional shareholders who also understood and supported the early-loss strategy. The conglomerates were affiliated with at least one of Japan's six corporate clans, called *keiretsu*, which revolved around the major Japanese banks [4]. Most U.S. chip producers, on the other hand, had no other businesses and product lines to carry them through chip slumps or price wars. The Japanese chip industry was also helped by the shift of electronics manufacturing from the United States to Asia.

In the face of the strong Japanese competition in high-volume, commodity-like, and price-sensitive memory chips, most loss-ridden U.S. chip firms turned to specialization in chip design or service. The conventional wisdom in the industry was that specialized or niche markets were not big enough to support all the existing companies. Customized design, production, and delivery could not provide the kind of wealth and industrial power, as well as military power, that the high-volume commodity-chip markets promised [32].

The minority view, however, stressed that the global chip industry was evolving away from mass manufacturing toward limited factory runs of many different types of expensive high-quality and high-performance customized memory chips, designed to meet the specifications of many different customers. The cost of designing chips was dropping more sharply than the cost of manufacturing them, with more functions squeezed onto single customized chips.

In December 1987, Congress earmarked $100 million for SEMATECH in the Department of Defense (DOD) appropriation for the fiscal year 1988 ending in October. The DOD would oversee SEMATECH's activities but would not set its research agenda. Although there is a sunset provision for U.S. Government funding to end in 1993, it is planned that SEMATECH will continue with the support of the U.S. electronics industry.

SEMATECH had asked all 50 state governors to submit site and funding proposals. Several states wooed it with various financial incentives. In January 1988, SEMATECH decided to base itself in Austin, Texas. It would use a vacant Data General Corporation wafer-fabrication plant offered by that city. It hoped to be building chips in that plant by the end of 1988. This plant would serve as a cutting-edge production unit, called *manufacturing proof facility*, in which new equipment and processes would be tested and standardized for use in member firms' factories. As a result, member firms, and the industry as a whole, would hopefully save millions of dollars in R&D costs by avoiding replication, would modernize their facilities, and would increase their competitiveness against their Japanese rivals [33].

SEMATECH had initially 13 members: Advanced Micro Devices, American Telephone & Telegraph Co., Digital Equipment Corp., Harris Corp., Hewlett-Packard Co., Intel Corp., International Business Machines Corp., LSI Logic Corp., Micron Technology Inc., Motorola Inc., National Semiconductor Corp., Rockwell International Corp., and Texas Instruments Inc. Foreign firms were not allowed to participate.

Although SEMATECH was incorporated as a not-for-profit corporation in Delaware, it has not qualified for tax-exempt status due to its limited membership receiving preferential licensing treatment. Special federal legislation would be required for its tax-exempt status and for its antitrust exemption [5]. The exemption for joint R&D projects from the treble damage and per se rules of antitrust law, under the 1984 National Cooperative Research Act, might, however, apply to SEMATECH [34].

Member-company annual assessments, for both merchant and captive producers, are based on semiconductor production values in the previous year. The minimum annual fee is $1 million. No member is assessed more than 15% of the total members' contribution. Fees are tax deductible as R&D expenses to the members, which have initial commitments of four years minimum. Membership is renewable annually and can be terminated with a two-year notice. Nonmembers will be able to license SEMATECH technologies for reasonable fees provided they are U.S.-capitalized companies [5].

SEMATECH, which chose Charles E. Sporck, president and chief executive of National Semiconductor Corp., as its chairman, planned to spend $1.5 billion over six years. One half of this amount would be provided by its members, with the other half coming from the U.S. Government. It aimed at developing, with exclusively U.S. materials, state-of-the-art chip-making processes by 1993 that could be transferred to individual companies. In order to arrive at its goal, besides carrying out its own activities in Austin, Texas, SEMATECH would establish "centers of excellence" in U.S. universities in specific areas of semiconductor manufacturing [5].

Some chip-industry analysts viewed SEMATECH with skepticism [35]. They argued that it had emerged largely as a proposal by U.S. firms for the government to bail out the domestic chip industry from its 1985–1986 depression. SEMATECH, preoccupied with the development of high-volume chip-making processes, was aiming at an outdated target. SEMATECH'S focus on mass-production memory-chip technologies would distract it from both the U.S. organizational deficiencies at the plant level and the trend toward small-scale flexible manufacturing of multiple customized products. Specialty chips such as ASIC (application-specific integrated circuit) devices, which were expected to reach 25% of the total market in 1990, required more frequent production-line changes, closer customer interaction, and hence greater factory integration.

SEMATECH was criticized even in terms of its chosen mission to restore U.S. leadership in commodity memory chips. SEMATECH, initially intended to be a joint venture in mass manufacturing, had instead emerged as an applied R&D consortium. Therefore, it could not directly enhance U.S. competitiveness in terms of higher yield and greater reliability— statistical measures that required high-volume production.

Furthermore, SEMATECH's plans to help the troubled U.S. semiconductor-equipment makers by providing them with a forum to develop state-of-the-art and standardized equipment and thus reducing their R&D costs met difficulty and generated controversy at the outset. SEMATECH's exclusion of foreign-owned companies, its restricted payments to vendors based on acceptance of orders, and its intention to deal with only a small group of equipment-makers caused concern and dissatisfaction in the equipment industry.

The views of these critics were supported by a U.S. government interagency report on the domestic semiconductor industry [16]. This report rejected the U.S. chip makers' basic claim that they needed direct government help to counter the harmful effects of Japanese government targeting. It argued that the structure of the U.S. industry had been unable to adjust to and cope with the highly cyclical demand for semiconductors. It also held macroeconomic factors largely responsible for the decline in the international competitiveness of the U.S. chip makers. It did, however, support the recent trend among U.S. firms toward more collaboration and cooperation in semiconductor R&D of the type with which Japanese firms have been successful. Nevertheless, it expressed skepticism about the specific role expected of the U.S. Government in SEMATECH [16].

In January 1988, SEMATECH announced that it would use IBM's four-megabit DRAMs and AT&T's 64-kilobit SRAMs as its test vehicles [36]. It chose these state-of-the art products in order to save both time and money in its quest to restore U.S. global dominance in memory chips by 1993. SEMATECH would receive from IBM and AT&T all the required specifications and tooling data in manufacturing these chips. IBM had never before shared any of its state-of-the-art chip technologies with an outside consortium [34].

Both IBM and AT&T were expected to benefit from their cooperation with SEMATECH in terms of the consortium's efforts to improve U.S. semiconductor-making equipment technologies. Those efforts would be based on the IBM and AT&T chips, offering the two large captive chip producers the prospect of both customized and standardized manufacturing equipment.

3.9. Semiconductor Research Corporation (SRC)

The SRC was established in 1982 by the Semiconductor Industry Association (SIA) as an affiliate nonprofit research cooperative, with 11 member companies. Its mission was to promote academic and generic research on silicon ICs through university contracts. The research involves IC technologies from architecture and design through devices and processes to manufacturing and testing. SRC, with 35 participating companies in 1986, has no laboratories of its own and does not perform any research itself. Instead, it channels funds from its member companies to academic researchers in areas of major interest to the SRC. In 1986, three U.S.

government agencies became SRC participants through a memorandum of understanding between the SRC and the National Science Foundation [37–38].

The SRC is now expected by the SIA to provide the interface between SEMATECH and the semiconductor research community [5].

3.10. Microelectronics and Computer Technology Corporation (MCC)

Another Austin, Texas-based consortium, the Microelectronics and Computer Technology Corporation (MCC), established in 1983, includes as shareholders 21 U.S. aerospace, computer, and semiconductor companies. Its mission as a private research corporation is to strengthen U.S. technological leadership in microelectronics and computers. The MCC, which has its own staff of engineers and scientists, works in software technology, VLSI/CAD, advanced computer architecture, and other areas besides semiconductors. However, almost half of the MCC's R&D has been centered on semiconductors. Unlike the SRC and like SEMATECH, the MCC develops technologies for its members, which then acquire the initial rights to those technologies. The MCC has a counterpart in Europe: the Munich-based European Computer Research Center (ECRC).

3.11. R&D Programs Organized and Funded by the Public Sector

During the 1980s, several governments have decided to encourage and support national and international cooperative R&D programs in electronics and information technologies. These programs emphasize basic or generic research. The major ones are the Fifth Generation Computer Project in Japan, the VHSIC (very-high-speed integrated circuit) Project in the United States, the Alvey Program in the United Kingdom, the Filiere Electronique in France, and the ESPRIT (European Strategic Program for Research and Development on Information Technologies) in the European Community.

These are similar to MITI's earlier cooperative R&D programs, such as the VLSI program, in Japan [1, 16]. They all assume that national competitiveness can be strengthened by publicly organized and funded R&D programs. They also overlook the fact that the globalization of the semiconductor and computer industries has made it increasingly difficult to distinguish national firms from foreign ones. Finally, they believe that their fruits can be kept within national or regional boundaries even when cross-country and cross-region private coalitions are rising in importance. In fact, in many cases these private coalitions are aimed at circumventing the neomercantilistic public policies [4].

4. Conclusions

The semiconductor industry has become a global one in which a firm's competitive positions in different countries are interdependent. The globalization of this highly innovative and cyclical industry has in turn increased the importance of coalitions or strategic alliances in the competitive strategies of firms, especially in their technology strategies. The increasing R&D and capital intensities of the industry, as well as the neomercantilistic efforts of national governments to create or preserve the international competitiveness of their firms, have also motivated chip firms in the United States, Japan, and Western Europe to conclude interfirm agreements.

The continued rapid innovativeness of the global semiconductor industry requires a combination of domestic as well as cross-border competitive and cooperative firm-specific strategies. The efforts of governments to restrict private interfirm arrangements for their national objectives are likely to be futile at best and at worst harmful from both national and global perspectives.

References

1. Hazewindus, N. *The U.S. Microelectronics Industry*. New York: Pergamon Press, 1982.
2. Malerba, F. *The Semiconductor Business*. Madison, WI: University of Wisconsin Press, 1985.
3. Dorfman, N. S. *Innovation and Market Structure*. Cambridge, MA: Ballinger, 1987.
4. Langlois, R. N. *Microelectronics: An Industry in Transition*. Center for Science and Technology Policy, Rensslear Polytechnic Institute, New York, 1987.
5. Semiconductor Industry Association. *SEMATECH*. Cupertino, CA: Semiconductor Industry Association, December 1987.
6. Nelson, R. R. *High-Technology Policies*. Washington, DC: American Enterprise Institute, 1984.
7. Erdilek, A. (ed.). *Multinationals as Mutual Invaders: Intra-Industry Direct Foreign Investment*. London: Croom Helm, 1985.
8. Porter, M. E. *Competitive Strategy*. New York: The Free Press, 1980.

COOPERATIVE RESEARCH AND TECHNOLOGY DEVELOPMENT 207

9. Porter, M.E. "Competition in Global Industries." In: M.E. Porter (ed.), *Competition in Global Industries*. (Cambridge, MA: Harvard Business School Press, 1986, pp. 15–60.
10. Porter, M.E. "Changing Patterns of International Competition." In: D.J. Teece (ed.), *The Competitive Challenge*. Cambridge, MA: Ballinger, 1987, pp. 27–57.
11. Porter, M.E., and Fuller, M.B. "Coalitions and Global Strategy." In: M.E. Porter (ed.), *Competition in Global Industries*. Cambridge, MA: Harvard Business School Press, pp., 315–343.
12. Ghemawat, P.; Porter, M.E.; and Rawlinson, R.A. "Patterns of International Coalition Activity." In: M.E. Porter (ed.), *Competition in Global Industries*. Cambridge MA: Harvard Business School Press, 1986, pp. 345–365.
13. Howell, T.R.; Noellert, W.A.; MacLaughlin, J.H.; and Wolff, A.W. *The Microelectronics Race*. Boulder: Westview Press, 1988.
14. Link, A.N., and Bauer, L.L. "An Economic Analysis of Cooperative Research." *Technovation* 6 (1987): 247–260.
15. Finan, W.M., and LaMond, A.M. "Sustaining U.S. competitiveness in Microelectronics." In: B.R. Scott and G.C. Lodge (eds.), *U.S. Competitiveness in the World Economy*. Cambridge, MA: Harvard Business School Press, 1985, pp. 144–175.
16. National Science Foundation. *The Semiconductor Industry*. Washington, DC: National Science Foundation, 1987.
17. *Financial Times* (November 16, 1987): 7.
18. *Wall Street Journal* (November 26, 1987): 8.
19. *Wall Street Journal* (December 5, 1987): 26.
20. *Wall Street Journal* (April 18, 1988): 6.
21. *Wall Street Journal* (April 19, 1988): 30.
22. *Financial Times* (April 26, 1988): 14.
23. *Wall Street Journal* (October 28, 1986): 34.
24. *Wall Street Journal* (September 25, 1987): 10.
25. *Financial Times* (November 24, 1987): 4.
26. *Wall Street Journal* (May 27, 1987): 6.
27. *Wall Street Journal* (July 30, 1987): 4.
28. *Wall Street Journal* (March 24, 1988): 12.
29. Link, A.N., and Tassey, G. *Strategies for Technology-based Competition*. Lexington, MA: Lexington Books, 1987.
31. *Barron's* (March, 9, 1987): 13.
32. Sumney, L.W., and Burger, R.M. "Revitalizing the U.S. Semiconductor Industry." *Issues in Science and Technology* 3 (4) (Summer, 1987): 32–41.
33. *Wall Street Journal* (January 7, 1988): 31.
34. Bureau of National Affairs. *Analysis and Reports* 37. Washington DC: Bureau of National Affairs, 1988.
35. *Wall Street Journal* (January 8, 1988): 6.
36. *Wall Street Journal* (January 27, 1988): 37.

37. Semiconductor Research Corporation. *Annual Report* Semiconductor Research Corporation, Research Triangle Park, NC, 1986.
38. Sumney, L.W., and Burger, R.M. "The Semiconductor Research Corporation and University Research in Integrated Circuits." *IEEE Transactions on Education* E-29 (2) (May, 1986): 61–68.

About the Authors

DAVID B. AUDRETSCH has been a research fellow since 1985 at the International Institute of Management of the Wissenschaftszentrum Berlin für Sozialforschung in West Berlin. Previously he taught at Middlebury College and at the University of Wisconsin, where he received his Ph.D. in Economics. He has also been a consultant at the U.S. International Trade Commission and the Federal Trade Commission.

BARRY L. BOZEMAN is Professor of Public Administration and Affiliate Professor of Engineering at Syracuse University, where he directs the Maxwell School of Public Affairs' Technology and Information Policy Program. Bozeman's interests are in the areas of R&D policy and technology development. Most recently, Bozeman's research has focused on an analysis of the political and economic environment of U.S. R&D laboratories. Bozeman received his Ph.D. in Political Science in 1973 from Ohio State University.

JOSEPH J. CORDES received his Ph.D. in Economics from the University of Wisconsin in 1977, and is a Professor of Economics at George Washington University. His current research focuses on the effectiveness of the R&D tax credit and the determinants of firm participation in publicly organized cooperative research programs.

DAVID H. COURSEY is a research associate in the Technology and Information Policy Program at Syracuse University. His major research interests include experts systems, organizational decline, and multiprogram research laboratory activities.

ASIM ERDILEK, Professor of Economics at Case Western Reserve University, received his Ph.D. in Economics from Harvard University in 1972. He has been a policy analyst at the National Science Foundation (1982–1984) and an Alexander von Humboldt Fellow at the Institute for World Economics, Kiel, West Germany (1977–1980). His research interests and writing are in the area of international economics.

ELIEZER GEISLER is Visiting Scholar at the Technology Institute at Northwestern University. He received his Ph.D. from Northwestern, specializing in the area of R&D management and entrepreneurship. His current research remains in these areas.

ALBERT N. LINK is Professor of Economics and Director of the Industrial Technology Program at the University of North Carolina at Greensboro. He received his Ph. D. in Economics from Tulane University in 1976 and has written extensively in the areas of productivity, technological change, and innovation policy.

DAVID C. MOWERY received his Ph.D. in economics from Stanford University. He has taught at Carnegie-Mellon University, served as the Director of the Panel on Technology and Employment of the National Academy of Sciences, and was a Council on Foreign Relations International Affairs Fellow in the Office of the U.S. Trade Representative.

GERHARD ROSEGGER is the Frank Tracy Carlton Professor of Economics at Case Western Reserve University. He has authored numerous studies in the fields of industrial economics and the economics of technological change. He has served as Fulbright Visiting Professor at the University of Innsbruck, Austria, and has held visiting appointments at the Technical University of Vienna and the University of Graz, Austria.

ROY ROTHWELL holds the Ph.D. in Solid State Physics. In 1971 he joined the Science Policy Research Unit (SPRU) at Sussex to work on issues relating to the industrial innovation process. He currently leads SPRU's Management of Technology Group. His research interests include innovation and the small firm; success and failure in innovation; comparative public innovation policies; technical change and international competitiveness; and technology and regional industrial development.

ALBERT H. RUBENSTEIN has his Ph.D. in Industrial Engineering from Columbia University. He was on the Industrial Engineering staff at Columbia from 1950–1953 and on the faculty of the School of Industrial Management at M.I.T. from 1953–1959. Since 1959 he has been Professor of Industrial Engineering and Management Sciences at Northwestern Univeristy, where he established and heads the Organization Theory area and the Program of Research on the Management of Research and Development. He is also Director of the Master of Engineering Management program and the Center for Information Technology at Northwestern.

L. FERNANDO RUIZ-MIER is Professor in Economics at the University of North Carolina at Greensboro. He obtained a Ph.D. in Economics from Purdue University in 1985. His major research interests are in the area of international trade. He is currently on leave as Assistant Secretary to the Ministry of Finance of Bolivia.

JOHN T. SCOTT is Professor of Economics in the Department of Economics at Dartmouth College. He received the Ph.D. in Economics from Harvard University in 1976. He has been an economist at the Board of Governors of the Federal Reserve System and the Federal Trade Commission. His writings are in the areas of technological change and industrial organization.

GREGORY TASSEY is senior economist at the National Institute of Standards and Technology in Gaithersburg, Maryland. Since receiving the Ph.D. in Economics from George Washington University in 1978, he has directed or served in research programs related to technology, innovation, and public policy. He has written extensively in these areas.

HARRY WATSON received his Ph.D in Economics from Indiana University and is now Professor of Economics at George Washington University. His research has concentrated on insurance markets, credit markets, tax evasion, social security, and the effects of taxation on charitable contributions, partnership behavior, research and development, and investment.

INDEX